Practically Macrobiotic

Ingredients, Preparation and Cooking of more
than 200 Delicious Macrobiotic Recipes

Written and illustrated by
Keith Michell

THORSONS PUBLISHING GROUP
Wellingborough, Northamptonshire
Rochester, Vermont

First published 1987

Published in the UK by
Thorsons Publishing Group
Denington Estate, Wellingborough,
Northamptonshire NN8 2RQ,
and in the USA by
Thorsons Publishers Inc.,
Park Street, Rochester, Vermont 05767.

British Library Cataloguing in Publication Data

Michell, Keith
Practically macrobiotic.
1. Macrobiotic diet — Recipes
I. Title
641.5'63   RM235

ISBN 0-7225-1140-X

Library of Congress Cataloging-in-Publication Data

Michell, Keith.
Practically macrobiotic.

Bibliography: p.
Includes index.
1. Macrobiotic diet — Recipes.   I Title.
RM235.M53 1986 641.5 86-5805
ISBN 0-7225-1140-X (pbk.)

Printed and bound in Italy
by Tipolitografia G. Canale & C. S.p.A. – Turin

208397

Practically Macrobiotic

In this very special cookbook, Keith Michell, the internationally acclaimed award-winning actor, artist and author, draws aside the curtain of mystery that tends to obscure macrobiotics, and in his inimitably entertaining style shows that being practically macrobiotic doesn't mean a life of strict diets. Instead it is a way to enjoy to the full and gain health benefits from the vast variety of foodstuffs that nature supplies.

Contents

*"It's a very odd thing—as odd as can be
That whatever Miss T eats turns into Miss T."*

—Walter de la Mare

Foreword

Following World War II, during the years 1945 to 1960, chemicalization, refinement, large-scale commercialization, and various types of artificialization of the food of the modern world became a standard. Trends leading to this state of affairs began in the early part of the twentieth century, together with the increased consumption of animal foods, including red meat, poultry, and dairy food. At the same time, the use of refined sugar, as well as tropical and semi-tropical fruits and their juices, increased. While consumption of meat and sugar rose, use of whole cereal grains, beans and legumes, fresh vegetables, and locally grown fruits decreased.

With these dietary trends came changes in the health patterns of our societies. Degenerative diseases such as cardiovascular disorders, cancer, arthritis, allergies, diabetes, hypoglycemia, and many others, including psychological disorders such as schizophrenia, paranoia, depression, anxiety, and other emotional afflictions, have escalated as a result of these transitions into the modern world. Individual and family life has become more and more unstable; we are now witnessing massive decomposition of the family as a unit, increased crime and antisocial behaviour, and a lack of cohesion in communities. These factors increase every year.

All of this indicates that modern society—its dietary habits, lifestyle, way of thinking, and other factors—is inadequate to sustain human health and maintain human spirituality on this planet.

For the past thirty years, the natural food movement, organic food movement, and holistic health advocates, especially those practicing the macrobiotic way of life, have been pioneering positive changes in diet, lifestyle, and way of thinking.

Modern macrobiotics, which draws upon the wisdom of ancient Greek, Judaic, and Oriental cultures and dietary practices, offers a positive solution for preventing various physical, psychological, and degenerative disorders, and offers possible recovery from them as well. Hundreds of thousands of people around the world who have begun the macrobiotic way of life have restored not only their physical health, but their psychological and spiritual health as well.

I take great pleasure in introducing this new cookbook, *Practically Macrobiotic* by Keith Michell, through the efforts of Thorsons Publishing Group. The author, a well-known actor who has contributed greatly to humanity through his artistic expression, has compiled in this book many recipes for delicious and healthy macrobiotic and natural food dishes. Many of them are particularly helpful for those just beginning the macrobiotic approach, or for sharing with those friends who are unfamiliar with natural food cuisine. While some recipes contain foods not usually used in macrobiotic daily practice, especially during times of recovering one's health, they are helpful for those who are in transition to macrobiotics.

We wish to extend our sincere thanks to both the publisher and the author with our hope that this book may be read and used by many people who wish to maintain their health, prevent degenerative disorders, and recover their well-being.

Michio Kushi
Brookline, Mass., USA

Introduction

Keith Michell has always put to best use an instinct for balance in his careers as artist and actor. No surprises, therefore, that he and macrobiotics should have embraced each other so closely. For macrobiotics is the way—or play—of harmony: the universal dynamics of change performed with graceful balance in our ever-evolving lives.

This is a book of fine arts created by a fine artist of canvas and cuisine — to say nothing of his acting talents! One of the best things about helping Keith was being inspired by his wonderful illustrations, completed enthusiastically by him so early in the project. I sometimes felt we should be weaving a text around the pictures rather than merely illustrating the words. The worst thing has been having to keep the recipes secret for so long! When he first showed them to me, a year before publication, I casually remarked how well they would supplement the cooking courses I was running at the time. The look he gave me would have been familiar to several of Henry VIII's wives! It was a wise rebuke; exposure to the public then would surely have made the recipes the subject of untimely culinary espionage!

While it is true that the world needs new cooks more than another cookbook, there are still an astonishingly small number of recipe collections in which health aspects are not compromised by the regular palate-placaters of dairy food and sugar. Twenty years ago, nutritional recommendations and macrobiotic dietary advice seemed poles apart; today they accommodate each other comfortably. Unsponsored voices in nutrition and medicine are calling for healthier diets based on whole grains, vegetables, seeds, nuts and fruit, and with a strong emphasis on reducing meat, dairy foods and sugar to minimal levels. But, still there remains massive ignorance about nutrition and diet, often (unforgivably) among the medical profession. This despite the dawning realization in the health sciences that malnutrition is now the most widespread background health disorder in our "developed" world.

It was with a sense of urgency more than novelty, therefore, that Keith decided to incorporate nutritional explanations and data into a book about macrobiotics. This has not been easy to do for several reasons. Science and macrobiotics view food from different perspectives. The quality of "energy" (ch'i or k'i) which is attributed to food in macrobiotics is not detected by nutritional analysis. For example, it is quite possible for a long-frozen sample of cabbage to show up equally as well in laboratory analysis as the freshly-picked version. We know instinctively that fresh is best for us. Nutrition doesn't. Food composition values are interesting and useful as long as they are not taken too literally. The data provided here will at least reveal how rich in nutrients and low in harmful aspects is the macrobiotic way of eating. A recent London University study shows that the macrobiotic diet is adequate in all nutrients and is full of those nutrients often lacking in the modern diet.

Macrobiotics has had quite a rough ride until recently. Misunderstandings and poor translations in the early days of its introduction to the West attracted a tiny but lunatic fringe of zealots who chose to interpret this gentle way of harmony as a kind of metabolic martial art — on one or two occasions even extinguishing themselves in the process. Secular medical judgment was, not surprisingly, fairly hysterical, which served only to compound the misunderstanding and delay progress towards a more "westernized" application of macrobiotic dietary principles. New research by Belgian doctors into the blood chemistry and tissue function of macrobiotic men and children has revealed a perfect picture of health. Other recent medical studies are similarly supportive.

INTRODUCTION

As governments are at last being forced by public opinion to take real interest in preventive health care, official recommendations for healthy eating are showing some hopeful trends. We should not, however, be complacent enough to believe that politicians in power hold the health of the people dearer to their hearts than they do the pressing attentions of the food, drug and agriculture industries. It is we, as individuals, groups and communities, who must spread the message — at least until it is received and understood by a critical mass of society. For the food/health connection is an absolutely crucial issue at this stage of humanity's journey, much as were public health and hygiene in relation to the killer epidemics of the nineteenth century.

The health of westerners has degenerated in this century to levels that would permit few of us to survive in the lifestyles of even our most recent ancestors. Modern medicine has little of use to offer beyond powerful painkillers and some effective emergency care. It continues to foster a mentality that seeks to blame illness on factors "beyond our control", rather than teaching us to accept responsibility for our disease and thus to learn something from it: but these latter days of the twentieth century are drawing us through the funnel of transformation into a brighter age. We have no alternative but to make this journey successfully, and we should be prepared to face a good deal of turbulence on the way. At this time our most valuable resource is sound health of body, mind and spirit.

How can macrobiotics help us in our progress? To move into a healthier future we need to rid ourselves of a sick past, to abolish old fears and build with the vision of uncluttered consciousness.

Macrobiotics does help transform worn-down health into welcome new potentials. It plays a powerful role in dissolving and eliminating the consequences of inappropriate habits accumulated in tissues, organs, muscles and joints through years of dietary and mental self-abuse. And it makes us feel good!—about ourselves, the world around us and our relationship with it.

Finally, and most importantly, macrobiotic food is delicious! At the risk of evoking another goodbye look from Keith I must admit to having tested these recipes, albeit in intimate company and in a far-off land. They are wonderful—among the best I have ever found. As you explore and enjoy them, please remember to give thanks that food of such quality, variety and goodness is available to be shared among us.

Richard Burton BSc
London, England

COPY OF THE CHARACTER *Shou (Long Life)* IN *grass script* SIGNED BY THE 85 YEAR OLD *Yeh Chih*. RUBBING DATED 1ST DAY OF THE 1ST MOON 1863

Introducing Macrobiotics

And what is your favorite food?

Macrobi-*what*-ics?

So you expect to live to a hundred, do you?

Who started it all?

And what is your favorite food?

There is no doubt that the subject of food can be a delicate one. In interviews, when a question like "And what is your favorite food?" is innocently asked, and a word like macrobiotics is uttered, interviewers tend to look startled. They could have a crank on their hands—a possibly dangerous one—who might try to convert them!

Let me say at once that I do not pretend to be an authority on the subject of macrobiotics. I don't think of myself as a cook—neither does anyone else as far as I know—and I never try to convert anyone. I'm not a particularly rigid practicing macrobiotic, which is probably the best sort to be. There are more extensive books written on the philosophy of the subject and several fine cookbooks. I am indebted to the authors of both categories. I eat my own *practically* macrobiotic way because I enjoy it. Being asked to write this book has been a good opportunity to find answers to many of the questions asked by interviewers, skeptics and friends over the last dozen years and, I might add, a chance to answer quite a few I have needed to ask myself about macrobiotics.

Macrobi-what-ics?

The word (it is *macro*biotics, by the way, not *micro*biotics) does conjure up the science laboratory rather than the humble kitchen, but it is not exactly a science because it is founded in philosophy. It is neither a cult nor a religion, but it can contribute to a good way of life. There are probably as many interpretations of it as there are people who practice it. Basically it is a practical way of selecting, preparing, cooking and eating food—not necessarily with chopsticks—based on the ancient and beautiful concept of *Tao*.

Tao is "the pursuit of the *natural* way of heaven and earth—the order of the universe; the Great Whole, containing all change."

The Chinese have a symbol or character called *shou*, which means longevity. This could be the origin of the word *macrobiotics*. The Greek translation of *shou* is *macro*, long (or great) and *biotic*, meaning life. (*Micro*biotics on the other hand means small or short life!)

 # So you expect to live to a hundred, do you?

Our body will survive on a physical level anywhere from forty to a hundred years however badly or well we treat it—but who wants a long life if it is a miserable or painful one? Personally I prefer the "Great Life" translation, in which it is not the quantity of life that is important but the quality of it. Whether it is *macro*, great, or generally unsatisfactory is mainly up to us.

Have you ever considered how meticulous we are about the fuel we feed our automobiles? Our bodies, on the other hand, are such infinitely more sophisticated pieces of machinery that by comparison they make satellites look like covered wagons. Yet we go on stuffing them with any junk we can find in the supermarket without so much as a glance at the labels.

One consequence of this treatment is that the use of tranquilizers alone has reached "epidemic proportions" according to a National Association of Mental Health report. One person in seven of the United Kingdom adult population takes these drugs every year.

What we eat and drink affects us physically, mentally and certainly spiritually. This is such a statement of the obvious and so simple that we tend to overlook it. Occasionally a hangover brutally brings the fact to our attention or sickness makes us recognize it. Both signal to us the fact that we are not eating naturally. Mind you, these days it is almost impossible to find food, water, salt or even air in its natural unadulterated state! Simply being aware of this danger is half way to dealing with it.

I was forcibly made aware of the importance of food when, in Australia as a teenager, just learning to stand on my own two feet, I landed in a hospital bed with a bad attack of quinsy—my tonsils and throat were so inflamed and swollen that I couldn't swallow. The effects of the illness were soon cured by injections of the latest drug—penicillin—and the doctor threatened to remove the offending tonsils as soon as the patient's condition improved. Fortunately, a far-seeing friend advised a visit to a naturopath instead. This man explained that the tonsils are one of nature's many ingenious warning devices used by the body to indicate an excess of toxins in the system. He advised cutting down on chocolates, cakes, sugary sweets and foods fried in recooked animal fats. It made sense.

Two decades or so later—1970—and the scene is New York, that city where a "healthy" diet can consist of synthetic food and vitamin pills. I was healthy enough—greedy but healthy and showing some overweight—but I seemed to have a continual hangover from which I never quite recovered. The food served in most restaurants was certainly boring. The menus were monotonous, overelaborate, overcooked and overpriced.

Then I was given a book as a joke, *You Are All Sanpaku* by William Dufty, about a man named Georges Ohsawa and his macrobiotics. It was a best-seller.

I was back in England trying out a new play before I got around to reading the book. Dufty, the author, had had every complaint you could think of, from headaches to hemorrhoids, and cured them all by this practical way of eating devised by Ohsawa. The book made startling, thundering sense to me. "You are what you eat," it said. "Physical and mental disorder comes from a disordered, unnatural way of eating."

The play settled down for a London run, and I settled down to eating "macrobiotically." This meant eating mainly brown rice and mixed vegetables with some fish and prawns, "real" soy sauce and sesame salt, no sugar or sugar products, and drinking less liquid. After three days I started losing weight—twenty pounds in ten days—and I could see muscles and things I'd forgotten I had! Best of all was a relaxation and mental clarity—a "high" you might say. Only I was kicking "drugs", namely sugar and chemicals, which gave me a strange new awareness and lack of anxiety—call it happiness—I hadn't experienced in years.

By the time we took the play to Los Angeles I was getting thin. My leading lady, Diana Rigg, remarked in her inimitable way that the audience wouldn't see me at all in our nude scene if I didn't do something about it! Actually I was the same weight I had been in my twenties.

I looked up the address of the Ohsawa Foundation and went along to ask a few questions. The woman I met there gave me an hour of her time and some valuable advice. *"Eat what you feel like but always remember the balance of yin and yang."* Cooking techniques from other countries, especially the Orient, can seem strange. Westerners are not used to the cooking methods, and eating nothing but rice and sea vegetables, however well cooked, seems a sacrifice which perhaps the body is not prepared to accept. It can, in fact, be dangerous to suddenly go on a diet of grains. If you feel like eating a steak do so—with green vegetables and a glass of wine to balance it! Just be aware of the balance. Above all, don't become a fanatic about it.

At that time Johnny (Tarzan) Weissmuller had a health shop named after him on Hollywood Boulevard, and there I found three of Ohsawa's original volumes. In his *Macrobiotic Guide Book* Ohsawa says the same thing: "Some people think that macrobiotics is no more than the eating of sesame seeds mixed with sea salt, carrots and brown rice. Others that it is summed up by 'Don't eat cake and sugar'. How far from the truth!. . . . I enjoy any cuisine—Western, Chinese, Japanese, Indian. I like fruit, candy, chocolate and whisky very much. If I choose to use these things now I am able to avoid harm because I can balance yin and yang. We must choose what is good for us—the art of making such a choice is macrobiotics."

I have stayed with this way of eating—or my interpretation of it—for a dozen years or so now, mainly for practical reasons. It is easy to prepare, tastes good and has stood me in good stead. An actor's life can be as vigorous and as stressful as an athlete's—physical and emotional demands and mental disciplines can be a heavier strain than people realize. More important, I love the grub and the way it makes me feel!

I really prefer grains to meat as a principal food. *Whole* grains, that is. There's such a choice! Millet is a good food, as are oats, barley, rye, wheat, buckwheat, corn and, of course, the good old standby, rice. I don't mean the cotton wool flakes of what is called "refined" rice but rich, chewy, short-grained brown rice. Seasonal vegetables in both England and the United States are superb, and seaweeds or sea vegetables eaten as laver, dulse, carrageen and kelp in parts of Europe are a rich source of minerals not as yet generally appreciated. There are a thousand new tastes to discover. Ohsawa says the food tastes of nature, and he's right! It is very exciting and never bland—unless it's badly cooked.

And in this day and age of neuroses and violence, macrobiotics helps bring some balance to life itself—the yin and yang balance of nature.

In this book I have tried to give you an idea of the sort of food there is to enjoy, new ingredients and recipes not only from the East but from other parts of the world. Most traditional dishes were originally macrobiotic when they were made from unrefined, whole ingredients and were balanced by man's and woman's intuition. Over the centuries, grains have long been the principal food of most civilizations, with vegetables, legumes or beans and, from time to time, some animal food, fish or meat, as supplements.

For those who are nervous about their vitamins, minerals, protein, etc, I have added lists of nutrient content of *whole* foods. Nutritionists approach the subject of diet analytically and scientifically but are, you will find, continually confirming the common sense of macrobiotics.

Assembling the material for this book has been one of life's adventures I would have not missed! I am grateful to John Hardaker of Thorsons Publishing Group for suggesting I write it and for his encouragement. I said yes to the idea without quite realizing what would be involved, and it wasn't long before I paid a long overdue visit to the Community Health Foundation at the East West Centre, Old Street, London. There they quickly summed me up as an "old-fashioned macrobiotic!" I'd like to thank those members of the foundation— Anna McKenzie, Montse and Peter Bradford, Lynne Stackhouse and Alastaire G. Drane for bringing my wife Jenny and myself up-to-date on the latest developments in the yin-yang kitchen. There are many new products on the market that make the cooking even more exciting, and many refinements of preparation I have tried to include in the following chapters. Jenny brings her own continental flair to cooking and, I am glad to say, patiently keeps me off the *too* straight and narrow culinary path by insisting on varying the menus.

Working in the theater meant traveling to the United States and Australia last year—equipped with pots, pans and *suribachi*. This is why the illustrations are done with felt pens. They are easy to pack and light to carry!

In New York I discovered a popular macrobiotic restaurant run by a young Englishman, Richard Markstein, who has great enthusiasm for and belief in the potential of macrobiotics. In San Francisco we found a young Argentinian, Louis Gutman, whose love for cooking and understanding of macrobiotics was really remarkable. Both Richard and Louis have generously contributed some of their own special recipes to this collection and encountering their freshness of spirit, which so many young macrobiotics seem to have, was a great pleasure. In Australia Brian and Anne Perkins and Suzan and Stefan Melkonian provided some fine meals and recipes with an Antipodean flavor.

I am particularly indebted to Richard Burton BSc, then nutritionist with the London Community Health Foundation; apart from his encouragement, Richard has painstakingly revised the text and has written the foreword to it. I would like to mention Angela Piscina, who has bravely applied her considerable skills experimenting with new dishes and ingredients, Roger Watson, PhD who has shared culinary secrets and offered valuable advice, and Bernie Echevarri who has expertly deciphered and typed innumerable handwritten drafts with hardly a demur. There are others—they will know who they are—who have provided help, recipes and encouragement. I thank them for their contribution to this book, which will, I hope, serve as an introduction to the subject of macrobiotics.

 ## *Who started it all?*

The first to use the word macrobiotics seems to have been a physician, Christopher Wilhelm Hufeland, who worked in Berlin and wrote a book called *Macrobiotik—The Art of Prolonging Human Life*. This was 150 years before George Ohsawa was to apply it in connection with food, cooking and Tao. Ohsawa also apparently introduced and first practiced acupuncture in Europe. He also brought the spirit of the Tao and of judo and kadu (flower arrangement) to the West.

To read his books is to encounter a somewhat stern, righteous, eastern prophet proclaiming to the western wilderness, in sometimes quaint English, his fervent faith in health or hell on earth. This, I suppose, is pretty much what he was.

Early this century he was a young Oriental student, and the East was becoming westernized. At that time natural whole food certainly hadn't the ring of sound common sense it begins to have today, nor was the situation of refined, convenience food as serious as it has more recently become. George Bernard Shaw advocated vegetarianism and was considered a crank, but then so had Buddha, Pythagoras, Plato, Plutarch, Ovid, Seneca, Milton, Pope, Shelley, Voltaire, Rousseau, Tolstoy, Newton and Gandhi! Obviously a thinking man's diet! Macrobiotics, although not strictly vegan, is, to my mind, a logical and natural progression from vegetarianism.

Ohsawa came from a westernized Japanese family and found his healthy way of eating through sickness. In fact he nearly died when he was only sixteen. His young mother, sisters and brothers were victims of tuberculosis, and he too was condemned as incurable by his western doctors. As a "poor orphan" he said he could no longer afford their treatment anyway. This was fortunate for him because he turned to a Japanese doctor in Tokyo, Sagan Ishizuka.

In those days nutrition was mainly concerned with the three organic ingredients—protein, fat and carbohydrate—but in Ishizuka's opinion the body's functions, organs and nervous system

Accept everything with great pleasure and thanks
ACCEPT MISFORTUNE LIKE HAPPINESS, DISEASE LIKE HEALTH,
POVERTY LIKE PROSPERITY. and if you don't like it or
cannot stand it, refer to your UNIVERSAL COMPASS
the UNIQUE PRINCIPLE. There you will find the
best direction. Everything that happens to you is what
you lack. all that is ANTAGONISTIC, unbearable
is COMPLIMENTARY THE MAN WHO EMBRACES HIS
ANTAGONIST IS THE HAPPIEST MAN — George Ohsawa.

were controlled by the *inorganic minerals*, in particular, potassium and sodium, and he divided foods into those two categories. Foods, he claimed, were the highest medicines, and all physical characteristics such as skin texture, overweight/underweight, good memory or bad, strength or weakness depended on environment *and* the intake of potassium and sodium. He wrote a book called *Chemical Diet for Longevity* and became very famous. A letter addressed to "Dr. Antidoctor, Tokyo" was delivered directly to him.

He cured Ohsawa, who studied his theory, related it to Oriental philosophy and realized that a concept explaining it has existed in the Orient for two thousand years. He lived to launch his macrobiotics, and for over fifty years advocated his reinterpretation of the "unique principle" of Tao as a basis for healthier and more peaceful living. Macrobiotics, he claimed, was a simple, practical discipline of life that anyone could observe with great pleasure to help restore health and harmony of soul, mind and body. "The theory is so simple," he wrote, "a child can learn it. There is only one principle to understand—*yin and yang*—a *universal compass, the heart of a world concept which can be applied throughout our daily life on every level.*"

During World War II Ohsawa was imprisoned in Japan for his antiwar activities. In 1946 he helped form the World Government Association in Hiyoshi under the splendid title of Center Ignoramus, where the principle of yin and yang was taught. In 1952 he and his wife Lima started traveling. They stayed in India, lived with Dr Schweitzer in Africa, then moved to France and Belgium teaching macrobiotics. In 1961 they went to the United States and established the Ohsawa Foundation in California, where his books were published. The clinic he ran was called Sanrant: *San*atorium + restau*rant*. There was no operating theater, no drug department: its center was the kitchen. "In macrobiotics our pharmacy is the kitchen," he wrote. "Our method is based on the potency of daily food."

His life was spent interpreting Oriental philosophy; and more than anything he wished to bring West and East together. This, as he saw it, was the world's chief hope of peace and freedom—two mighty words—which only faith in man's oneness with nature could achieve. Having taught his methods for fifty years, he admitted that although he was convinced of its great value, there was still a chance that he might be wrong. "Why otherwise," he asked, "in all these years have I been able to find so few western doctors or philosophers who can understand the writing and philosophy that were taken for granted in the East centuries ago?"

Time seems to be answering his question. Nearly twenty years after his death the spirit of macrobiotics—the oneness of man, nature and the universe, seems to be surviving! Yin and yang are being integrated into western thinking. After some initial vehement resistance, Oriental philosophy is influencing Occidental medical treatments, nutrition and what we eat perhaps more than Ohsawa ever imagined it would and more than we ourselves realize. In recent years the great increase in the number of shops supplying health products throughout England, the United States and parts of Europe and Australia is a response to a greater public dissatisfaction and demand. Most such shops successfully stock macrobiotic supplies. Natural eating is definitely coming back!

Everything changes and, as I discovered in those cooking classes, the concepts of macrobiotics are continually being revised to suit other new decades. Our scientists' ventures into space have accustomed us to universal awareness and, according to Michio Kushi, Ohsawa's successor, macrobiotics is a way of life according to the largest possible view. "One day," he says, "future generations will look back at the cult of our modern civilization's artificial food as a fad ... under many names and forms macrobiotics will continue as long as human life continues to exist".

 # Yin and Yang

What is this yin and yang?

So which foods are yin and which are yang?

Do yin and yang mean acid and alkaline?

What is this yin and yang?

The question requires an answer. Now *that* is yin and yang!

Yin and yang are complementary opposites, which together make a whole. Understanding this, the Unique Principle, is what Tao is all about. "Wholeness," said George Ohsawa, "is the highest wisdom . . . everything can be understood the better through an awareness of this harmony of opposites."

We in the West tend to think of natural opposition as absolute, different and separate. Good *versus* bad, rich *versus* poor, left wing *versus* right wing. But yin and yang coexist as two sides of oneness, of the universe—of god or what you will.

The earliest idea of complementary opposites was probably that of the Earth Mother—the Tellus Mater—who provided life by her fertility, and of the Sky Father, who controlled the sun and elements necessary for growth and fertilization. In Greek mythology there were Chaos and Earth. According to Indian mythology Shiva is the destroyer—the male power—and Vishna the preserver, the female power. In the beautiful Chinese book of changes, the *I Ching*, Ch'ien represents the sky power, Father and Heaven, while K'un is the yielding Mother and Earth. To the ancient Chinese the calm, receptive, peaceful and earthly powers were yin. Strength, aggression, violence and clamor were heavenly powers and yang!

Yin and yang. The Mother and Father who bring about all changes. These forces are still discussed quite seriously today in Somerset, where the Glastonbury Tor is set in the Valley of Avalon. It is a mysterious, spiraling mound, the center of a vast "round table" with its Glastonbury Giants spread for miles around—zodiac symbols so large that they are visible only from the air. Sun-God-Sagittarius (King Arthur) and the Earth-Mother-Virgo (Guinevere) are outlined by natural contours, roads and waterways. Were they conjured up by nature across the landscape or by the power of Celtic mythology and man's fertile imagination?

Yin and yang are equally important, let me hasten to add! Each has its natural place. They can only survive in relationship; they mutually attract, depend on and influence one another. Neither is totally yin nor completely yang. They achieve oneness in the natural order of things. The yin-yang of female and male, the passive-receptive and active-creative energies are only one tiny balance in the mighty scale. The number of yin-yang opposites is infinite.

You will find yin and yang everywhere, at all times. Breathing out follows breathing in, expansion eases contraction, separates gather together, silence quietens sound, stillness stays activity, outward embraces inward, negative discharges positive, weakness shall overcome strength, high rests upon low, water quenches fire, shadow is cast by light, striving up touches bearing down, day is changed by night, space is measured by time. They oppose and complement each other and will eventually mutually transform each other. Summer changes to winter, youth to age, matter to energy. Every beginning has an end. Yin and yang. Even the colors of the spectrum are a facet of it. The cooler colors of Yin—purples, blues and greens—contrast their complements, the warmer reds, oranges and yellows which are yang. Together they make light.

Foods are also carriers of these two powerful forces, and when we eat food we produce cells, muscles, nerves, hormones, enzymes, genes, organs and thoughts that are antagonistic and complementary. Both yin foods and yang foods are needed by our bodies. Being aware of this provides a quite remarkable compass when cooking! Yin and yang balance seems to help maintain a balance in one's attitudes, too.

Try it and see. Your body—and your mind—will be grateful.

☯ So which foods are yin and which are yang? ☯

There are a number of factors that influence the yin-yang of food. Generally speaking, as you see on the charts, fruit and vegetables are more yin, grains and legumes more balanced (slightly yin), animal products more yang. You can eat more or less what you wish, but avoid extremes of yin or yang whenever possible.

The old maxim "You are what you eat" is so astonishingly simple that the usual reaction is to joke about it. But take a good, hard look at people who are compulsive pork or beef eaters! Meat is an elaborate, expensive and painful (not only for the animal!) way to obtain protein that is available directly from grains and beans. I am convinced that most of the senseless violence in the world is caused by the growing fad of prosperous societies who insist on meals predominantly comprising animal flesh every day.

In time you will come to judge food quality for yourself. Being aware of yin-yang properties can help you to recognize their presence in food, and you will enjoy playing the yin-yang game.

Generally speaking, whatever contains water is more yin. However, there are other indications of yin and yang. Colors can help identification: violet, indigo, blue, green or white show yin, while yellow, orange, red and brown or black generally show more yang. (There are exceptions—tomatoes are red and extremely yin!) The taste can range from yin-spicy, sour and sweet to yang-salty and bitter. Fat and protein content makes for yin, carbohydrates and mineral content for yang.

Fruit and vegetables, being more yin, grow upward and expansively. Their effect on body temperature is cooling: Those which have violet, blue, green, or white colours are more yin, and those with yellow, orange, brown or red colors are usually more yang. Those grown in hot, tropical regions are more yin than are those grown in the colder climates. They tend to have a stronger odor and taste, to be juicier and softer, to grow faster and cook more quickly, which are properties of more yin.

Vegetables grown in spring and summer are more yin than those grown in autumn and winter. If they grow vertically and expansively above the earth they are more yin than those growing under the earth and downward. Carrots, for example, are orange in color, are harder, drier, more compact and more yang than most other vegetables, but are more yin than grains.

Grains are very small and compact, ripen slowly, are dry, hard and brown, gold or yellow in color, with little odor or taste. They are more yang than are most other vegetables but are more yin than meat.

Animal foods are much more yang. They form separate, compact unities with a more compact inward formation of organs and cells. They have warm body temperatures, and they move about, some faster (the more yang ones) than others. Their color is generally that of hemoglobin (yang) red.

White, cold-blooded fish, shellfish and so on are less yang than are warm-blooded meat, bird and fowl. Freshwater fish are less yang than saltwater fish.

Vegetables being more yin tend to produce a more overall relaxation in the body's functions. Animal foods, on the other hand, being more yang, make for tenseness. Yin foods and yang foods are complementary, and they mutually attract. If you eat salty (yang) food, you will tend to crave sweets (yin).

Ideally, food should be mainly vegetable quality, selected from the middle of the yin-yang scale.

21

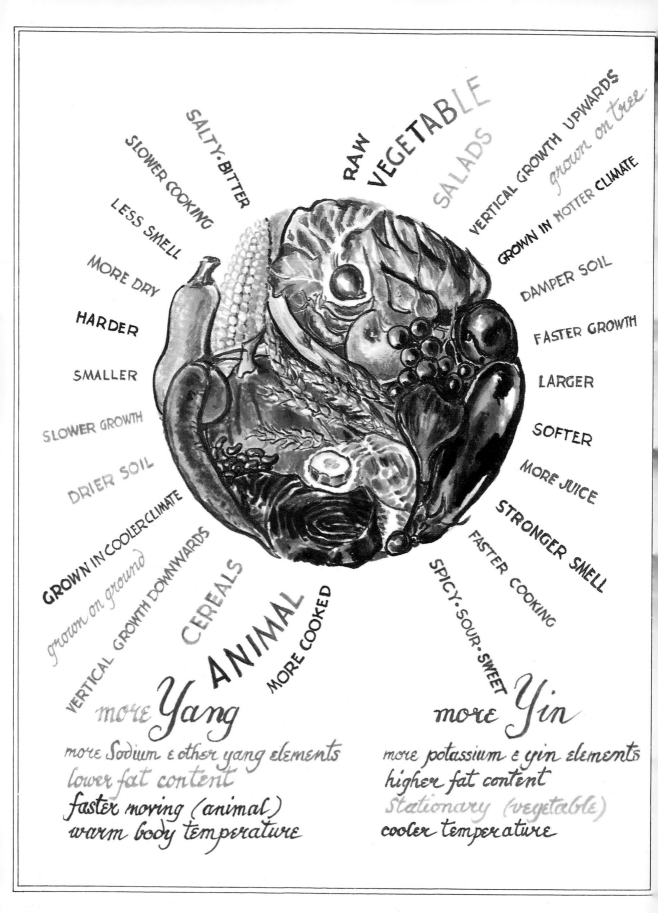

Yin and yang correspond to the seasons. In spring and summer in hot, tropical climates we tend to eat more yin foods. We prefer salads, lightly cooked vegetables and some fruit as dessert. Because hot weather is yang, we need the yin food as a balance, and nature supplies it. In cooler seasons like autumn and winter in cold climates, we crave more yang foods— grains such as millet, buckwheat, short-grained rice, root vegetables, slightly more salt and even some animal food. These help warm us and keep out the cold.

Always try to buy vegetables in season. They are cheaper then anyway, because they are more plentiful. In this day and age of export and import, choose your vegetables from a climate similar to your own or from the same geographical latitude. Treat those exotic delicacies from the tropics with some restraint. Such foods are yin and will cool you down, which you don't need in the middle of a freezing winter. They make you feel the cold and generally prevent your body from adapting to your natural weather conditions.

Cooking affects yin and yang. Cooking can transform a meal. Grains, beans, vegetables, seaweeds and nuts—some more yin than others—may need to be made more yang, especially in winter or in a cold climate. Fire, pressure, salt and time are the chief yang factors. Baking, roasting, grilling, pressure cooking, sautéing and the use of sea salt, tamari, soy sauce, miso and pickles all help to yangize and energize food. Animal foods, fish, shellfish and poultry need less yang treatment. Boiling, steaming and the use of fresh salads, some spices, fruit and desserts help yinize a meal. Raw fish is less extreme yang than is cooked (see SASHIMI). Cooking is the art of adjusting these factors and adapting food to the season, time, and place and the needs of the individual. When you know your yin from your yang you will enjoy balancing a meal, and you and yours will feel a great deal better for it.

☯ *Do yin and yang mean acid and alkaline?* ☯

This question is often asked, and the answer is yes—and no!

When Ohsawa studied Ishizuka's theory that sodium and potassium were the most important inorganic minerals in the body, and related it to the Unique Principle and Tao, he realized that he needed to categorize acid and alkaline in relation to yin and yang. In what was probably his first book, *Lecture Series in Shokuyo*, published in 1928, he called acid yang and alkaline yin. By the sixties, however, when he first lectured in New York, acid had become yin and alkaline yang. Yin or potassium-containing foods were acidic, he claimed, and yang or sodium-containing foods were alkaline. He set the desirable ratio of yin (potassium) and yang (sodium) at something between 3:1 and 7:1.

But potassium and sodium are two metallic elements with such very similar characteristics that it is often difficult to tell them apart—and both are alkaline! Once in the body, however, as electrically charged ions, they are completely complementary *and* antagonistic to one another. Their yin-yang relationship is essential to the body's proper functioning.

Nutritionists, however, talk about two types of food. First, acid or alkaline foods—how acidic or alkaline the *food* is. Second, acid- and alkaline-*forming* foods—the condition the foods cause in the body after they are eaten. Biochemically, the chief alkaline-producing elements are calcium, potassium, sodium and magnesium. These balance the main acid-forming elements of phosphorus, sulfur and chlorine. The alkaline-producing elements keep the blood and intercellular fluids alkaline, in spite of the body's continuous metabolic production of large amounts of acid.

Yin ▽

Fruits
TROPICAL
LEMONS
PEACHES
PEARS
ORANGES, LIMES
WATER MELON
APPLES, CHERRIES
STRAWBERRIES

Beverages
SUGARED DRINKS
FRUIT JUICES
COFFEE
DYED TEAS
MINERAL WATERS
SODA WATER
WELL WATER
HERBAL TEAS
KOKKOH
DANDELION ROOT
BANCHA TEA
BURDOCK ROOT
MU TEA
GINSENG ROOT

Alcoholic Beverages
VODKA
WINE
CHAMPAGNE
WHISKY
SAKE
BEER

Vegetables
POTATOES
EGGPLANT TOMATOES
SHIITAKE PEPPERS
CUCUMBER
SWEET PEPPERS
SPINACH
ASPARAGUS
ARTICHOKE
BAMBOO SHOOTS
MUSHROOMS
RED CABBAGE, BEET
BRUSSELS SPROUTS
CAULIFLOWER
BROCCOLI, CABBAGE
DANDELION LEAF
LETTUCE, ENDIVE, KALE
ONION, GARLIC
PARSNIP, TURNIP.
DAIKON RADISH
LEEKS
PUMPKIN SQUASH
MARROW COURGETTE
WATERCRESS
BURDOCK
DANDELION ROOT
CARROT
JENINJO

Dairy Foods
ICE CREAM
YOGHURT
MILK

GOAT'S MILK

SOFT CHEESES
HARD CHEESES

Sea Vegetables
NORI
HIZIKI
WAKAME
KOMBU

Nuts & Seeds
CASHEWS
PEANUTS
ALMONDS
CHESTNUTS

SQUASH SEEDS
PUMPKIN SEEDS
SUNFLOWER SEEDS
SESAME SEEDS

Beans
SOYA BEANS
GREEN PEAS
WHITE
PINTO
KIDNEY
LENTILS
BLACK
CHICK PEAS
AZUKI

Grains
CORN
OATS
BARLEY
RYE
WHEAT
RICE
MILLET
BUCKWHEAT

Animal Food
SHELL FISH
WHITE MEAT FISH
FOWL
MEAT
RED MEAT FISH
EGGS

Condiments
GOMASIO
TEKKA

TAMARI
MISO

SALT

Yang ▲

This chart, showing the yin-yang relation between the various food categories, is adapted from Ohsawa's original table.

High protein foods, and especially animal foods, contain abundant quantities of sulfur and phosphorus which in the body are acid forming.

Grains also contain some sulfur and phosphorus, and most of them are considered acid forming.

Most fruits and vegetables contain potassium, sodium, calcium and magnesium. They may have a sharp "acidic" taste—but they neutralize body acid!

Ohsawa never classified the difference between acid-forming and alkaline-forming foods, but Herman Aihaha sums it up in his book on the subject: "The characteristics of acid and alkali are very similar to the Oriental concept of Yin and Yang—which is a whole concept of life. Yin and Yang are always changing in our life just as acid and alkali work in us."

Ohsawa classified the yin-yang of elements by using spectroscopy. All elements radiate specific wave lengths: long-wave radiation is yang, and short-wave is yin. According to Ohsawa, sodium has a long-wave radiation and is therefore yang, while potassium produces short-wave (yin) radiation. The spectroscopic colors are interesting—sodium is orange (yang) and potassium violet (yin):

RED $6500\overset{\circ}{A}$	ORANGE	YELLOW	GREEN	BLUE		VIOLET $4289\overset{\circ}{A}$
Hydrogen						
Carbon	Sodium					
		Magnesium			Oxygen	Nitrogen
		Chlorine		Phosphorus		
				Sulfur		
				Calcium		Potassium
						Manganese
			Iron			
			Copper			

YANG ACTIVITY ──────────────────────────── YIN ACTIVITY

Ishizuka and Ohsawa set the ideal ratio of potassium to sodium in man's food at 5:1. It is interesting to note that in a list of food compositions published by Ohsawa in 1938 rice was considered to have the perfect balance of yin and yang; the potassium-sodium ratio was K23:Na4.6, that is 5:1. In 1970 this ratio, according to "Food Values of Portions Commonly Used", Bowes and Church, had changed to K112:Na9, i.e., 12:1. Two other sources, including the United States Agriculture Department, give the potassium-sodium ratio of rice as K214:Na9, which is nearly 24:1! Herman Aihara conjectures that this increase in potassium may be because foods are now much more yin as a result of the fertilizers and chemicals used to grow them.

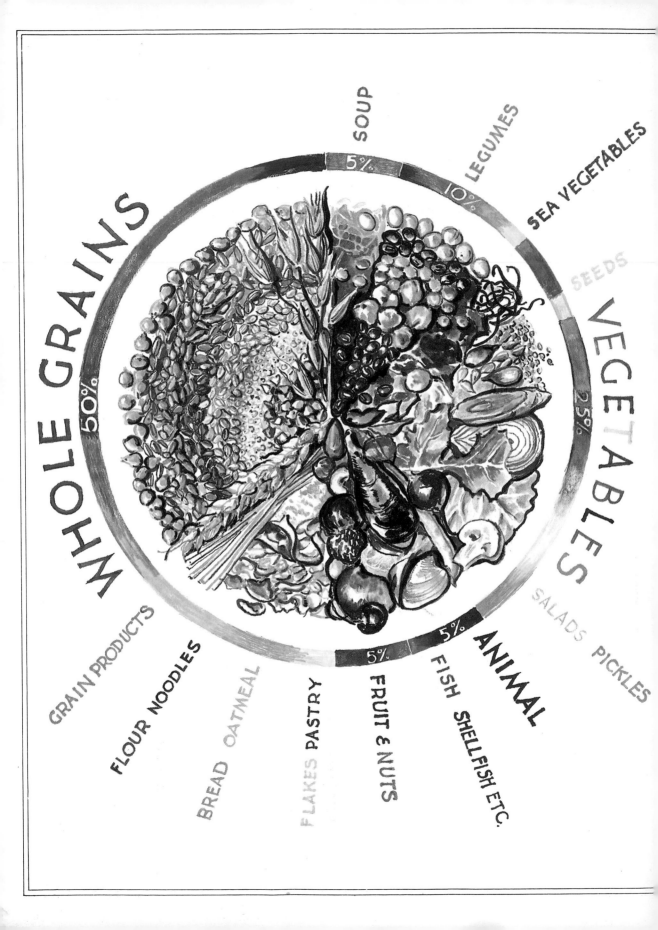

Putting a Meal Together

Soup, approximately 5 percent

Grains, 50 percent or more

Legumes (and Seeds), more or less 10 percent

Vegetables (and Sea Vegetables), about 25 percent

Animal-quality Food, 5 percent or no more than 10 percent

Seasoning

Desserts, Fruits and Nuts, a moderate 5 percent

Drinks

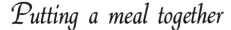

Putting a meal together

This chart is intended to give some idea of the proportions in which each food type can be used when preparing your menus for the day. It is to suit a temperate climate and does not have to be adhered to rigidly. Relax and enjoy preparing and varying your meals. Many hundreds of different meals can be created (and created is the word!) by using different combinations.

Food categories may overlap. Soup to begin a meal might contain grains or beans, certainly sea vegetables or land vegetables and/or fish. Miso soup made from noodles with tofu can contain a little of everything and be a quick meal in itself. Vegetable courses may include salads and pickles when the weather is warmer. Try to use mainly vegetable-quality food, with animal food as an occasional supplement. It's not that you can't eat meat or anything else you wish, but once you get used to the clean, natural taste of vegetables and grains you will find meat rather heavy going. "Man is the prince of animals," said Ohsawa, "We have no need to feed ourselves with meat . . . too much meat protein (yang) results in thrombosis, cruelty and violence . . . vegetables are the supreme food, the normal, logical and pure source of food. Without vegetable life no animal on earth could survive. Our hemoglobin is derived from chlorophyll." And he sums it all up with, "If it can protest or run away—don't eat it!"

Many factors will control the nature and content of your meal. You, the cook, will feel different each time you prepare food, as will your family or your friends. The weather will also be different and the seasonal vegetables available will give you new ideas about putting the ingredients together.

One thing is certain: If you cook calmly and with loving care, taking pleasure in the doing, it will be reflected in the results. Care is probably one of the most important ingredients of any meal.

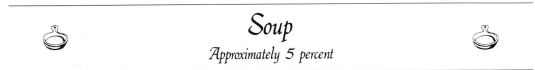

Soup
Approximately 5 percent

Soup is an excellent start for a meal—it can also begin a day well for that matter. You should need no more than one or two cups or bowls of it each day. Good seasonings to use are tamari soy sauce or miso.

For soup stock always keep the water after steaming or boiling vegetables, or make some by bringing water to a boil with a piece of kombu in it. Other sea vegetables can be used, or bonito flakes—to give flavor and texture to soups (see INGREDIENTS—SEA VEGETABLES).

Miso soup can be a meal with a selection of grains or noodles, beans or tofu, with land and sea vegetables. There are several different types of misos (see INGREDIENTS—MISO).

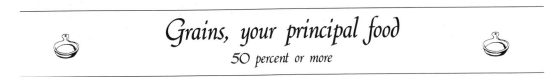

Grains, your principal food
50 percent or more

The principal food—whole cereal grains and their products—should ideally make up 50 percent or more of your day's food and the volume of each meal.

Grains have served mankind for thousands of years and have been the principal food of practically every civilization. They need to remain man's primary food. The length of the human digestive tract is apparently more suited to dealing with grains and vegetables than with animal food.

But how modern man abuses his grains! He refines them, he predigests them, he knocks the life out of them and leaves the polishings rich in nutrients to the animals—who thrive! He then sells his refined grains in the supermarkets—poor, incomplete, unbalanced and unnatural shadows of their former selves! No wonder they are not as popular as they used to be!

Get used to whole grains: They are alive and full of life energy and they are a richer food than the cereal and flour products made from them. When grains are crushed or ground, they lose some of their vitality, especially if stored for any length of time. Flour products also tend to cause mucous in the body.

Chief Grains: Brown rice, millet, barley, whole wheat (bread, pastry, crackers and noodles), oats (oatmeal), maize or corn (cornmeal), buckwheat groats (noodles), rye (bread), etc. (see also INGREDIENTS—GRAINS).

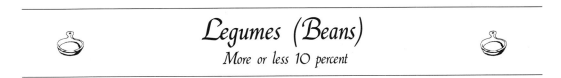

Legumes (Beans)
More or less 10 percent

Beans can be used as a side dish or can be mixed or cooked with your grain. They are useful for soups. There are a number of soybean ferment products such as tamari soy sauce, tofu and tempeh, which bring new flavors to a meal.

The serving of grains and beans together is important. The useable protein is increased considerably when the two are combined.

Beans blend well with sea vegetables. Cooking the beans with some seaweeds such as kombu strips or wakame helps to digest them. The sea minerals tend to balance the fat and protein of the beans.

Chief Beans: Aduki, chick peas, lentils, black turtle and, for less frequent use, pinto, kidney beans, split peas (see also INGREDIENTS—LEGUMES).

Seeds

Seeds can be used sparingly as condiments. They should be washed and roasted or baked briefly, first with some salt or soy sauce; *never* use oil—they already have a high oil content. They are tasty and crunchy sprinkled on grains, beans or vegetables. Try roasted pumpkin seeds sprinkled over your freshly steamed kale. Roasted sesame seeds ground with a small amount of sea salt (gomasio) are often used. Sesame paste is used as a spread (see INGREDIENTS—SEEDS).

use
VEGETABLES
in SEASON
or from a
CLIMATE similar to
your own & preferably
ORGANICALLY GROWN

Vegetables and sea vegetables
About 25 percent

Vegetables range from more modern land varieties down the evolutionary cycle to fungi, sea vegetables and sea moss—all mainly cooked.

Land vegetables: The leaf and root varieties can be used in soups, can be served as separate side dishes or can be cooked with the main grain. They can be sautéed in water (or a little oil), steamed, boiled, baked, fried (using unrefined vegetable or seed oils). Some vegetables need only to be immersed briefly in boiling water. They can be served raw in warmer weather or as a lightly boiled salad or pickles.

Chief Vegetables: More modern species of temperate origin: carrot, burdock, parsnip, daikon (mooli), salsify (and their leaves), cabbage, Chinese cabbage, lettuce, spinach, kale, parsley, watercress, arugola, Swiss char, collard greens, mustard greens, cauliflower, celery, cucumber, squash, pumpkin, onion, leek, scallion (spring onion), green peas, string beans, dandelion, clover, beansprouts, grain sprouts, etc.

More ancient or tropical species: potato, sweet potato, yam, tomato, eggplant, asparagus, green pepper, artichoke, bamboo shoot, okra, beets, lotus root, etc.

More primitive origin: mushroom and other fungi species.

In temperate climates it is not a good idea to use too many of the tropical species. Macrobiotics generally avoid potatoes, tomatoes, and eggplant. These are members of the *solanaceae*, or nightshade family, as are chili, cayenne pepper, tobacco, belladonna and several other poisons and drugs.

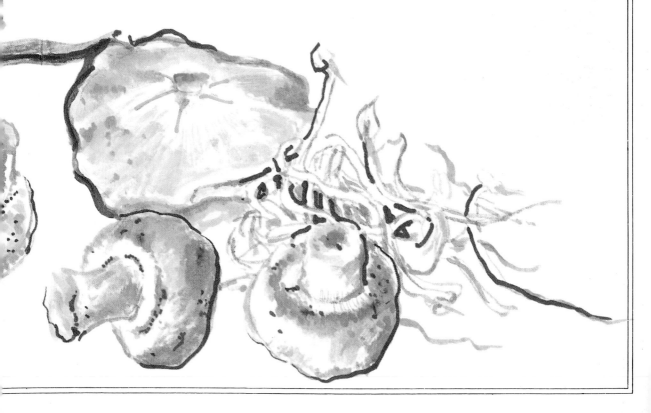

Sea vegetables

About a quarter of your vegetables can consist of sea varieties, which are a very special part of a macrobiotic meal. Incredibly rich in minerals, they can be served as a separate side dish, but they can also be combined with beans and are excellent for soups. Dulse and ulva are delicious in salads. Fresh Welsh laver (same family as nori) can be used as a spread or to make oatcakes.

Before cooking, most dried sea vegetables need only be immersed in water for a minute or two until soft. Soaking in water too long may extract minerals. Always use the same water for cooking the seaweed unless, as with some uncultivated species, deposits of sand or tiny shells remain after soaking.

Sea vegetables can also be roasted over a flame or in the oven, then ground to make condiments to flavor food. Agar-agar and carrageen make fine jellies (kanten), aspic or jellied soup.

Chief Sea Vegetables: agar-agar (kanten), arame, dulse, carrageen (Irish Moss), dulse, hiziki, kombu, laver, nori, wakame (see INGREDIENTS—SEA VEGETABLES).

Animal-quality food
5 percent or not more than 10 percent

If we choose to eat animal food—and in certain colder climates and polar regions man needs to do so—the less highly evolved species such as shellfish and fish are more suitable than are wild bird, chicken, turkey, etc., which in turn are preferable to mammal meats like lamb, beef and pork.

Once or twice a week then, but as a complementary side dish, *not* as a principal food, have some fish or shellfish. Faster moving, dark-meat fish are more yang than are slower-moving white meat fish and shellfish varieties.

Nearly all cultivated animal produce—chicken, pork, beef, butter, eggs and milk are to some extent artificially produced and chemically treated. Wild, free-range birds are less likely to be so than domestic birds, and lamb is preferable to beef or pork for the same reason.

Always serve animal foods with plenty of vegetables to balance the yang.

Chief Fish species: sole, halibut, hake, cod, salmon, trout, snapper, bluefish, whiting, flounder, haddock, smelt, carp, swordfish, tuna, shark, mackerel, sardine, anchovy, eel, etc. and their roes.

Other Seafood: oyster, clam, scallop, mussel, shrimp, lobster, crab, etc.

Chief Amphibian Species: frog, snail, turtle (eggs), etc.

Chief Bird Species: chicken, turkey, duck, pheasant, partridge, etc., and their eggs.

Chief Mammal Species: rabbit, hare, boar, pig, goat, cattle, sheep, their milk and milk products.

Natural Enzymes and Bacteria: Enzymes are produced by the body during digestion. Fermented foods can be used to help this digestion process. The vegetable-based fermented foods are dealt with under the next section on condiments. Enzymes are also present in beer, whisky, wine, sake, and other fermented alcoholic drinks. Chief animal-fermented products are cheese, yoghurt, buttermilk, etc.

Seasoning your food

Food should never taste salty. Use condiments only to bring out the natural flavors. When cooking in a temperate climate, the best seasoning to use is a pinch of *unrefined* sea salt or rock salt, which contains a correct balance of minerals invariably removed from "table" salt. Natural salt is an off-white color because of its mineral content. Refined salt is 99 percent sodium chloride; it is usually iodized and may even contain sugar to make it pour, or magnesium carbonate to bleach it white; phosphate of lime and other substances are also often added.

There are several other vegetable-based fermented foods that are useful for seasoning. Tamari, soy sauce, miso and umeboshi plums are some of these. Each is to be used carefully.

Chief Condiments: sesame salt (gomasio), umeboshi plums, tekka, tamari soy sauce, miso, roasted seaweed powder (see under INGREDIENTS).

FRUIT is the edible flesh around the seeds of plants & contains a great deal of SUGAR.

Desserts, fruits and nuts
A moderate 5 percent

Fruit needs to be used carefully even when in season. Fruit is the edible flesh around the seeds of plants and contains a great deal of sugar. Because of this we tend to devour it in large quantities. Apples, the most yang of fruits, are still much more yin than are vegetables and grains. They are delicious lightly cooked with agar-agar, to make a kanten or jelly. Tropical fruits eaten in cold weather won't help keep you warm.

Natural desserts can be made by using more yang, sweet vegetables—pumpkin or squash pie for example. Sweet brown rice, aduki beans and chestnuts can also be used. Dried fruits and raisins are useful for sweetening or you can use small quantities of barley malt or rice syrup.

Grain products and beans can be used to make rice cakes, puddings, popcorn, pastry, cereals and cookies or crackers.

Chief Temperate Zone Fruits: apples, cherries, peaches, plums, apricots, strawberries, blueberries, blackberries, raspberries, etc., canteloupes and various local melons; watermelon; pears; peaches; grapes; mandarin oranges.

Chief Tropical Fruits: oranges, lemons, limes, pineapple, coconut, mango, papaya, banana, avocado, etc.

A few roasted ground or whole nuts are delicious served over desserts, cooked in cakes or biscuits and added to muesli. Like seeds, nuts taste much better fresh from the shell and roasted. Use sea salt or a little tamari soy sauce to season them from time to time. Don't use oil as they have a high oil content. Nut butters such as peanut butter should be used sparingly. Sesame seed paste (tahini) is preferred, but it also has a high oil content.

Chief Nuts: almonds, walnuts, hazelnuts, chestnuts, pine nuts, cashews, peanuts. The more oily nuts are Brazil nuts and pecans (see INGREDIENTS—NUTS).

What to drink

Macrobiotics emphasizes the fact that we all tend to drink too much liquid. This makes sense when you consider that cooked grains and vegetables contain a great deal of water, which reduces the need for extra liquid.

Try not to drink with your meal—it dilutes the digestive juices, which can cause trouble. Beverages, the last part of the meal, may be taken with dessert or alone when needed.

I think one of the turning points in my drinking career was a moment during a rehearsal break when I found myself throwing several large spoons of white sugar into a cup of the BBC's finest rehearsal-brewed coffee—just to make it palatable. That bitter, milky, chemical taste just wasn't good enough—and it was hard to disguise!

There are no chemical additives in macrobiotic teas or coffees. They are made from herbs and roasted roots, and once you are used to the flavor of nature you will wonder how you could ever have put up with anything else.

Bancha and twig tea are the most refreshing drinks for all occasions. They taste very much like "ordinary" or what some call "normal?" tea but, being free of the additives, they taste cleaner —and do you more good. *Green tea* is more bitter (see INGREDIENTS—BANCHA, GREEN TEA). *Dandelion and burdock roots* and grains can make excellent coffees or teas when roasted. *Mint tea* is not used often, but it is a good digestive and is a refreshing summer drink. *Camomile* tea is good for the vocal chords—by inhaling the steam or as a gargle. *Mu tea* is a combination of herbs and is delicious served with a dash of apple juice (see INGREDIENTS—MU TEA).

Apple juice should be the main summer fruit juice used. Make sure it has no additives. Apples are a fruit local to most temperate climates. Juices are, however, only part of the whole fruit and even sweeter!

Mineral water with a squeeze of fresh lemon juice is a drink for very hot weather. Needless to say, however, carbonated drinks and alcohol are not encouraged! Ohsawa apparently enjoyed his drop of whisky. In fact, different macrobiotic books suggest different alcoholic beverages. They seem to vary according to the preference of the author! Some suggest a good-quality beer or cider, while others advocate sake, and Ohsawa ordered his whisky neat—they *are* mainly grain products I suppose! Michio Kushi advises that, "Small amounts of fermented or alcoholic beverages may be taken *before* the meal if the first part is soup . . . to smooth the appetite and digestion!"

Chief Beverages: bancha tea, twig tea (*kukicha*), maté tea, green tea, mu (herb) tea, dandelion tea or coffee, burdock tea, comfrey tea, unsweetened grain coffee, roasted barley tea (*mugicha*), rice or other grain teas and other traditional nonaromatic teas.

Fermented Alcoholic Beverages: beer, cider, sake, whisky, wine, etc.

Any Questions Before Cooking?

Why Organic Foods?

Why Fruits and Vegetables in Season?

Why Whole Foods?

Why Less Animal Foods?

Which Pots and Pans?

What Other Utensils?

Preparing Vegetables

Serving and Eating the Meal

Why organic foods?

Vegetables grown organically are sometimes difficult to find in big cities. Such vegetables can cost more, too, if they aren't covered with insecticides—"artificial protection science misguidedly offers us"—but if the insect won't eat these products, why should we?

Some people say you can't tell the difference between an organically and a chemically grown product, but you generally can. The larger, more colorful and shinier the fruit, the more likely it is to be puffed up with fertilizers or sprayed with hormone mixtures. It may look appealing on the supermarket shelves, but the natural flavor will almost certainly be missing. Smaller fruits and vegetables are more yang—Ohsawa says that a small red apple has a lower potassium-sodium ratio than a large green one. Those highly colored carrots (probably dyed!), straight and clean (probably grown in fertilized sand), and probably waxed to make them shine will have to be scraped thoroughly. If they are crooked shapes, are somewhat dusty with tops attached (valuable greens—use them!) they are probably organic as advertized and only need a rinse or gentle scrub with your bristle brush before cooking.

Why fruits and vegetables in season?
(Or from a similar climate?)

Tropical fruits and vegetables are fine when eaten where the sun blazes down, but in the depths of an English winter or a New York snowstorm they can make us feel the cold. They are more yin, designed by nature to balance the yang, hot weather conditions in which they grew. Eating them continually—and people who come from tropical climates to live in colder places tend to do so—can cause a great deal of unhappiness and sickness. Imported foods also need to be treated with preservatives in order to travel. Fruits and vegetables are allowed by law to be washed with retarding agents, to be treated with anti-sprouting agents or with enzyme inhibitors to prevent further growth.

Fruit juices come under this category. They are generally synthetic anyway, with chemical flavorings to delight the palate. Even real, fresh orange juice may be alright for a Spanish or Moroccan summer or a Florida beach (in moderation!) but should not become a daily habit. Pure apple juice made from organically grown apples is a better fruit drink for a summer—but check the labels for additives and use it moderately. Remember, there are quite a few parts of the fruit missing from the juice.

Why whole foods?

There are huge vested interests in converting natural whole foods into precooked, processed food in order to make your life simpler in the kitchen and to control the shelf life of the product. During processing, however, literally thousands of chemicals, drugs, preservatives, stabilizers, softeners, sweeteners, alkalizers, acidifiers, emulsifiers, hormones, dyes, anti-oxidants and hydrogenants all find their way into our diets without our realizing it. According to the London Food Commission Food Report, Autumn 1985, two thousand tonnes of additives are now used each year by British manufacturers alone—over eight pounds annually per consumer! Dietary diseases resulting, it claims, from our consumption of so much processed starch, fat and sugar, cost the National Health Service over £1 billion a year. They will go on doing so unless we consumers do something about it! Such foods include those brightly colored bottles of soda, soft and iced drinks, sugared sweets, saccharine syrups, all artificially flavoured, those crisps, jellies and incandescent iced lollies (popsicles) we ply our kids with to please them. ("They might as well eat their school chemistry set," the above Food News report dryly observes.) The TV commercials for all these products are lavish because the manufacturers are very rich.

The food value of such products is, on the other hand, usually very poor. Perhaps one of the most serious causes of deprivation in our affluent society is the removal of vital nutrients from our chief food sources: bread, flour and grains. White bread, white flour, white rice and—the worst of all—white sugar! Ohsawa said that the harmfulness of white sugar is much more terrible than is imagined. Try to avoid sugar and sugar products. The natural sugar content of fruits and vegetables is really sweetness enough (see VITAMINS, CARBOHYDRATES, SUGAR).

Why less animal foods?

There is a seventeenth-century English proverb: "Much meat, much maladies," and today's nutritionists are practically unanimous about the effects of eating too much meat. It does contain protein, but fish or grains with beans can contain as much, if not more. Michio Kushi suggests that of the thirty teeth in our head twenty of them are premolars suitable for grinding grains and cereals, eight are incisors for cutting vegetables and four are canines for tearing at food. He thus arrives at the proportion of twenty-eight teeth for vegetable-quality food to four for animal quality—his golden ratio of 7:1! While total vegetarians may need to watch their vitamin B_6 and B_{12} supply, meat eaters need to exercise their own form of caution: Nearly all cultivated animals or their produce—chicken, pork, beef, butter, eggs and milk—are chemically treated at some stage. If you ever go in a shed full of caged, drugged chickens with their beaks cut, you will wonder about the quality of the meat and eggs being mass-produced there for you.

"Animal meat," said Ohsawa, "is the ideal composition for an animal unaccustomed to thinking . . . cow's milk is, after all, intended to be nourishment for calves!" Milk intake is now being associated with some alarming diseases. Meat, milk and eggs are high in cholesterol and saturated fats (see THE BODY—A LABORATORY? PROTEIN, CALCIUM and SATURATED FATS).

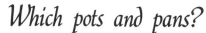

Which pots and pans?

One nutritionist writes, "Copper can neutralize and aluminum poison your vitamin supply." Macrobiotic cooks Wendy and Edward Esko recommend heavy cast iron pans and skillets. The latter are certainly extremely useful, but a strong right arm is sometimes needed to handle the larger ones. They do distribute the heat evenly, but there is a possibility that too much iron may be served with the food if iron pots are used exclusively (see MINERALS—IRON).

Ceramic pots are good for cooking grains and beans. They need a flame deflector or cast-iron stand to prevent strong direct heat, and sudden temperature changes can crack them. Any pan needs to be left to cool before pouring cold water over it. Even cast iron will suffer from this treatment.

Stainless-steel pots, especially with reinforced heavy bottoms, are practical. Use lower heat, though, as they absorb heat directly and can burn the food. A stainless-steel pressure cooker is usually recommended: They save fuel and cook food quickly. Pressure yangizes the food, too.

Pyrex pots and ovenware are more fragile, but they are light, clean and pretty to handle. You can see what is going on while the food is cooking.

Enameled iron pots are useful, but they do chip, and the enamel scratches if metal or wire wool pads are used to clean them.

What other utensils?

There are several other items you can buy for the kitchen. Some you will own already if you enjoy cooking.

Wooden spoons and ladles won't scratch your pans and are kind to the food.

A natural bristle brush is ideal for gently scrubbing your root vegetables under water.

A good vegetable knife with a carbon steel blade is probably the best investment. It cuts cleanly and helps you make attractive patterns of your vegetables to decorate a meal. You will need a sharpening stone, which is quite therapeutic to use. The carbon steel blade needs sharpening only along one side of the cutting edge. Stainless steel blades are fine, but they can chip.

A wood chopping block—a good sized one—for your vegetable cutting is a must. Oil it with sesame oil from time to time and try not to wash it with soap. Just wipe it with a wet cloth before starting and between each differently flavored vegetable.

Glass or ceramic jars, or even wooden ones, are useful for storing your grains, beans, nuts, etc. Make sure the tops are an airtight fit.

A grinding bowl or suribachi, with a wooden pestle for grinding your sesame salt, mixing your miso thoroughly, making salad dressings, creams, puréeing food for babies, etc., are also useful—and decorative.

Sushi mats are helpful not only for making sushi but for covering your pots to keep the food warm or cool.

A bamboo strainer is available to strain your bancha or twig tea.

A stainless steel steamer is one of the best instruments for preparing vegetables. After a minute or two, greens turn a vibrant, chlorophyll color, which means they're ready to be eaten.

A grater. A flat one for general use is the most practical. There are also some attractive China ones for grating ginger that are now available.

Preparing vegetables

Vegetables need to be kept alive and fresh until the moment you cook them. First wash them carefully—roots need a gentle scrub—but soaking them for hours in gallons of water destroys their vital nutrients.

Cutting vegetables can add to their appearance and help balance their yin-yang quality. That sharp knife is needed, but be careful of your fingers! Keep them out of harm's way by curling them under at the first knuckle of the fingers holding the vegetable. Place the side of the blade against your knuckle and the front end of the cutting edge gently on the vegetable and push smoothly away from you the full length of the blade. Try not to saw backward and forward or to treat the vegetables too roughly. Roots are usually sliced on the diagonal, and vegetables such as onion, for example, from top to bottom rather than across to include as much of their yin-yang property in each portion as possible. The top of a root is more yin than is the base. There are several patterns you can make—triangular, half moon, diced, matchsticks, chrysanthemums, rectangles, quarters and flowers. Roots such as carrots and

burdock also can be shaved as you would sharpen a pencil or rolled as you cut them. Keep the pieces small.

It has been said before and will be said again—keep your vegetable water after cooking and use it for soup stock, sauces, etc. Most leaf vegetables need only to be boiled briefly in a little water or steamed for a minute or so and they are ready. It's a good idea to plunge vegetables quickly into boiling water to seal them and protect water-soluble vitamins as much as possible.

Never use too much oil either when sautéing. You generally need only brush the pan or skillet with oil and use low heat. Avoid commercial cooking oils, recooked animal fats, lards, margarines, etc. Sesame oil, corn oil, soy, sunflower or safflower oils are the best to use. Make sure they are cold pressed or unrefined. Extracted oils have usually been subjected to high temperatures, which changes the quality of the oil. Heating your pan until the oil smokes can mean a loss of vitamin E (see THE BODY—A LABORATORY? FATS. For deep-frying see INGREDIENTS—TEMPURA, OILS).

Serving and eating the meal

Having prepared your meal with care, be careful now not to pile the plates high with mounds of grains or to fill the bowls to the brim: large portions can be daunting. "Sometimes," said Ohsawa, "when confronted by an Occidental vegetarian meal I feel as sad as if I had been turned into a horse because of the coarse consistency of the food." ... "The quantity of the food changes the quality," he said. "You can have too much even of a good thing." Ohsawa took the view that every disease is caused by excess in diet, and he claimed he never saw one patient who was suffering from lack of food. Grains in particular can look and taste unappetizing if not served well. They generally need a sauce of some kind. Always prepare *and* present the food with an awareness of the yin-yang balance of textures, tastes and colors.

Before eating the meal you have prepared—or that has been prepared for you—give yourself a moment's calm to think and to be grateful. Don't rush at it.

Gandhi said, "Chew your drink and drink your food." Chew each mouthful of food at least thirty times. Ohsawa suggests fifty—even a hundred or more—as stress on the jaws might help curb excess indulgence! This makes good sense, as saliva lubricates and begins breaking down our food before it is swallowed, and the pressure of chewing is also yang. Chewing helps calm your body as the miracle of digestion begins.

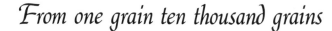 *From one grain ten thousand grains*

I was staying in a large and luxurious hotel on film location for a few weeks where the chef kindly cooked some brown rice for me. Being greedy, I asked if I could have a second helping, but the waiter said it had already been thrown out. "Everything," he said, "*had* to be."

This brought home the incredible waste of food that must take place daily in hotels and restaurants all over the world. I thought of the macrobiotic maxim, a small voice in a big world, "*From one grain ten thousand grains.*" If everyone in the world threw away just one grain of rice we would lose enough grains to feed a million, and from each of these grains might grow ten thousand to feed some billion more.

My arithmetic isn't all that good, but the maxim brings with it a sudden sharp awareness of how precious food is. Prepare natural food carefully, eat it with gratitude and appreciate it to the last grain.

The names of some of these new, natural ingredients may sound strange to you, but don't be discouraged! They have been introduced from different parts of the world and from different cultures—some from the Orient, some from the Middle East, Europe and Russia; the Welsh and the Irish still use sea vegetables, and the Scots know their oats—or did before oats were refined and packaged! Properly prepared, these new supplies are a real food source and have been used as such for centuries in their places of origin. Most traditional foods were in fact originally well balanced—and macrobiotic!

The better cook you are the more fun you are going to have experimenting with them, and the better your cooking will be because the quality of your raw materials is vastly improved. The difference it can make to the texture, flavor—and benefit—of your meals is unbelievable.

The food content lists are averages of different food samples and the absence of a particular nutrient (—) by it does not necessarily mean that it is not in that particular food but that reliable information may not be available. (See *About the food contents lists* at the end of this section, p. 93.)

AGAR-AGAR (See SEA VEGETABLES and KANTEN.)

AMAZAKE

Amazake is a sweet rice ferment sold as a drink now. It has the texture of milk because it is blended and strained and can be used to make jellies and creams. Unblended, it has the texture of rice pudding and is, in fact, delicious as such.

Here is a recipe for homemade amazake.

1 cup brown rice
4 cups water
1 cup sweet brown rice (koji)
Pinch salt
1 cup warm water

1. Bring 1 cup brown rice to a boil in 4 cups of water. Turn heat down and simmer gently for an hour, or until the water has been absorbed. The rice should be soft. Let cool for 10 to 15 minutes.
2. Mix the koji and rice in a glass or ceramic bowl with a pinch of salt, and add the warm water (1 cup) to keep the mixture from sticking to the pan.
3. Cover the pot and incubate at body temperature (95°) for 6 to 8 hours, either by leaving on a "low" electric plate or covered in a very low oven or even in a warm cupboard.
4. After it has incubated, the amazake should taste sweet. Bring to a boil (add a little more water if necessary but only to keep it from sticking). Boil for 5 to 10 minutes.

> 5. Let cool. Refrigerate in a glass bowl or jar.

Amazake can be used to make rice pudding by adding a teaspoon of lemon peel, ½ teaspoon cinnamon and ½ cup raisins. It will serve 6 to 8. It can also be blended if a smoother texture is desired (see also INGREDIENTS—KOJI).

ADUKI BEANS (AZUKI) (See LEGUMES.)

BARLEY MALT

Barley malt is a sweetener or grain honey made from sprouting barley that is cooked into a sweet syrup. Nothing else is added: The barley is steeped in water to soften it, is germinated and then heat is applied to dry the malt and bring out the flavor. A syrup is produced that contains dextrins, maltose, dextrose, minerals and protein.

Because it is less sweet than either honey or maple syrup, you may be tempted to use too much when cooking (see also CHEMISTRY OF CARBOHYDRATES, p. 219).

Food Content of Barley Malt (per 100g): calories, 295; protein, 3.5g; carbohydrates, 67.5g; calcium, 80mg; phosphorus, (−); iron, 2.0mg; sodium, (−); potassium, (−); vitamin B_1, 0.04mg; vitamin B_2, 0.035mg; niacin, 4mg; vitamin C, 8mg. (*Source: USDA*)

BANCHA TEA

Bancha is sometimes called *kukicha* and sometimes *three year tea*. Bancha, in fact, means "three tea," i.e., the plant from which it was picked was at least three years old when harvested. *Kukicha*, on the other hand, means "twig tea" and this tea is made mainly from the twigs of the same plant. It is harvested late in the year, when the caffeine content is at its lowest level. It is roasted three times or more to improve the flavor and to reduce the tannic acid content. The twigs of kukicha have an even lower caffeine content than do the leaves of bancha.

They are both good, general purpose drinks. They will give you a gentle lift at any time of the day. Bancha (and kukicha) are prepared like ordinary tea, a teaspoon per person and one for the pot, but it is more economical if boiled for ten minutes in a stainless steel or enamel pot on the stove. You have only to add water and reboil it to make further supplies.

BONITO FLAKES

Paper-thin flakes shaved from the dried fermented bonito fish (*hanakatsuo*) are used for soup stocks or to garnish soups or noodles.

BROWN RICE (See GRAINS.)

BROWN RICE VINEGAR

This is vinegar made from fermented brown rice in agricultural communities of Japan. Organic brown rice is used with a white rice *koji*, seed vinegar from the previous year and well water. The fermentation takes nine or ten months. Brown rice vinegar is sharp in flavor and is useful for salads and for keeping vegetables fresh. It is good sprinkled over grated daikon radish or on a sea vegetable salad. A salad dressing can also be made by mixing it with apple juice or lemon juice and a little olive or sesame oil. It will add piquancy to sauces.

BUCKWHEAT or KASHA (See GRAINS.)

BURDOCK ROOT (*Artium lappa*)

This wild, hardy, thistlelike plant is common to the Northern Hemisphere—England, northern Europe and the United States. The Japanese name for it is *gobo* and the entire plant—young leaf, stems and the root—can be used. The leaves for salad and greens and the root will give your cooking a rich, earthy flavor. According to herbalists the long, black root is one of the finest blood purifiers, and is of benefit to rheumatism sufferers; used externally, it will help skin ailments. It is even claimed to be a sexual restorative in the Orient. It is certainly one of the most yang roots.

Before cooking, burdock root will need washing and a gentle scrub. Slice it diagonally or in matchsticks or whatever pattern you decide, then soak the sections in water for ten to fifteen minutes to prevent discoloration (the water will go green). Burdock needs to be cooked longer than do most root vegetables. It can also be purchased as an unusual and invigorating herbal tea. Boil the dried, dark brown chips in water (1 teaspoon per cup) for five to ten minutes.

Food Content of Burdock (per 100g): calories, 75; protein; 4.1g; fat, 0.1g; carbohydrate, 16.3g; calcium, 47mg; phosphorus, 71mg; iron, 0.8mg; sodium, 45mg; potassium, (−); vitamin B_1, 0.3mg; vitamin B_2, 0.05mg; vitamin C, 2mg.

CAROB (ST. JOHN'S BREAD)

Carob is a legume or bean and belongs to the locust family. The edible pods and beans from this tall, green, shady tree have been a source of food for thousands of years for humans and animals. When St. John the Baptist lived in the wilderness on locusts and wild honey it was the dark, purple carob or locust bean—not the insect—he was enjoying! And a very "yin" diet it would seem to be! The use of carob is increasingly recommended in place of chocolate which contains caffeine and needs to be artificially sweetened—usually with white sugar—which carob does not. Carob flour is regarded as interchangeable with chocolate powder and is a good substitute for it in cooking cakes and desserts.

Food Content of Carob (per 100g): calories, 175; protein, 5.0g; fat, 1.25g; carbohydrate, 81.3g; fiber, 8g; calcium, 350mg; phosphorus, 75mg; iron, 4.25mg; sodium, (−); potassium; (−).

DAIKON OR MOOLI

This long, white radish root is sold by many greengrocers now and is used by Chinese cooks. It makes a delicious side dish or a salad served grated with a few drops of tamari soy sauce or umeboshi vinegar or grated with carrot. It also makes a refreshing pressed salad, or it can be cooked in soups, stews, etc. It is good for the digestion of oily foods and is said to "cut" fat and mucous deposits in the body.

Daikon greens are also a rich food source. Boil them quickly as green vegetables, or steam them.

Food Content of Daikon (per 100g): (greens in brackets) calories, 19 (49); protein, 0.9g (5.2g); fat, 0.1g (0.7g); carbohydrates, 4.2g (8.5g); fiber, 0.7g (1.4g); calcium, 35mg (190mg); phosphorus, 26mg (30mg); iron, 0.6mg (1.4mg); sodium, (−) (100mg); potassium, 180mg (−); vitamin A, 10, IU (3,000 IU); vitamin B_1, 0.03mg (0.1mg); vitamin B_2, 0.02mg (0.3mg); vitamin B_3, 0.4mg (0.5mg); vitamin C, 32mg (90mg).

DASHI

Probably the most important ingredient of noodle dishes is the broth in which they are served. Here is a recipe for "dashi," which is a clear soup made as follows:

8 cups water
2 strips kombu, each 6" long
2 teaspoons bonito flakes
3 shiitake mushrooms
½ cup water
2 tablespoons tamari soy sauce
2 tablespoons mirin (optional)

1. Place kombu in water and bring to a boil.
2. Add bonito flakes and simmer for 10 minutes.
3. Soak mushrooms for 10 minutes in water. Remove stalk ends and slice finely. Add mushrooms and soaking water to kombu and bonito flakes.
4. Simmer for 30 minutes. Add tamari and mirin. Serve with noodles.

Serves 4 to 6

48

Oats

DENTI
This is black tooth powder made of sea salt and charred eggplant (aubergine). The powder is used as a gargle before brushing the teeth. It will also stop bleeding if applied to cuts.

DULSE (See SEA VEGETABLES.)

GENMAICHA
This is a green tea mixed with roasted, puffed rice. It has a unique sweet flavor.

GINGER
Ginger is a golden-colored, pungent, spicy root vegetable with a multitude of uses as a condiment in cooking. This tropical plant is now grown in many hot countries such as Australia. Because of its shape the root is called "hand" or "finger" and is said to have medicinal properties. A compress made with grated ginger and very hot water will stimulate circulation, "dissolve stagnation" and help kidney problems, stomach aches and intestinal problems such as constipation and diarrhea (*not* appendicitis), stiffness of shoulders and joints, sinus troubles, cysts and neuralgia—even toothache.

Here is a recipe for making a ginger compress:

8 cups water
3 tablespoons grated, fresh ginger
1 piece cheesecloth, 6" square

1. Bring water *almost* to a boil and remove from heat.
2. Tie the cheesecloth around the ginger and drop it into the hot water.
3. Let the ginger stew, covered, for 10 minutes. The water will become milky.
4. Squeeze the juice from the cheesecloth and remove it from the hot water.
5. To apply a compress, roll up a cotton towel or cloth. Hold each end and dip the center into the hot ginger water. Keeping the ends dry will enable you to wring out excess water without burning your fingers.

    Place the hot compress over the affected area. It should be as hot as you can stand it. Cover with a thick, dry towel to keep in the heat. When the compress has cooled (5 minutes or so), repeat the process several times until the skin has become red.

Food content of Fresh Root Ginger (per 100g): calories, 49; protein, 1.4g; fat, 1.0g; carbohydrates, 9.5g; fiber, 1.1g; calcium, 23mg; phosphorus, 36mg; iron, 2.1mg; sodium, 6mg; potassium, 264mg; vitamin A, 10 IU; vitamin B_1, 0.20mg; vitamin B_2, 0.04mg; vitamin B_3, 0.7mg; vitamin C, 4mg.

GOMASIO (See SEEDS—SESAME SALT.)

GRAINS

Grains are the edible fruit seeds of cereal grasses. To many people they are synonymous with animal fodder, but in fact until a couple of hundred years ago, when industrialization began, whole grains had been the staple food of all major civilizations. They have always been of first importance in supporting life and were always eaten whole. However, particularly over the last thirty or forty years, there has been a drastic increase in commercial processing. Natural nutrients are extracted from grains, depleting our supply and upsetting the natural fundamental balance in our diet, depriving us of a rich source of vitamins and minerals. Refined grains are generally pretty tasteless, far less satisfying to eat and certainly less nourishing. The insecticides, additives, bleaches and dyes used on them in the various processes they undergo haven't improved them either!

The rediscovery of the whole and vital grain is perhaps the most exciting aspect of macrobiotics; certainly no meal seems complete without them. However, you need to learn to cook them well and serve them with some seasoning, vegetables or sauce. I had a woman come to my dressing room one night complaining that she'd tried "my" brown rice. She had, she confessed, only cooked it for fifteen minutes! Whole grains take rather longer to cook than the processed, precooked stuff—usually about forty minutes to an hour. Put them on while you prepare the rest of the meal. Remember that grains contain that vital force of new life and are better eaten whole than as flakes or flours which, if eaten too often, tend to cause mucous in the body. One macrobiotic cook I met referred to flour as "dust!" Even the simple process of milling grain into flour can destroy its natural balance and some of the nutrients it contains. The whole grains also last longer than when ground into flour. They can be kept for up to a year or more in airtight containers in a cool, dark place. Flours need to be used within a few months. For this reason hand grinding mills are becoming popular. The flour is made when needed.

There are several types of grains and many delicious ways to prepare them as the main course of your meal.

BARLEY (Hordium vulgare)

Barley is believed to be the oldest cultivated grain. It is a relation of the rice plant and a native of Mesopotamia, where it was used to make breads and was fermented to make beer. There are traces of barley cultivation at neolithic sites dated 8000 BC in the Middle East, and there are numerous references to it in the Bible. Ancient settlements in Egypt (4500 BC) and Switzerland (3000 BC) show how long it has been used by mankind. In the Sumerian civilization, from around 4000 BC, it was used as monetary currency—so many sacks for a day's work. By the Middle Ages in Europe, it was chiefly replaced by wheat and rye, but as barley is an adaptable grain that grows in different climates, it is still the staple food of many countries in the Far East, Asia, Middle East and parts of Europe and South America. The people of Tibet consider it their most important food. In North America it is used mainly to make beer and alcoholic drinks or to feed livestock. In Scotland it is still used today for cooking the classic Scotch broths, and malted barley is used to make whisky, gin and beer. In Japan barley is called *mugi* and a tea made by roasting the grains and then boiling them in water is called *mugicha*. There is also a delicious *Mugi*-miso. Barley cooked by itself has a rather bland flavor but when combined with rice or other grains it makes them much lighter in texture. Barley is an excellent food that is high in nutrients and lower in fat than most other grains. Pot or Scotch barley is less refined than is light, pearled barley, which is the partially polished berry. Barley is delicious in soups, of course, or in vegetable-grain dishes, pies or stuffings. You can roast the grains and grind them into flour to make bread or pastries.

To cook barley:

1 cup barley
4-5 cups water
Pinch salt

1. Wash the grains and soak overnight— some cooks soak barley for two days.
2. Place grains in pot and add a cup of water and salt. Bring to a boil.
3. Turn down heat, cover and simmer gently for 1½ hours. Add more water if necessary.
4. Serve hot, garnished with chopped scallions or parsley and gomasio or tahini sauce.

Barley can be roasted before cooking for a change of flavor. It will then cook a little faster.

Food Content of Barley (pearled) (per 100g): calories, 349; carbohydrates, 79.0g; fiber, 0.4g; fat, 1.4g; protein, 8.2g; calcium, 16mg; phosphorus, 189mg; sodium, 3mg; potassium, 160mg; iron, 2.0mg; sulfur, 240mg; magnesium, 35.7mg; vitamin A_1, nil; vitamin B_1, 0.17mg; vitamin B_2, 0.05mg; niacin, 3.1mg; vitamin C, nil.

BUCKWHEAT (*Fagopyrum esculentum*)

Buckwheat was probably first cultivated in central Asia, north of the Himalayas and from there was taken westward to eastern Europe and eastward to China and Japan. It is also known as Saracen corn and is thought to have been brought to Europe by the Crusaders. It has been common in Japan for 2,500 years. Buckwheat is not, in fact, botanically a grain: the plant is related to dock and rhubarb, and its fruit is a small, dark, three-sided nut which resembles a miniature beechnut. In Britain until recently it was cultivated mainly to feed pheasants and livestock, but in Russia and central Europe *kasha* is a popular staple food. There is a story told of a Russian Olympic team who arrived in Paris, couldn't find any buckwheat and caught the next plane back to Moscow! One of my favorite dishes is buckwheat "burgers" or croquettes, but it also makes a good porridge.

Buckwheat flour is difficult to extract from its sheathlike husks. As it is a heavy, dark flour it is often mixed with lighter rice or wheat flours, and is used for muffins or biscuits. In Japan the flour is used chiefly to make noodles called *soba*. These noodles are sometimes made from 100 percent buckwheat flour or more traditionally from 80 percent buckwheat and 20 percent whole wheat flours. They are a useful standby for your menus and can be added to soups (see INGREDIENTS—NOODLES). There has recently been an increase in the popularity of buckwheat pancakes. These are made in restaurants in France and other countries, but the batter is often prepackaged and can contain white sugar.

Buckwheat contains more protein than other grains as well as the amino acid lysine in which grains tend to be low. It is rich in iron and the B complex vitamins and is the best natural source of rutic acid, which helps arteries and circulatory ailments: For this reason homoeopathic doctors prescribe it for high blood pressure and chilblains. It is also reportedly good for the lungs, kidneys, bladder and water retention. It is one of the more yang of the cereals, as it grows in very cold climates and the groats are small and compact. Evidently, insects do not attack it, and it fares poorly if chemicals are used on it. Although noodles can be eaten all year round, it is better to eat buckwheat groats more in the cooler seasons, as they generate body heat. Buckwheat is available in a roasted or unroasted form. To help the flavor, re-roast for five minutes before cooking. The unroasted grains should be roasted in a dry skillet for ten to fifteen minutes. Stir to avoid burning.

Food Content of Buckwheat (per 100g): calories, 335; protein, 11.7g; fat, 2.4g; carbohydrates, 72.5g; fiber, 9.9g; calcium, 33mg; phosphorus, 282mg; iron, 3.1mg; sodium, 6.1mg; potassium, 235mg; vitamin A, nil; vitamin B_1, 0.6mg; vitamin B_2, 0.15mg; niacin, 4.4mg; vitamin C, nil.

CORN or MAIZE (*Zea Mays*)

Corn is native to South America, where it has been used domestically for 10,000 years and has become the staple grain food and a source of flour or meal for the entire American continent. The name "corn" can cause confusion. To the English corn means wheat, to the Scots corn means oats, to the Americans it means corn on the cob. The reason for this is that when the early English settlers saw it they christened it Indian corn. The Indians worshiped the *Zea Mays* plant and called it "seed of seeds." Christopher Columbus introduced it to Europe where it became known by a variety of names: "Rhodes corn" in Lorraine, "Syrian *doura*" in Bayonne, "*il gran tusco*" in Italy, "Turkish corn" in Germany and Holland and "Christian Corn" in Turkey! Other voyagers took corn to Africa, India, Japan and China, and today it is grown all over the world, from Argentina to Queensland, from Asia to the plains of Lombardy. Corn needs hot sun and summer rainfall to flower and is more yin than the other cereals. It's a miraculous plant for it grows quickly, virtually producing itself, but bread from cornflour, cornmeal cakes or popped corn do not make adequate staple food. The niacin content of corn is bound to other substances and is not released in the body. The Indians in Mexico and Peru eat beans with *tortillas* and treat their corn with lime, which makes the niacin more readily available and adds to the calcium content. In times of famine in Europe during the Napoleonic wars, corn was the only food available and came to be associated with an epidemic of pellagra, a niacin-deficiency disease. This probably accounts for the fact that European farmers still regard corn mainly as animal food.

Corn makes corn syrup, corn oil, corn on the cob and one particular variety is used to make popcorn. Bourbon is a product of fermented corn. Sweet corn (as it is called in England and Australia) or corn on the cob (in America) is grown as a vegetable but is much too sweet to be dried and ground into flour. There is also *flint corn*, the successor to the original "Indian corn," which is hard and difficult to grind and is used mainly to feed animals. *Dent corn*, which "dents" on the top when it dries, is used to make flour and cornmeal although it is considered nutritionally inferior to other types. The poorest corn, foodwise, is the most popular—popcorn.

The flour made from corn is often white and processed and although it is a good thickening agent it is not, nutritionally, of much value. Stoneground, whole-grain, unsifted (unbolted) cornmeal is the type to buy. If it is whole-grain it has not had the valuable germ removed. "Sifted" or "bolted" means it has been put through a mesh to produce a finer-textured product. Cornmeal can be used as a supplementary grain to make desserts, breads, muffins, sauces, gravies, corn fritters, tempura batter and a variety of other dishes.

Food Content of Corn (per 100g): calories, 96; protein, 3.5g; fat, 1.0g; carbohydrates, 22.1g; fiber, 0.7g; calcium, 3mg; phosphorus, 111mg; iron, 0.7mg; sodium, trace; potassium; 280mg; chlorine, 112mg; sulfur, 368mg; vitamin A, 400 IU; vitamin B_1, 0.15mg; vitamin B_2, 0.12mg; niacin, 1.7mg; vitamin C, 12mg.

MILLET (Panicum miliaccum)

A native of Asia, millet once rivaled barley as the chief food of Europe and was more widely grown than wheat in the seventeenth and eighteenth centuries. In China it was a popular food before rice was introduced there, possibly around 2000 BC. It is still a staple food in northern China, India, Korea and Ethiopia. In Japan where it is also a traditional food it is called *awa* but is now used mainly for making millet *mochi* or to feed the parakeets! The most common millet in Britain is the bead-shaped, foxtail, Italian or yellow millet. Again it is the birds who benefit but in the West today millet is now coming under closer scrutiny as it is an essential food of the Hunzas, a remarkable tribe living in the Himalayan foothills, famed for their longevity and fitness.

Millet is a small, hard and round grain; it is grown in cold climates and is the only yang, alkaline-forming grain. It is good for spleen or pancreas disorders and settles an acid stomach in no time! Millet lacks gluten, so that bread made from the flour does not rise very high but does have a good protein content, although not as high as wheat. It contains more iron than any other cereal and is well balanced in amino acids.

Millet is a very versatile food and especially long lasting. It will keep for at least two years—some reports say up to twenty—and can be used in vegetable dishes, soups, stuffings or cabbage rolls. It makes excellent croquettes (particularly with aduki beans), muffins and pastries, or it can be eaten as a cereal. Its color is attractive and complements other foods well. As with most grains, millet should be washed and can be toasted before cooking.

To cook millet:

1 cup millet
4-5 cups water or vegetable stock
Pinch salt (per cup of millet)
1 teaspoon tamari soy sauce

1. Place in pan, add water and salt and bring to a boil.
2. Boil vigorously for 5 minutes. Lower heat, cover and simmer for 30 to 40 minutes, or until water has disappeared. Do not stir or disturb grain.
3. Diced vegetables can be added—carrots and parsley for color, or onions.

Food Content of Millet (per 100g): calories, 327; protein, 9.9g; fat, 2.9g; carbohydrates, 72.9g; fiber, 3.2g; calcium, 20mg; phosphorus, 311mg; sodium, (−); potassium, 430mg; magnesium, 162mg; iron, 6.8mg; silicon, 160mg; vitamin A, nil; vitamin B_1, 0.73mg; vitamin B_2, 0.38mg; niacin, 2.3mg; vitamin C, nil.

OATS (Avena sativa)

Oats have been harvested since Neolithic times. They are native to Central Europe, and the wild oats common in Britain are thought to be the original ancestors of the modern cultivated variety. They are a staple food in Scotland, where they are thought to be good for the eyes. They are, in fact, rich in inositol, a B complex vitamin. Oats have one of the highest protein contents of all the grains. They are rich in calcium and iron. One brawny young Scot interviewed on TV declared that he ate oat porridge (flavored with salt) every day because it made him sexy! Oats do contain some zinc, which can help the male in that respect. Carl C. Pfeiffer gives the zinc content of oatmeal as 14mg per 100g. Oats have a high fat content, but they also contain soluble gums which bind cholesterol in the intestines, thus preventing its absorption.

Oats have, in fact, been found effective in lowering the amount of cholesterol in the blood.

Oatmeal or rolled oats are generally eaten as porridge. If they are marked "quick cooking," they are usually smaller and have been preheated before they were rolled. The larger "hulled" or "gritted" oatmeal has not been heated. Steel cut oats are better, but whole oats are by far the most satisfying. Oat flakes may be used for cereals, as a basis for summer breakfast muesli, for crumbles, cakes and puddings. Whole oats combine well with other cereals such as rice or millet to make a smooth mixture for croquettes, and are beautiful in soups. Oatmeal can be used to make breads and desserts.

To cook whole-oats porridge

1 cup whole oats
5-6 cups water
Pinch salt (per cup of oats)
½ cup soy milk

1. Wash the oats.
2. Place in a pot and bring to a boil; add salt.
3. Reduce heat to low and cover. Use a flame deflector mat to prevent sticking and simmer for 2 hours. Add more water if necessary.
4. Add soy milk and stir in.

The oats can also be placed in boiling water and left, covered, in a very low 210°F oven overnight to be ready in the morning. Use 1 cup oats to 4 cups boiling water. This makes really beautiful cereal.

Food Content of Oats (per 100g): calories, 313, protein, 13.0g; fat, 5.4g; carbohydrates, 66.1g; fiber, 10.6g; calcium, 55mg; phosphorus, 320mg; iron, 4.6mg; sodium, 10mg; potassium nil; zinc, 14mg; vitamin A, nil; vitamin B_1, 0.30mg; vitamin B_2, 0.10mg; niacin, 1.5mg; vitamin C, nil.

RICE (*Oryza sativa*)

"Brown rice should be the staple of your diet. It is an excellent food, low in fat and rich in vitamins and minerals," says nutritionist Nan Bronfen. She is speaking from a scientific, not a macrobiotic point of view. Rice, like wheat and many other cultivated grains, is native to the dry valleys of Central Asia. Interestingly enough early Chinese civilization didn't know rice at all—their staple grains were sorghum, wheat and millet in the North, and yams in the swampy south. Aquatic rice is thought to have become established in India and to have reached China by 2000 BC, spreading from there to Indonesia. Rice did not play a particularly important part in Japanese diet either until as late as the seventeenth century. Today more than half the world's population lives mainly on rice, and it is incredible that the rice grown and eaten in many overpopulated areas should be commercially refined "white" rice, and that those people continue to be deprived of the many natural nutrients that whole grain rice contains. In its whole grain form rice is high in nourishing protein, calcium, iron, B vitamins, etc., but many of these are lost in processing and polishing, when the valuable outer layers are removed (see HOW VITAL ARE VITAMINS?, p. 226).

I remember craving a bowl of brown rice and vegetables during a stay in Hong Kong. I couldn't get it anywhere. I finally found a shop selling whole-grain rice, took it back to the hotel and asked the waiter if they could cook some in the kitchen for me to eat in an hour's time. He looked astonished and explained that it would take much longer as he would have to polish each grain before it could be eaten! A Dr. Williams, who first extracted Vitamin

B_1 in an oil from rice bran, said, "Man commits a crime against nature when he eats the starch from the seed and throws away the mechanism necessary for the metabolism of that starch."

Whole-grain or brown rice is referred to as "soul food" by Ohsawa who said it had the perfect balance of yin and yang. You are not expected to live on rice alone, but it will certainly be an important, central part of your diet. It is convenient for daily use, and it will help calm you when you are feeling edgy from dietary overindulgence or in times of stress or sickness. Learning to cook it well is, of course, one of the first lessons of macrobiotics. The principal varieties of rice available at most wholefood stores are short-grain rice, medium grain and long grain. The harder, more compact short-grained rice is the more yang and is better suited for eating in cooler and temperate climates. The long-grained rice is better for warmer regions and hot weather. Cooked rice can be stored in a cool place or can be refrigerated, reheated, steamed, baked or fried, made into rice balls (croquettes), used in soups, salads, desserts, breads, for sushi rolls, vegetables pies, casseroles or pilaf, paella or stuffings.

There are a multitude of uses for rice on the menu. There are even crisp rice cakes on the market, which make an excellent alternative to bread.

Make sure your rice is whole grain and be careful when buying it—a large percentage of green grains means the rice is not ripe. Broken or chipped rice has been badly milled and cannot be stored for long as it will readily oxidize. Use organically grown rice if possible. It should say if it is organic on the package. If it doesn't, it isn't!

Whole grain rice takes longer to cook than do the commercial "white" varieties packaged for you in the supermarkets. The time it is cooking can be spent preparing the rest of the meal the vegetables or sauce to go with it.

To cook brown rice:

1 cup whole-grain brown rice
3 cups water
Pinch sea or rock salt (per cup of rice)

1. Wash the rice quickly and immediately before cooking it.
2. Place in a ceramic, stainless steel, cast iron or enamel pot—with a heavy lid preferably. A flame deflector mat is useful to keep the rice from sticking. Add water and salt. Bring to a boil.
3. Let the rice boil vigorously for 5 to 10 minutes, then cover with the lid, lower the heat and simmer gently for 30 to 40 minutes, or until the water has disappeared. Do not stir or disturb the grain. If the heat is very low it will not burn.
4. Turn off heat and let stand for 10 minutes, or until ready to serve. Use a wooden ladle or spoon to serve.

Serve with a little tamari soy sauce and sesame salt or a sauce made with sesame butter and miso.

To make the rice fluffier, the grains can first be dry-roasted in an iron skillet or can be plunged directly into boiling water. In both cases the cooking time is slightly shorter.

To pressure-cook rice:

1 cup brown rice
2 cups water
Pinch sea or rock salt

1. Wash the rice quickly just before using it.
2. Place in pressure cooker and add water and salt (never fill cooker more than half full with grain).
3. Cover and turn heat to high. When the gauge begins to hiss, turn heat to medium low. Place a flame deflector mat under pan.
4. Cook for 40 to 45 minutes. Remove from heat and leave to depressurize (15 to 20 minutes).
5. Lift gauge gently to check that pressure is down before removing lid.

Food Content of Brown Rice (per 100g): calories, 360; carbohydrates, 77.4mg; fiber, 0.9g; fat, 1.8g; protein, 7.5g; calcium, 32mg; phosphorus, 220mg, sodium, 9 mg; potassium, 216mg; iron, 1.6mg; sulfur, 10mg; magnesium, 88mg; selenium, 39mg; copper, 0.2mg; manganese, 1.6mg; zinc, 1.8mg; silicon, 40mg; iodine, 0.002mg; vitamin A, nil; vitamin B_1, 0.34mg; vitamin B_2, 0.04mg; vitamin B_6, 0.5mg; niacin, 4.7mg; vitamin C, nil.

RYE (Secale cereale)
Rye is probably of south west Asian origin. In fertile soil it grows to 7 to 8 feet in height. To the Greeks it was a vigorous weed. The Romans began cultivating it. By the Middle Ages it was the staple grain throughout Europe, and the basic English loaf was made from roughly ground rye and barley! Germans still use it to make pumpernickel bread, and both Russians and Scandinavians prefer the flavor of dark rye bread. Whole rye flour is dark in color. There are also "light" and "medium" rye flours available, which have been sifted and contain less bran. Commercial pumpernickel breads are often made with the "light," refined flour and are colored darker by the addition of caramel, molasses, instant coffee or coffee substitues. Always choose the least processed darker flour. In Scandinavia rye is used for crisp bread. Early settlers from Holland took rye seeds with them to America, where it is now used chiefly for animal food and is fermented to produce whisky. The Russians make beer from it.

Rye is similar in composition to wheat but is less glutenous; it is, though, more resistant to cold, disease and pests. These are the only two grains that can be used by themselves to make bread. The protein in rye is less elastic, and the bread is heavier. But rye scores highly for taste. It is often mixed with wheat flour in bread recipes, and such bread is better if naturally leavened—up to twenty hours of slow rising. Rye can be made indigestible by leavening agents. There is a new high-protein grain called *triticale*, which is a cross between wheat and rye.

Rye is delicious mixed with rice. It is cooked the same way as rice and may be cracked with a rolling pin for faster cooking.

Food Content of Rye (per 100g): calories, 334; carbohydrates, 73.4g; fiber, 2.0g; protein, 12.2g; fat,

1.7g; calcium, 38mg; phosphorus, 376mg; sodium, 1mg; potassium, 467mg; iron, 3.7mg; sulfur, 28mg; magnesium, 115mg; silicon, 30mg; iodine, 0.001mg; vitamin A, nil; vitamin B_1, 0.43mg; vitamin B_2, 0.22mg; niacin, 1.6mg; vitamin C, nil.

WHEAT (*Triticum aestivum/durum*)

Said to be native to Mesopotamia, wheat has been the "staff of life" and main food of temperate regions since recorded time. Egyptians, 4,000 years ago, isolated yeast and baked exotic, high-domed, coiled and plaited breads. Most of Cleopatra's "treacherous vessels" were used for carrying bread to Rome. Wheat seeds were taken to Britain and Gaul by the Romans, and a primitive variety of it, called *emmer* has been found in prehistoric village excavations in Britain. Columbus, in 1492, took wheat with him to the West Indies. Cortes, in 1519, took it to Mexico. The English distributed it to their colonies and shipped it to Australia, North America and South Africa—and that versatile grass has flourished in all climates! There are many different varieties. In Canada the hard, red winter wheat, developed in drier areas and containing 11 to 15 percent protein, has the type of gluten best for making bread. The softer wheats from more humid areas, contain less protein (8 to 10 percent) and are usually used for cakes and pastries. Naturally, only flour from whole grains and preferably stoneground should be used. Macaroni, spaghetti and pasta products are made from the hard *durum* wheat semolina (semolina flour refers to the large particles left after sifting out the fine white flour). *Cous cous*, which is popular in North Africa, is made from wheat that is refined (but not bleached) and then cracked. It cooks very quickly. *Bulghur* is a form of whole wheat berries from which the outer, tough bran layer has been removed. The grain is then partially boiled, dried and cracked; as it is partially precooked it can be eaten after boiling for 10 minutes or so. It is used extensively in the Middle East and features in salads. Bulghur and cous cous are more yin and are better suited to hot climates. They have lost some of their nutritional value in processing and are better used only as supplementary foods.

White flour: Vicki Peterson in *The Natural Food Catalogue* tells of white flour, which was popular in the Middle Ages, when bakers treated it with chalk, alum, arsenic powder and even ground-up bones from the graveyard! Today it is likely to be bleached with chlorine dioxide, which is also used to clean household drains!

Wheat germ: is *not* now generally recommended by nutritionists. It deteriorates rapidly, being high in fat, and is very likely to be rancid even if you purchase it freshly processed. Being a plant extract, it is yin and causes imbalance (see VITAMINS).

Whole wheat grains can be cooked. Soak them first, overnight, then bring to a boil in four or five times their volume of water. Simmer for one and a half hours, or until the grains have split open and are soft. They can then be made into croquettes, they can be mixed with rice or vegetables or simply added to soups. A traditional English dish called *frumenty* uses currants boiled with the cooked wheat.

Food Content of Hard Spring Wheat (per 100g): calories, 330; carbohydrates, 69.1, fiber, 2.3g; fat, 2.2g; protein, 14g; calcium, 36mg; phosphorus, 383mg; sodium, 3mg; potassium, 370mg; iron, 3.1mg; magnesium, 160mg; sulfur, 9mg; silicon, 46mg; iodine, 0.001mg; bromine, 0.15mg; vitamin A, nil; vitamin B_1, 0.57mg; vitamin B_2, 0.12mg; niacin, 4.3mg; vitamin C, nil.

GREEN TEA

All teas, in their numerous forms, come originally from the same plant; various blends derive their different flavors and fragrances from the way the tea leaves (or twigs) are processed and cured. The tea plant was transplanted from China to India by the English, and Japanese tea also had its origins in China. A priest named Eisai, a Zen Buddhist of the twelfth century, was apparently evangelical in his enthusiasm for tea and attributed to it such benefits as clearness of thinking and longevity. Tea grew well in Japan, where Eisai took it, and it became so popular there that the mystique attached to it, influenced by Zen, became formalized in the practice called *sado*, or the tea ceremony.

Green tea can be harvested at any time of the year. The leaves picked are the young ones, but the later in the season they are picked the less caffeine and tannin they contain. *Green tea should not be boiled*. It needs only to be steeped for several minutes in hot water in a pot. A quarter of a cup of dried tea leaves will provide enough tea for four people. The tea need not be dark in color, and the leaves can be steeped three or four times. It is, of course, not drunk with milk and sugar, but its slightly bitter taste is good at the end of a meal or with desserts.

Green tea mixed with roasted, puffed rice is called *Genmaicha* and has a special, sweet flavor.

HATCHO MISO (See MISO.)

HIJIKI (See SEA VEGETABLES.)

KANTEN (AGAR-AGAR)
This is jellied dessert or aspic made from agar-agar, which sets firmer than gelatin and does not melt as readily.

Seasonal fruit can be used in the kantens—strawberries, cherries, blackberries, blueberries, peaches, pears, apples, raisins, etc. Melon should not need to be cooked—simply pour the hot juice and agar-agar mixture over it and allow it to set. Kanten is also made as a savoury aspic by using vegetable stock or water and tamari soy sauce with sliced vegetables, sea vegetables, fish or even aduki beans (See also SEA VEGETABLES).

KASHA or BUCKWHEAT (See GRAINS.)

KOJI (*Aspergillus oryzea*)
This is a light green mold widely used for fermenting food products such as miso, shoyu, amasake, sake and koji pickles. The role of koji is to trigger fermentation by providing nutrients needed by yeasts and bacteria. During its growth it produces enzymes that convert proteins, fats and starches to simpler and more readily fermented substances. Koji is sensitive and reacts to small temperature and humidity changes. It thrives best at about 95°F, which is close to body temperature, and prefers a humidity of 80 percent. Koji can be purchased in some whole food stores.

KOME MISO (See MISO.)

KUKICHA
This is a Japanese twig tea (see also BANCHA TEA).

KUZU
Kuzu is high-quality starch used like arrowroot or as a very effective medicine. It is made from the root of the kuzu plant, which is native of the mountains of Japan and now grows

wild in the southern United States, where it is called *kudzu*. It grows like a vine, wrapping itself around trees, often to a height of 30 feet. The tough roots grow deep into the ground, and the extraction of the starch from them is done by hand, which is a long and expensive process.

During early winter, when the sap and vitality of the plant is concentrated below, its roots are pulled from the soil. This work requires men, picks, shovels, winches, levers and, at times, oxen as well, as some of the roots have grown straight into mountains to a depth of fifteen or twenty feet. They can be several yards long, and some are as wide as a man. From them soft, white, chalklike kuzu is made; it contains more calories per gram than honey, but unlike honey, which is quick-burning sugar, kuzu is a long-sustaining source of energy and is easily digested. Although in appearance it resembles arrowroot, which is indigenous to tropical areas, it is a quite different product. It is usually packaged in small irregular lumps, which disperse quickly in cold water to make a milky liquid. When heated and stirred over low heat the liquid suddenly becomes clear. It makes an excellent thickener for Chinese-style vegetable sauces, it can be used in soups or in sweet jellies with kanten (see AGAR-AGAR). Kuzu helps digestion, and since ancient times it has been popular in Japan as a treatment for colds and intestinal ailments. Here are some recipes for kuzu remedies:

Kuzu, Umeboshi and Ginger: A drink to combat colds and the flu.

3 cups cold water
1 teaspoon kuzu
1 umeboshi plum
Juice of 1 tablespoon grated ginger

1. Dissolve the kuzu in the cold water and add the ginger juice and umeboshi plum.
2. Bring gently to a boil, stirring until the liquid clears.
3. Cover and simmer for 20 minutes. Add more water if mixture becomes too thick.
4. Serve as a hot drink, or sprinkle on a little tamari soy sauce and eat as a soup.

Kuzu, Umeboshi and Soy: For digestive disorders, diarrhoea, etc.

2 cups water
1 teaspoon kuzu in ½ cup of cold water
1 umeboshi plum
1 teaspoon tamari soy sauce

1. Dissolve kuzu in a little water and mix with the water and umeboshi plum.
2. Bring to a boil, reduce heat and simmer for 5 minutes. Stir to avoid lumps.
3. Add tamari soy sauce and serve hot.

Food Content of Kuzu (per 100g): calories, 336; protein, 0.2g; fat, 0.1g; carbohydrates, 83.1g; fiber, nil; calcium, 17mg; phosphorus, 10mg; iron, 2mg; sodium, 2 mg; potassium, (−); vitamin A, nil; vitamin B_1, nil; vitamin B_2, nil; niacin, nil; vitamin C, nil.

LAYERING METHOD (*NICHIME STYLE*)

This is a method of cooking vegetables, soups and stews in which the ingredients are placed in the pan with the more yin ones at the bottom and the more yang at the top. They are then allowed to cook, in a little water, undisturbed.

LEGUMES

Leguminous plants include peas and beans—seeds from a pod that opens lengthwise when ripe. Next to cereals they are the most vital human food source. They contain many nutrients and more protein than any other vegetable product—often more than meat, fish and eggs. They are a great protein booster when eaten with grains as they contain amino acids that cereals lack (see PROTEIN). They are useful in farming, as their roots harbor bacteria which convert nitrogen into nutrients that in turn enrich the soil. Members of the legume family include aduki beans, soybeans, blackeyed peas, pinto, mung, lentils, black turtle, red kidney, navy, pink, lima, split peas and garbanzos (or chick peas). Peanuts are botanically classified as legumes, as are olives, the wisteria vine, some poisonous weeds such as loco weed, laburnum, wild lupins and ornamentals such as the sweet pea.

Beans are also a good source of calcium, iron and vitamins B_1 and niacin. Germinating bean sprouts, when the life force is activated within the seed by moisture and warmth, manufacture a rich source of nutrients needed for growth: amino acids and vitamins A, E and B, including possibly Vitamin B_{12}, which is so difficult to find in plant life. After a few hours of germination, a seed develops vitamin C, which was completely lacking in its dry state. Certain beans can manufacture six times more vitamin C than can an equivalent amount of citrus fruit.

People sometimes complain that beans are difficult to digest, and there is a proverb in China that says, "A man who eats too many beans becomes a fool!" Too many can lead to intestinal problems, irritability and unclear thinking, but if prepared and eaten properly, digestibility should really be no problem. The amount of water and salt used, the soaking time (and changing the soaking water before cooking), the cooking time and, as with all food, the *chewing time* are all important for proper digestion. Serve as a side dish rather than as the main food of the meal, or try adding them to grains, noodles, vegetables or sea vegetables, even to fruit or raisins to make a dessert. They are interesting, too, when cooked together.

If they are properly stored in airtight containers in a cool place away from moisture and insects, beans can keep well for several years.

Cooking Legumes

You are your own processor when it comes to preparing wholefoods and, before cooking, beans should be spread on a cloth and sorted for any stones or bits and pieces, washed thoroughly and soaked for some hours, sometimes overnight. *Discard the soaking water.* Another aid to their digestion is to place one or two strips of kombu or wakame sea vegetable in the pan. The beans should then be placed in fresh water (1 cup beans to 4 cups water), brought to a boil, covered, the heat reduced to low and cooked for anything from 40 minutes to 3 hours (depending on the type of bean—soybeans may need 4 hours or more!). Then add 3 tablespoons of tamari soy sauce or ¼ teaspoon of sea salt or rock salt per cup of dry beans and cook, uncovered, for another 15 minutes to an hour, or until they are soft and most of the water has evaporated. If salt is added to the beans too early when cooking, the skins will harden.

When pressure cooking beans use only three cups of water to one cup of beans, and generally cook for around 45 minutes; remove the cover and add salt or tamari soy sauce and cook, uncovered, until the liquid evaporates.

Legumes can also be "shocked" during cooking. To avoid this barely cover them with water, and while they are cooking keep adding just enough cold water to keep them covered. Pour the water slowly down the side of the pan.

Beans may also be baked. Boil them for 20 minutes first in 4 to 5 cups of water for each cup of beans. This will loosen their skins. Place a kombu strip in the baking dish, add water and beans, cover and cook in a 350°F medium oven for 3 or 4 hours. You may need to add more water after a couple of hours. You can also add diced onions, carrots or other root vegetables and can season with miso or tamari soy sauce. If you want to make a dessert, add raisins, apples, etc., during cooking.

ADUKI or AZUKI BEANS (Phaseolus angularis)
The seeds of a "bushy" annual that is native to China and Korea were little known in the West until the advent of macrobiotics, but they are now being grown organically in Europe and America. In Japan the small, compact bean is called the "king of beans" and is said to be good for the liver and kidneys. Aduki is considered one of the more yang beans and can be used in soups, pies, pizzas, to make patés or can be served with vegetables, sea vegetables, roasted pumpkin or sunflower seeds, etc. They make a nourishing and satisfying side dish, or they can be used with grains for croquettes.

Soak aduki for at least an hour or two before cooking. This will save cooking time. Cook as described above, with a strip of kombu, for 1¼ hours, then uncover, sprinkle with tamari soy sauce and salt, increase heat and cook another 20 minutes, or until most of the water has evaporated. Try diced carrot, pumpkin or squash (marrow) added with the tamari for variety. In China and Japan aduki are used in desserts—try cooking them with 1 cup raisins per 1 cup of aduki. This makes a delicious kanten.

For kidney complaints boil 2 tablespoons of beans in 8 cups of water until soft (1½ hours). Add a dash of tamari soy sauce, drain and drink a little three times a day.

Food Content of Aduki Beans (dry) (per 100g): calories, 326; protein, 21.5g; fat, 1.6g; carbohydrates, 58.4g; fiber, 4.3g; calcium, 75mg; phosphorus, 350mg; iron, 4.8mg; sodium, 20mg; potassium, 1,500mg; vitamin A, 6 IU, vitamin B_1, 0.5mg; vitamin B_2, 0.1mg; niacin, 2.5mg; vitamin C, nil.

BLACKEYED PEAS (Vigna unguiculata)
This bean has many names: cowpea, kaffir bean, Hindu cowpea or yard-long bean (the asparagus cowpea, which has pods up to 3 feet in length). This legume has a distinctive black eye and originated in Africa, where it is still a staple food. Explorers took it to America and the West Indies in the seventeenth century, and it is very popular throughout the southern states of the US. Today it is cultivated all over the tropical world. In Africa the dried seeds are roasted and ground into a coffee substitute, the young shoots eaten like spinach and the pod used as a green vegetable. Blackeyed peas become tender with cooking and absorb other flavors well.

Food Content of Blackeyed Peas (cooked) (per 100g): calories, 108; carbohydrates, 18g; protein, 8.1g; fat, 0.79g; fiber, 4.3g; calcium, 24mg; phosphorus, 146 mg; sodium, 1.2mg; potassium, 379mg; iron, 2.1mg; zinc, 1.8mg; magnesium, 55mg; vitamin A, 351 IU; vitamin B_1, 0.3mg; vitamin B_2, 0.1mg; niacin, 1.4mg, vitamin C, 17mg.

GARBANZOS/CHICK PEAS (Cicer arietinum)
Garbanzo is the Spanish name for chick pea. They are also known as *Egyptian peas, Bengal gram, pois chiche* and *ceci* (in Italy). These peas grow in curious hook-shaped pods and can be white, yellow, brown, red, or almost black. Their origin is rather uncertain. Chick peas

grew wild in Egypt at the time of the pharaohs. They are thought to have originated in western Asia and to have been introduced from there to Palestine and Mesopotamia and eastward to India. Explorers and merchants took them to Africa and South America. Today they are grown commercially as far abroad as Australia. They are a staple of the Middle East and are milled into flour, are roasted whole or are ground after cooking and used to make *hummus* and *falafel*, or deep-fried patties. Chick peas also appear in many European and Oriental recipes.

Chick peas need soaking for a long time—overnight is best. Use 2 cups of water per cup of peas. Pour away the soaking water and pressure cook in 3 cups of fresh water for an hour and a half (three hours in 4 cups of water without a pressure cooker). Add salt and simmer another hour. Be sure the water level is always above the beans otherwise they can be difficult to soften. It is a good idea to use a large strip of kombu when cooking them. As a variation, add diced onion with the salt for the last half hour.

Food Content of Garbanzo (dry) (per 100g): calories, 360; carbohydrates, 61.0g; fiber, 5g; protein, 20.5g; fat, 4.8g; fiber, 4.9g; calcium, 150mg; phosphorus, 331mg; iron, 6.9mg; sodium, 26mg; potassium, 797mg; sulfur, 110mg; zinc, 2.7mg; vitamin A, 50 IU; vitamin B_1, 0.31mg; vitamin B_2, 0.15mg; niacin, 2.0mg; vitamin C, 5mg; folic acid, 0.19mg.

KIDNEY BEANS (*Phaseolus vulgaris*)

There are hundreds of different varieties of kidney-shaped beans: French beans, haricot beans, calico beans, navy beans, pinto beans, green and wax beans, snap beans, common beans, red kidney beans, black turtle beans, *frijoles* or *spoca*. The American invention, baked beans in tomato sauce, sold in cans the world over, are haricot beans. "Boston beans" are a recipe made with pork by early American settlers from beans given to them by the friendly Indians who had cultivated kidney beans or French beans since prehistoric times. Columbus gave detailed descriptions of them growing in Cuba in 1492 and later, in Honduras, he saw the same plant with red or white seeds. These beans became a valuable source of nonperishable protein for sailors and explorers on such expeditions. The kidney bean was brought back to Europe in the sixteenth century and reached England through France in 1589 to be christened the French bean. These are the young pods and are prepared as a green vegetable. Snap beans have fibrous strings along the pod, which need to be removed before boiling. Navy beans are dry, mature seeds and have been developed to be resistant to disease. They are usually white in color. Black turtle beans are a shiny, black variety of the common kidney bean. They are a staple food throughout the Caribbean, Central and South America and Mexico. Fried black beans and rice are the national breakfast dish of Costa Rica and are known as *galli pinto*. Cook with kombu to keep the skin from becoming too soft. All dried varieties of *Phaseolus vulgaris* are better cooked with kombu. Red kidney beans will have a creamier texture too if instead of adding tamari soy sauce and salt for the last twenty minutes you place one or two teapoons of miso (per cup of cooked beans) on top and cover with a lid. Mix only when cooking is completed.

Food Content of Red Kidney Beans (cooked) (per 100g): calories, 117; carbohydrates, 21.4g; protein, 7.8g; fiber, 1.5g; fat, 0.5mg; calcium, 37.8mg; phosphorus, 140mg; sodium, 3.2mg; potassium, 340mg; iron, 2.4mg; copper, 0.34mg; vitamin A, 5.4 IU; vitamin B_1, 0.1mg; vitamin B_2, 0.05mg; niacin, 0.7mg; vitamin C, 3mg; folic acid, 0.03mg.

Food Content of Black Turtle Beans (dry) (per 100g): calories, 339; carbohydrates, 61g; protein, 22.3g; fat, 1.5g; calcium, 135mg; phosphorus, 1,038mg; sodium, 25mg; potassium, 1,038mg; iron, 7.9mg; vitamin A, 30 IU; vitamin B_1, 0.56mg; vitamin B_2, 0.2 mg; niacin, 2.2mg; vitamin C, (–).

LENTILS (Lens esculenta)

The biblical "mess of pottage" that Jacob gave Esau was made of lentils, one of the earliest cultivated crops in the East. It would seem that a traveling Seventh Day Adventist from Germany introduced them to America when he gave some to an obviously enterprising farmer who proceeded to cultivate them.

There are many different varieties of lentils, usually identified by their color—green, red, orange, yellow, brown or black. They play an important part in Indian cooking in various types of *dal*. Lentils are richer in protein than any of the other legumes except soybeans. The pink and red varieties from India contain more protein than do the other types. In third world countries their calorific value has earned them the name of "poor man's meat."

Lentils do not need much soaking, although it is said that soaking helps to digest them. They cook comparatively quickly—in 45 minutes to an hour. Remember that the longer you cook beans and the softer they are the more easily they are digested. Add ¼ teaspoon of sea salt (per cup of lentils) and cook a further 20 minutes, or until most of the water has evaporated.

Food Content of Lentils (cooked) (per 100g): calories, 106; protein, 7.8g; fat, trace; carbohydrates, 19.3g; fiber, 1.2g; calcium, 25mg; phosphorus, 119mg; iron, 2.1mg; sodium, 30mg; potassium, 249mg; copper, 0.27mg; zinc, 1.0mg; vitamin A, 20 IU; vitamin B_1, 0.07mg; vitamin B_2, 0.06mg; niacin, 0.6mg; vitamin C, nil.

LIMA BEANS (Phaseolus lunatus)

There are several varieties of lima bean and they come in two sizes: the larger is the butter bean and the smaller is called the sieva bean. Other names for it are curry bean or pole bean. Apparently, lima beans were discovered in pre-Inca tombs in Peru dated 5000 BC and were common in America when Columbus arrived there. The Spanish *conquistadores* took them to the Phillipines, and by the seventeenth century the lima bean was growing in hot areas all over the world. It is still, today, the main legume crop of tropical Africa and is called Madagascar bean there. It has never survived colder regions and has to be imported into the U.K. and Europe, where "butter beans" have long been popular canned, dried or frozen. The white beans are usually preferred, probably because raw lima seeds contain a poisonous element, *organogenetic glycoside*, and the white bean is considered less toxic than the darker types. *Prolonged soaking and boiling removes this toxin.* Being a tropical bean it is considered, with soy beans, the most yin of the legume family. It is a good idea to roast them in a dry skillet and soak them overnight before cooking with a yang vegetable such as burdock root or lotus root. They shouldn't be eaten too often and must be chewed well.

Food Content of Lima Beans (cooked) (per 100g): calories, 138; carbohydrates, 25.6g; protein, 8.20g; fiber, 1.6g; fat, 0.6g; calcium, 29mg; phosphorus, 154mg; sodium, 2.7mg; potassium, 612mg; iron, 3.1mg; zinc, 0.89mg copper, 0.57mg; vitamin A, 30 IU; vitamin B_1, 0.13mg; vitamin B_2, 0.05mg; niacin, 0.68mg; vitamin B_6, 0.18mg; vitaming C, 1mg; folic acid, 0.04mg.

MUNG BEANS (Phaseolus mungo or vigna mungo)

In India, where this bean was cultivated before recorded history, it is known as *moong dal* and is used to make flour. This bean is popular throughout Asia today. In the East it is made into porridge with a little glutinous rice. Indonesians use it against protein deficiency and, in Malaya, large quantities of mung bean gruel are consumed after the Ramadan month of fasting. In China it is the small green type that is commonly sprouted and used to make noodles.

As they can contain up to 37 percent protein and are considered a rich source of vitamin B$_2$ and vitamin C, mung bean sprouts are useful—and delicious—served cold in salads or cooked with vegetable dishes. In India the rare *black gram bean* is important among the high castes, and the golden seed is gaining popularity in America and Europe.

Food Content of Mung Bean Sprouts (raw) (per 100g): calories, 35.2; protein, 3.8g; fat, 0.2g; carbohydrates, 6.6g; fiber, 0.67g; calcium, 19mg; phosphorus, 64mg; iron, 1.3mg; sodium, 5mg; potassium, 223mg; zinc, 0.86mg; vitamin A, 19 IU; vitamin B$_1$, 0.13mg; vitamin B$_2$, 0.13mg; niacin, 0.76mg; vitamin C, 19mg; folic acid, 0.008mg.

PEAS (*Pisum sativum*)

The common garden pea, *petit pois*, *mangetout*, snow pea or marrow fat pea, is marketed according to its size and sugar and starch content. Split peas are the dried peas without their skins. This annual climber prefers northern climates but can also be grown in more tropical areas. The history of the pea is, in fact, one of the longest and most illustrious of the legumes. Some historians even believe it originated in the Garden of Eden—that is, between the Euphrates and Tigris rivers. Remains of it have been found in the ruins of Troy, in predynastic Egyptian tombs and at the site of a Neolithic lake village in Switzerland dated 4500 BC. The Greeks prized it, the Romans cultivated it, it spread to Abyssinia and Africa, reaching Asia by 400 AD. From there it was taken east to India and west to Europe where, by the Middle Ages, it was one of the most important legumes. In the seventeenth century, at the court of Louis XIV, aristocrats were consuming large platesful of fresh, young green peas after visiting the theater, according to Madame de Maintenon's diary! The French fashion caught on in England and peas are popular as a green vegetable to this day. Unfortunately they are more often canned or frozen and are likely to contain green coloring and sugar. This is because of "popular demand" say the manufacturers! Split peas have held their own and cook more quickly than other legumes. Soak them overnight. *Petit pois* are the very young, small peas that have a lower sugar content. They are used in freezing and canning.

Food Content of Split Peas (cooked) (per 100g): calories, 115; protein, 8g; fat, 0.15g; carbohydrates, 20.8g; fiber, 0.4g; calcium, 11mg; phosphorus, 89mg; iron, 1.7mg; sodium, 13mg; potassium, 296mg; copper, 0.25mg; vitamin A, 40 IU; vitamin B$_1$, 0.15mg; vitamin B$_2$, 0.09mg; niacin, 0.9mg; vitamin C, nil.

Food Content of Green Peas (cooked) (per 100g): calories, 71.3; protein, 5.4g; fat, 0.4g; carbohydrates, 12.1g; fiber, 2g; calcium, 23mg; phosphorus, 98.8mg; iron, 1.8mg; sodium, 1.3mg; potassium, 136.3mg; copper, 0.15mg; zinc, 0.75; vitamin A, 538; IU; vitamin B$_1$, 0.28mg; vitamin B$_2$, 0.11mg; vitamin B$_6$, 0.15mg; niacin, 2.3mg; pantothenic acid, 0.34mg; vitamin C, 20mg.

SOYBEANS (*Clycine max*)

The seeds of the soybean are small and oval in shape and vary in color from yellow through grey and brown to black. The bean, also known as *haba soya* or *preta*, is native to China and for thousands of years has been called "the meat of the earth" in the Far East. Modern analysis has proved the title an apt one: the soybean is one of the few sources of so-called high-quality protein. It is an outstanding protein booster and can increase usable protein substantially when eaten with grains, which have a shortage of lysine (see THE BODY—A LABORATORY? PROTEIN COMPLEMENTS). Soybeans were first recorded in 2800 BC by the Emperor Shen Nung, who described them as one of the most important crops in his country. Use of the bean spread to Japan and Korea. It was taken to Europe in 1712 by a German botanist, Engelbert Kalmpfer, and samples were grown in the hothouses of Kew Gardens in England. As early as the eighteenth century its nutritional qualities were appreciated but not until the twentieth century did the bean begin to be produced commercially in the West. By 1969 the American government had subsidized over 41 million acres for soybean cultivation. America now leads, with China, in commercial soybean production, which has become big business not only as food but for industrial use as well. Paint manufacture, the plywood industry, brewing, pharmaceutical and cosmetic products all utilize the natural emulsifying and binding properties of soybean extracts, while their natural preservative qualities are valuable in prolonging the shelf life of various foodstuffs. Soybeans are used to produce flour, oil, textured vegetable and meat-substitute protein as well as the valuable traditional fermented foods such as miso, tofu, tempeh, tamari, etc. (see INGREDIENTS). Soy milk is often made with added sugar, so check your labels. Soy yoghurt, whipped cream and even cheese are also now available on various world markets.

The soybean is considered the most yin of the pulses and is not recommended for frequent use. Nutritionist Nan Bronfen warns that it is higher in fat than most legumes and has a rich lecithin level (see FACTS ABOUT FATS, p. 220). Soybean sprouts should never be eaten uncooked (steam or stir fry for 6 or 8 minutes) because the raw bean contains a substance known as *trypsin inhibitor*, which seems to interfere with protein digestion and the assimilation of the amino acid *methionine* in the body. This also applies to sprouted peas, chick peas, beans, fenugreek, alfalfa and lentils. Grain sprouts can be eaten raw.

Before cooking soybeans it is a good idea to roast them in a skillet and soak them for 24 hours (3 cups water per cup of beans), bring to a boil in fresh water with a strip of kombu and simmer for 2 to 4 hours. Add flavorings during the last hour. If pressure cooking soybeans, add a teaspoon of vegetable oil (corn, soy, sesame or sunflower) to keep the skin from clogging the gauge! Black soy or Japanese beans can be soaked with a half teaspoon of salt added to the water to prevent the skin coming off the beans. Change the water, bring to a boil and simmer. Skim off any gray foam that floats to the top. When foam no longer appears, cover the pot and cook for 2½ to 3 hours. Add a little tamari soy sauce and shake the pot.

Food Content of Cooked Soybeans (per 100g): calories, 130; protein, 11.0g; fat, 5.7g; carbohydrates, 10.7g; fiber, 1.7g; calcium, 72.8mg; phosphorus, 179mg; iron, 2.7mg; sulfur, 265mg; sodium, 2.2mg; potassium, 540mg; vitamin A, 27.8 IU; vitamin B_1, 0.21mg; vitamin B_2, 0.1mg; niacin, 0.6mg; vitamin C, nil. (The vitamin C content of Soybean sprouts is 13.3mg.)

LOTUS ROOT (*Nelumbium muciferum*)

The lotus is a sacred plant in India and China and is used extensively for cooking in the Far East. The lotus root is actually a tuber which grows horizontally in the mud bottoms of murky ponds and mysteriously retains pockets of air. The root is brown outside, the hollow-chambered inside is off-white. The perforated pattern is decorative for many dishes. Lotus is one of the more yang roots and is especially good for respiratory problems. It is traditionally used for colds, sinus and lung congestion, etc. Lotus root tea is made by grating the fresh root and squeezing out the juice, adding an equal quantity of water, a pinch of grated ginger and a pinch of sea salt. Bring these ingredients to a boil and simmer for 2 to 3 minutes. Powdered lotus tea from a wholefood store may be used instead. Dried roots are available for cooking but need soaking in water first.

Food Content of Fresh Lotus (per 100g): calories, 62; protein, 2.4g; fat, 0.1g; carbohydrates, 14.3g; fiber, 0.9g; calcium, 20mg; phosphorus, 80mg; iron, 0.5mg; sodium, 30mg; potassium, (−); vitamin B_1, 0.05mg; vitamin B_2, 0.03mg; niacin, 0.5mg; vitamin C, 20mg.

MAPLE SYRUP

Maple syrup is made from the sap of maple trees in North America and Canada. It takes about 200 quarts (200 liters) of sap to make 4 quarts of syrup. It is a natural sweetener, but use it in moderation. It is useful when changing from sugars to something less sweet.

Food Content of Maple Syrup (per 100g): calories, 250, protein, nil; fat, nil; carbohydrates, 6; calcium, 165mg; phosphorus, 15mg; iron, 1mg; sodium, 15mg; potassium, 130mg; copper, 0.45mg; vitamin A, nil; vitamin B_1, (−); vitamin B_2, (−); niacin, (−); vitamin C, nil.

MIRIN

Mirin is a natural sweetening agent used in cooking and made from sweet rice, rice koji (a cultivating rice mold) and spring water. It is used in broths, dips, salad dressing and marinades for tofu or fish. It is sometimes served hot with Mu tea.

MISO

Miso is a naturally fermented food made from cooked soybeans and cooked rice, barley, wheat, buckwheat, whole rice, white rice, etc., that has been impregnated with the organism *Aspergillus oryzae*. This is called koji. Sea salt and spring water are added during a long fermentation process in wooden vats. Miso paste is an essential ingredient in macrobiotic cooking, and you will soon grow very fond of it. It is high in protein, including all the essential amino acids and calcium, it is free of toxins, while the enzymes and bacteria in it help proper digestion. Miso is also a source of vitamin B_{12} (0.17 micrograms per 4 ounces) and is an important supplement for vegetarians.

The story of a whole culture is contained in the name miso. There are early references in Chinese literature to a type of miso which could contain a mixture of meat or fish and sometimes sweet, wild fruit. It was eaten in the Orient long before the Christian era. The first reference to soybeans used as a protein source was in 500 AD, by which time Buddishm was encouraging a meatless diet and the monks developed a process of salt pickling and fermentation which showed a remarkable understanding of microbiology. Some scholars maintain that the origins of miso are in the heartland of North Japan, where ancient homemade miso traditions are still very much in practice. The miso is still allowed to age in cedar vats without haste for 18 months to 3 years by the same process of enzymatic fermentation that has been used for centuries. After World War II, stainless steel, fast fermentation and mass production drastically changed the quality—and flavor—of miso. However, there were men in Japan who fortunately, like the many small vintners in France, held on to the natural and traditional production methods. These men waited patiently for the fad for fast food to pass. As people have begun to object to the taste of chemicals and synthetics, traditional miso is again becoming popular. Misos, like soy sauce, tamari, sake and rice vinegar, are made by using the mold culture *Aspergillus oryzae*. Salt also quickens the growth of the fungus which produces enzymes that digest starches and proteins. The difference between types of miso is partly due to the different kojis used to make them. The most popular types of miso are the following.

Hatcho Miso: This is a soybean miso made from soybean koji. Known as the food of the samurai warriors, it is made according to a recipe more than 400 years old. The cooked soybeans are inoculated with an *Aspergillus oryzae*. Hatcho is very dry miso and is made in enormous cedarwood kegs with less water and less salt than red or barley misos. It ferments slowly and needs over three years to mature under heavy pressure. Hatcho is the thickest in texture of the misos and has a rich, almost chocolate-like taste that goes well with the darker, heavier root and winter vegetables. It is an excellent base for miso soups, or it can be mixed with other kinds of miso to subtly change flavors.

Mugi Miso: This means barley miso and is made with barley koji. It is called the "country-style" miso and is popular because it is suitable for both summer and winter cooking. The pleasing aromas of mugi may also account for its popularity: The barley koji is mixed with the soybeans in kegs to ferment. Barley, which contains both proteins and starches, produces the enzymes to reduce protein to amino acids and produces other enzymes to convert starches to sugars, which are further fermented to produce alcohols and ethers—which is why mugi smells go good!

Kome Miso: *Kome* means "rice" and, in most cases, white rice. There are several different kinds of kome miso, and they are the most generally used in Japan. Rice koji works primarily to convert starches to sugars, and the fermentation is more active and rapid. It is the same kind of koji as that used to make amazake, sake and rice vinegar. Kome is the sweetest of the misos. There are many different varieties: *Shiro* (white) miso is the sweetest and can be made in one or two weeks. It spoils quickly if not refrigerated but is a beautiful summer miso and can be used for salad dressings, sauces and spreads. There are other types of rice misos, all various shades of red (*aka* miso), orange and brown and each with a different flavor. Kome misos go well with lighter vegetables and greens in the spring and summer.

Genmai Miso: This is a kome or rice miso but a more modern type, which has been produced since brown rice came into demand. *Genmai* means brown rice. Traditionally, white rice is used to make nearly all rice misos because the outer bran of brown rice is resistant to any kind of spoilage or molds—including koji! The result of recent experimentation is the richly flavored genmai miso.

Natto Miso: This is made from soybeans and ginger.

Soba Miso: This is made from buckwheat.

Miso soup makes a light and nourishing meal at any time of the day but, before being added to soups, casseroles, stews, etc., miso needs to be ground into a purée. Your suribachi is perfect for this. Add a little soup stock or hot water (½ cup to a tablespoon of miso) and stir it well before pouring it into the soup.

There is a theory that miso should not generally be boiled and that the pot should be taken off the heat when the miso is added or, preferably, the miso puréed with a little hot soup or water, added to each bowl and stirred into the soup when serving. I find that if the miso has boiled the soup can taste sour when reheated later. Manufacturers certainly recommend that it is not boiled for long periods except in special kinds of cooking.

Try to resist the temptation to use too much miso. It is delicious but is also a very yangizing ingredient.

Food Content of Hatcho Miso (per 100g): calories, 180; protein, 16.8; fat, 6.9g; carbohydrates, 15.8g; fiber, 2.2g; calcium, 140mg; phosphorus, 240mg; iron, 6.5mg; sodium, 3,800mg; potassium, (−); vitamin B_1, 0.04mg; vitamin B_2, 0.12mg; niacin, 1.2mg; vitamin B_{12}, 0.17mg. vitamin C, nil.

MOCHI
Mochi is rice cake generally made from cooked, pounded sweet rice, which is more glutinous

than regular brown rice. In Japan sweet rice is traditionally used to make the alcoholic drink sake and is used in making mochi.

Mochi can also be made from a sweet millet or millet and sweet rice mixture, or by adding dry-roasted black soybeans during the final stages of pounding. Fresh mugwort may also be pounded into the rice. Mochi can be purchased ready-made in a variety of flavors in certain markets.

Pan-fry squares of Mochi over low heat or bake in the oven until it puffs up. Serve with a seasoning of tamari soy sauce and ginger juice. Delicious served on top of miso soup.

Food Content of Rice Mochi (per 100g): calories, 336; protein, 7.6g; fat, 2.3g; carbohydrates, 73.2g; fiber, 1.2g; calcium, 10mg; phosphorus, 290mg; iron, 1.1mg; sodium, 3mg; potassium, (–); vitamin B_1, 0.36mg; vitamin B_2, 0.10mg; niacin, 4.5mg.

MUGICHA
Mugicha is tea made from roasted, unhulled barley boiled in water. It is usually sold preroasted and prepackaged in wholefood stores, but barley can be roasted in a dry skillet until dark brown. Store in an airtight container.

MU TEA
Mu tea—which one lady journalist thought was our family name for tea with milk!—is in fact a blend of some sixteen different herbs. Mu means "unique", which Mu tea certainly is! It is a product of George Ohsawa's studies and combines herbs according to their yin and yang properties. Ginseng is one of them and is one of the most highly regarded Chinese herbs. Other herbs included can be peony root, Japanese parsley root, cinnamon, licorice, peach kernels, ginger root, rhemannia or even mandarin orange peel, atractylis, cloves, montan and coptis.

This invigorating drink is delicious with a dash of apple juice and is good for the stomach. Mu tea is yang and should not be used regularly or in large quantities. It is usually sold in sachets, each sachet making 4 or 5 cups of tea when boiled in water for 10 minutes. The sachets can be used a second or third time, and the contents can help flavor pastries.

NATTO
Natto is another soybean-ferment product high in protein, calcium and iron, which aids the digestion of food in the intestines. Wendy Esko, in *Introducing Macrobiotic Cooking*, says that she notices that eating natto also makes the skin feel smooth and young. "A person who has eaten much dairy food," she observes, "is more likely to dislike natto than someone who has been macrobiotic for several years and has discharged much of his past dairy food intake."

Natto can be served on buckwheat noodles or with tamari soy sauce over a bowl of rice. It is sold in small frozen packets.

Food Content of Natto (per 100g): calories; 167; protein, 16.9g; fat, 7.4g; carbohydrates, 11.5g; fiber, 3.2g; calcium, 103mg; phosphorus, 182mg; Iron, 3.7mg; sodium, (–); potassium, 249mg; vitamin B_1, 0.07mg; vitamin B_2, 0.5mg; niacin, 1.1mg.

NATTO MISO
This is not actually a miso but is a condiment made by briefly fermenting soybeans, grains, ginger and kombu.

NIGARI

Nigari is hard, crystallized salt made from the droppings of dampened sea salt. It is used in making tofu.

NORI (See SEA VEGETABLES.)

NOODLES

The Japanese, like the Italians, have a passion for noodles, and shops selling them are apparently numerous in every Japanese town and city. Peddlers set up stalls in the streets rather like they do on New York City streets, where you can buy those salty pretzels made of white flour and covered in table salt!

It is said that Marco Polo took the idea of kneading dough, stretching it, rolling it and cutting it into long strands from China to Italy and started the Italian craze. Before that though, traveling monks in the ninth and tenth centuries brought the idea from China to Japan, and Japanese noodles emerged to stay. They are made using buckwheat flour, which is certainly hardier and healthier than the white flour spaghetti products in our western supermarkets.

Noodles are quickly and easily prepared and just what you need for unexpected guests; they are a favorite, all-year-round food that can be used for breakfast, lunch, dinner or as a snack. They can be eaten hot or can be served cold, fried with vegetables, tempuraed, served simply with tamari soy sauce and chopped scallions or in a broth. There are several varieties of noodles.

Soba Noodles: *Soba* means "buckwheat". It also means "close by". In Japan it is a custom to present soba noodles to new neighbors as a gift of welcome. The shape of the noodles is popularly associated with longevity, and a bowl of soba is traditionally eaten at the New Year. Soba is so popular though, that the demand for it exceeds its domestic production, and a great deal of the flour is imported from Canada and Brazil. As buckwheat contains almost no gluten and does not lend itself to the making of pasta, soba noodles are normally made from about 80 percent buckwheat flour with 20 percent whole wheat flour, but there is a 100 percent buckwheat noodle that is made. Other soba noodles are *ftoh* soba, a short, thin soba noodle, *jenenjo* soba, which contains *jenenjo* flour made from a mountain potato of that name; *cha* soba, which contains tea leaves; and *youmugi* soba, which is made by using mugwort.

Cooking soba properly requires a good-sized pot so that the noodles won't stick together. They already contain salt, so very little needs to be added.

1. Bring water to a boil and add noodles. Bring to a boil again. Stir to keep them from sticking together. After a minute a head of foam will begin to rise.
2. Add a small amount of water to stop the boiling. Bring to a boil again.
3. Repeat this 3 times. Reduce heat and allow the noodles to simmer for about 7 minutes. Stir well.
4. Strain them under running cold water to prevent sticking. Reheat by using a little soy or sesame oil in the bottom of the pan.

An alternative method is to place soba in boiling water, bring to a boil again, lower heat and simmer for 10 to 15 minutes. Strain in running, cold water. When cooked, the noodle should be the same color throughout when broken. Or try the old Italian spaghetti test of throwing a piece against a smooth wall—if it sticks it's cooked! The water used for cooking soba can be seasoned and served as a drink (*sobaya*), either hot or cold.

Food Content of Soba (per 100g): calories, 360; protein, 10.8g; fat, 1.8g; carbohydrates, 73g; fiber, 0.4g; calcium, 30mg; phosphorus, 210mg; iron, 5.0mg; sodium, 700mg; potassium (−); vitamin B_1, 0.2mg; vitamin B_2, 0.88mg; niacin, 1.2mg; vitamin C, nil.

Udon Noodles: *Udon* is plain wheat pasta and comes from the wheat district, the island of Shikoku. Fresh udon is thick and fleshy. Dried udon, which is most often used in the home, is thinner. It is traditionally made from refined, "sifted" flour but is obtainable now from 80 percent whole wheat and 20 percent "sifted" flour. There is also a 100 percent whole wheat udon noodle.

Udon, like soba, is best cooked in plenty of water and in the same way. It takes a little longer, say five more minutes, to cook. It need not be washed but can be scooped straight from the pot. If cooked too long, however, it may need to be rinsed in cold water.

The noodle water from cooking udon can be used for noodle broth, stews, etc.

Food Content of Udon (per 100g): calories, 116; protein, 2.6g; fat, 0.3g; carbohydrates, 24.9g; fiber, 0.1g; calcium, 5mg; phosphorus, 25mg; iron, 0.3mg; sodium, 120mg; potassium, 1; vitamin B_1, 0.04mg vitamin B_2, 0.01mg; niacin, 0.2mg.

Somen Noodles: These are a light, very thin noodle. They are dried outside in the icy cold of winter and are usually served cold in the summer.

Food Content of Somen (per 100g): calories, 341, protein, 8.4g; fat, 1.3g; carbohydrates; 71.8g; fiber, 0.3g; calcium, 24mg; phosphorus, 110mg; iron, 1.8mg; sodium, 1,200mg; potassium, (−); vitamin B_1, 0.12mg; vitamin B_2, 0.04mg; niacin, 1.0mg.

Ramen Noodles: These are Chinese-style noodles that have become popular. There is an instant variety, precooked in hot oil and sometimes chicken fat, which makes them unable to qualify as natural food!

Saifun Noodles: These are a clear "cellophane" noodle made from mung beans.
There are of course other whole grain noodles available that will add variety to your menus: spaghetti, shells, rigatoni, spirals, flat noodles, lasagne and so forth. They are sometimes available made of whole wheat flour and are generally made without salt.

Probably the most important ingredient for noodle dishes is the broth in which they are served (see DASHI). There are several other sauces that can be made.

NUTS
Botanically, nuts are the single seeds or edible kernels of plants and have a hard or brittle shell. Since ancient times they have been gathered as a source of food and oil. The Greeks used them, the Romans cultivated them and sugared them. Medieval Europeans learned from the Arabs to use them for sweetmeats, and the Moors taught the Spanish, who in turn took their recipes to the Americas after the conquest where the Aztecs were already using pumpkin seeds, peanuts and probably pecans to thicken sauces. Nuts contain rich quantities of minerals and vitamins, they are high in protein but have a large stock of oil to be used as energy needed by the new plant life that will spring from them.

Their shells protect them from heat, air, light and moisture almost indefinitely. Once shelled, on the other hand, the oil in them quickly oxidizes and becomes rancid. They should be stored, tightly covered, in a cool, dark, dry place. It is advisable to buy them unshelled as packaged, commercial nuts can be treated with preservatives, dyes and inhibitors and are often fried in saturated or rancid fats. Try to find a reputable organic source. Nutritionists advise against eating too many—no more than half a dozen a day. Some can be shelled more easily (pecans, for example) by standing them in boiling water for 5 minutes. Roasting the kernels is a good idea. Nuts are more yin, and roasting or toasting is yang and certainly brings out their flavor. Use the skillet (no oil) for 5 to 10 minutes, or place them in a medium oven for a quarter of an hour.

Use nuts sparingly as a condiment, for decoration or to flavor kantens, cakes, etc.

ALMONDS (Prunus dulcis)

Almonds are the seeds of a tree of the peach family, native to the eastern Mediterranean. In early spring groves of the pink and white blossoms adorn the landscapes of the regions in which it grows. The ladies of Rome used almond oil as a favorite skin moisturizer and today it is still an ingredient in beauty creams. There are two varieties: sweet and bitter. Sweet almonds are used whole or ground or are pounded into a milky paste. They can be sliced or "slivered" and added as a flavoring for soups or fish dishes. Almonds also combine well with chicken and rice or they can be baked and salted with tamari soy sauce. Bitter almonds are broader in shape and their powerful flavor, similar to peach or plum kernels, is due to an enzyme reaction that produces prussic acid. This poison fortunately evaporates when heated, but raw bitter almonds should be avoided.

Food Content of Almonds (per 100g): calories, 598; protein, 18.6g; fat, 54.2g; carbohydrates, 19.5g; fiber, 2.6g; calcium. 234mg; phosphorus, 504mg; iron, 4.3mg; sodium, 4mg; potassium, 773mg; magnesium; 271mg; copper, 0.83mg; manganese, 1.9mg; vitamin B_1, 0.2mg; vitamin B_2, 0.92mg; niacin, 3.5mg; vitamin B_6, 0.1mg; biotin, 17.6mg; folic acid, 0.1mg; pantothenic acid, 0.47mg; vitamin C, trace, vitamin E, 15.0mg.

BRAZIL NUTS (Bertholettia excelsa)

These are the seeds of a tall forest tree in South America, and collecting them can be a risky business. In high winds those who gather them need to wear protective headgear as each shell, the size of a coconut, can weigh up to four pounds. Inside this shell the Brazil nuts are packed away neatly like chocolates in a box! Surprisingly few of the nuts are, in fact, consumed in Brazil where, to quote "Charley's Aunt," "the nuts come from!" Half the crop goes to the US, where their popularity continues to increase, and they have been taken to Europe since 1633. They can be roasted, and, used in cakes or grated on vegetables or kantens.

Food Content of Brazil Nuts (per 100g): calories, 654; protein, 14.3mg; fat, 66.9mg; carbohydrates, 10.9g; fiber, 3.1g; calcium, 186mg; phosphorus, 693mg; iron, 3.4mg; sodium, 1mg; potassium, 715mg; magnesium, 251mg; copper, 1.5mg; manganese, 2.8mg; zinc, 5.1mg; silenium, 102mg; vitamin B_1, 0.96mg; vitamin B_2, 0.12mg; niacin, 1.6mg; folic acid,. 0.004mg; pantothenic acid, 0.23mg; vitamin C, 10mg; vitamin E, 6.5mg.

CASHEW NUTS (Anarcardium occidentali)

The South American Indians called the fruit of this tree native to Brazil *acaju*, which Portuguese colonists heard as *caju*. The Portuguese took the cashew to their Indian colonies in the sixteenth century, and India is now one of the biggest exporters of the nut. The fruit of the cashew is fleshy, tart, reddish and pear-shaped and is called an apple. The nut grows as a hard protruberance under this fruit, and although the kernel is edible, there is a toxic oil in the outer layer which produces blisters on contact with the skin. The skin must be removed and the nut roasted before it is eaten. In fact, many Brazillians simply detach the cashew nut and eat the fruit! Cashew nuts are mainly used salted (and roasted), in baking or to make cashew butter or cream. They are also tasty as a condiment on green vegetables or as a decoration for meat dishes.

Food Content of Cashew Nuts (roasted) (per 100g): calories, 561; protein, 17.2g; fat, 45.7g; carbohydrates, 29.3g; fiber, 1.4g; calcium, 38mg; phosphorus, 373mg; iron, 3.8mg; sodium, 15mg; potassium, 464mg; magnesium, 267mg; zinc, 4.35mg; vitamin A, 100 IU; vitamin B_1, 0.43mg; vitamin B_2, 0.25mg; niacin, 1.8mg; folic aicd, 0.06mg; pantothemic acid. 1.3mg.

CHESTNUTS (*Castanea sativa*)

Sweet chestnuts should not be confused with horse chestnuts (*Aesculus hippocastanum*), which are more suitable as squirrel food. *Castanea sativa* is native to the Mediterranean and belongs to the same family as the oak and beech. Roman legions carried it to colder, northern regions beyond the Alps, where it grows quite happily, but the fruit will not ripen. Spain being the traditional source of the sweet chestnut in Britain, it is known there as *Spanish chestnut*. In France, where probably the highest quality of nut is produced, it is called *marron*, and *marron glacé* is a famous sweet. In Italy, however, it is a staple food and is ground into a flour, *farina dolce*, which is used to make bread and gruel.

The chestnut does not keep well at room temperature. In fact, it is the only nut that can be treated more like a vegetable. It contains more carbohydrates and much less oil than do most nuts. It can be cooked quite differently and can be served roasted, boiled, steamed, puréed or used in pies or stuffings; the flour makes delicious bread. To peel sweet chestnuts, place them in boiling water, turn off the heat and let stand for five minutes. Remove and allow to cool. Then peel with a sharp knife. To roast them, remember to slit the outer casing on the flat side and place on a baking tray, flat side up, in a medium oven (or in front of a wood fire!) for twenty minutes or so. Test for tenderness by prodding a knife through the slit.

Food Content of Chestnuts (per 100g): calories, 194; protein, 2.9g; fat, 1.5g; carbohydrates, 42.1g; fiber, 1.1g; calcium, 27mg; phosphorus, 88mg; iron, 1.7mg; sodium, 6mg; potassium; 454mg; magnesium, 53.6mg; copper, 3.6mg; vitamin B_1, 0.22mg; vitamin B_2, 0.22mg; niacin, 0.6mg; vitamin A, 89 IU; vitamin B_6, 0.33mg; biotin, 1.3mg; pantothenic acid, 0.47mg; vitamin O, 6mg; vitamin E. 0.5mg.

HAZELNUTS (*Corylus avellana*)
FILBERTS (*Corylus maxima*)

The name "hazelnut" is from the Anglo Saxon word *haesil*, which means headdress; this describes precisely how this nut fits into its cupule or covering. Filberts, on the other hand, which are longer and more robust, are named after a French abbot, St. Philbert, whose feast day in August coincides with their time of ripening. The *Corylus* tree adapts to differing conditions, producing varying types of nuts. Hazelnuts are more common in Europe, and filberts more usual in the US. Both hazelnuts and filberts are high in oil and are used commercially in butters and chocolate manufacture. They can be roasted and chopped to decorate desserts. To skin them, bake first in a moderate oven for 15 to 20 minutes. When cool, the skin can be easily removed with your fingers.

Food Content of Filberts (Hazelnuts) (per 100g): calories, 634; protein, 12.6g; fat, 62.4g; carbohydrates, 16.7g; fiber, 3.0g; calcium, 20.9mg; phosphorus, 337mg; iron, 3.4mg; sodium, 2.0mg; potassium, 454mg; magnesium, 233mg; copper, 1.28mg; manganese, 4.8mg; zinc, 2.6mg; vitamin A, 107 IU; vitamin B_1, 0.46mg; niacin, 0.9mg; vitamin B_6, 0.5mg; folic acid, 0.07mg; pantothenic acid, 0.96mg vitamin C, trace.

PEANUTS (*Arachis hypagae*)

Peanuts are the seeds of an annual plant native to South America. They have been discovered in Peruvian tombs dated 950 BC. They are also called groundnuts because they grow on long tendrils below the ground. Another name for them is monkey nuts. They are, strictly speaking, legumes, as the shell is the dried pod of the plant. Portuguese explorers took them from Brazil to East Africa during the sixteenth century. Traders fed them to African slaves on the sea voyages from Africa to the shores of the US, where nuts left over were planted to start a major industry. Peanuts are used mainly to make peanut butter, although sesame butter is probably of better food value. The flavor of peanut oil is considered rather overpowering for cooking, and the methods of extraction are sometimes dubious. Nut butters are usually hydrogenated to keep them from becoming rancid, and the extra hydrogen renders them useless as essential fatty acids. Do not eat too many too often.

Food Content of Peanuts (roasted) (per 100g): calories, 564; protein, 26g; fat, 47.5g; carbohydrates, 18.6g; fiber, 2.4g; calcium, 69mg; phosphorus, 401mg; iron, 2.1mg; sodium; 5mg; potassium, 674mg; magnesium; 175mg; copper, 0.44mg; manganese, 1.59mg; vitamin A, trace; vitamin B_1, 1.14mg; vitamin B_2, 0.13mg; niacin, 17.2mg; biotin, 34mg; folic acid, 0.1mg; pantothenic acid, 2.08mg; vitamin E, 6.5mg.

PECANS (*Carya illinoensis*)

Pecans—and hickory nuts—are the pits of fruit from the *Carya* family of trees. Pecans, indigenous to the southern states of America, are generally considered superior. They are cultivated in Texas and Oklahoma and are now being exported to Europe. Hickory nuts grow wild in the northern states of the US. Both were a vital staple food for the American Indians. Pecans are, of course, used in the famous pecan pie; they are also used in nut breads and salads or for decorating kantens and sweets. Pesto sauce can also be made with pecans.

Food Content of Pecans (per 100g): calories, 687; protein, 9.2g; fat, 71.2g; carbohydrates, 14.6g; fiber, 2.3g; calcium, 73mg; phosphorus, 289mg; iron, 2.4mg; sodium, trace; potassium, 603mg; magnesium, 131mg; copper, 1.05mg; manganese, 1.42mg; zinc, 3.0mg; vitamin A, 130 IU; vitamin B_1, 0.86mg; vitamin B_2, 0.13mg; vitamin B_6, 0.169mg; niacin, 0.9mg; folic acid, 0.024mg; pantothenic acid, 1.6mg; vitamin C, 1.85mg.

PINE NUTS (*Pinus pinea*)

The seeds of the stone pine, which is a native of Italy, are packed into the hard, mosaic casing of the pine cone. The trees are now cultivated all around the Mediterranean coast and the nuts are used in many recipes—in Italy, for example, *pesto Genovese* is a popular sauce. They are also chopped and used in stuffings, sweet and sour sauces and rice bases. In the middle East they are a popular addition to dolmades. They have a distinctive and pleasant taste but need long storage and cooking time to help dissipate the somewhat "turpentine" flavor.

Food Content of Pine Nuts (per 100g): calories, 642; protein, 13.2g; fat, 51.1g; carbohydrates; 20.7g; fiber, 1.1g; calcium, 10.7mg; phosphorus, 610mg; iron, 5.36mg; sodium, (–); potassium, (–); vitamin A, 35.7 IU; vitamin B_1, 1.3mg; vitamin B_2, 0.25mg; niacin, 4.7mg; vitamin C, trace.

PISTACHIO NUTS (*Pistacio vera*)

The pistachio is the seed of the fruit from a small tree native to Syria. The Roman epicurian Lucius Vitellus developed a pistachio passion when he was governor there and had large quantities of them shipped back to Rome. From there they were taken to the rest of the known world. The pistachio has been cultivated for thousands of years in Syria, Turkey, Israel, Greece and Italy and is today grown in California and Texas. It is one of the most popular nuts in

America today. It is eaten raw or is mixed with commercial ice creams, used in puddings and cookies, stuffings, sauces, baking and for sweet dishes. It is sometimes an ingredient of *halva* or *locoum* (Turkish delight). The natural nuts have a delicate green color. The bright red ones are, of course, dyed and usually have refined salt all over them.

Food Content of Pistachio (per 100g): calories, 587; protein, 13.3g; fat, 53.5g; carbohydrates, 18.7g; fiber, 2.0g; calcium, 130.7mg; iron, 7.3mg; phosphorus, 500mg; potassium, 967mg; magnesium, 158mg; copper, 1.12mg; vitamin A, 229 IU; vitamin B_1, 0.7mg; vitamin B_2, (–); niacin, 1.4mg; folic acid, 0.06mg; vitamin C, nil.

WALNUTS (*Juglans regia*)
The walnut tree is also of Middle Eastern origin and was called the Persian Tree by the Greeks who described the nut as *karyon* (*kara* means head) because its convolutions resembled those of the brain. The walnuts grown in the Northern Hemisphere are called English walnuts in America but are known also as French or Italian walnuts in Europe. Black walnuts, which are native to North America, have very hard shells and were stored by the Indians as an important food supply. Walnuts are used as a flavoring or topping in western cooking. In the Middle East they are pickled or used for making stuffings and sauces. In Italy they are sometimes used to make *pesto*.

Food Content of English Walnuts (per 100g): calories, 651; protein, 14.8g; fat, 64g; carbohydrates, 15.8g; fiber, 2.1g; calcium, 99mg; iron, 3.1mg; phosphorus, 380mg; potassium, 450mg; sodium, 2mg; magnesium, 131mg; copper, 1.39mg; manganese; 1.8mg; zinc, 2.26mg; vitamin A, 30 IU; vitamin B_1, 0.33mg; vitamin B_2, 0.13mg; niacin, 0.9mg; vitamin B_6, 0.73mg; biotin, 37mg; folic acid, 0.066mg; pantothenic acid, 0.9mg; vitamin C, 2mg; vitamin E, 1.5mg.

OILS
Most plant foods—vegetables, grains, legumes, nuts and seeds—contain varying proportions of oil, some more than others. Carrots, for example, have 0.2 grams per 100 grams. Avocado, which is botanically a fruit, has an oil content as high as 16 percent. Brown rice contains 1.8 percent, aduki beans 1.6 percent, and soybeans a high 10.3 percent. Nuts and seeds are much higher: walnuts are one of the richest in oil at 64 percent and safflower seeds have 65 percent fat. Coconut contains 35 percent fat, 30.4 percent of which is saturated. Most of the oils extracted from plant sources are polyunsaturated but are, nevertheless, only part of the whole food and are therefore more yin. Nan Bronfen recommends using them as little as possible and eating the whole foods instead, which contain a more natural balance of oil, vitamins—in particular vitamin E—and the essential linoleic acid. Extracted oils are invariably subjected to heat of some kind during processing and are potentially more toxic than oil fresh from natural, whole sources. Rancid oils can cause a loss of vitamins in the body. Even cold-pressed oils are usually run through steel mills which can become hot. Heat generates peroxides which destroy the vitamin E in the oil needed to prevent oxidation. The more vegetable oils we use the more vitamin E we need. It is better generally to sauté vegetables in water, as frying food increases the fat content of your meal, and at extreme temperatures fat decomposes to produce irritants such as *acrolein*, which can affect skin and mucous membranes. Use oils sparingly for flavor rather than swamping the food with them. Buy them "unrefined" and cold pressed whenever possible and store them in a cool, dark place.

CORN (MAIZE) OIL
Corn has been pressed for its oil since the Peruvians began cultivating it many thousands

of years ago. It is relatively easy to extract by centrifrugal force, and some doctors advise using it externally for skin disorders. It is also a good, general purpose oil for light cooking. It is, however, more yin than most other oils and boils over if used for deep frying (see GRAINS—CORN).

Food Content of Corn Oil (per 100g): calories, 900; protein, nil; fat, 10g (saturated); 78.6g (unsaturated); carbohydrates, nil; fiber, nil; calcium, trace; phosphorus, nil; sodium, trace; potassium, nil; zinc, 0.18mg; vitamin A, trace, vitamin B_1, trace; vitamin B_2, trace; niacin, trace; vitamin C, trace; vitamin E, 77.8mg.

OLIVE OIL

Homer and Pliny praised the virtues of olive oil and the Hebrews used it for ancient anointing ceremonies and regarded the olive as a symbol of prosperity. Olives are more easily cold pressed without heat or chemical processing. The first cold pressing produces *virgin* or *Lucca* oil, which may have a greenish tinge and a rich olive scent. Other olive oils are a blend of this oil with hydraulic extractions. Olive oil gives a distinctive flavor to your cooking and makes salads reminiscent of sunny Mediterranean holidays! It can be combined with an oil such as safflower, which is richer in linoleic acid, for use as a salad oil or cooking medium.

Food Content of Olive Oil (per 100g): calories, 885; protein, trace; fat, 10.7g (saturated), 80g (unsaturated); cholesterol, trace; carbohydrates, trace; fiber, nil; calcium; 0.5mg; phosphorus, nil; sodium, 0.007mg; potassium; trace; iron, 0.07mg; copper, 0.07mg; zinc, 0.18mg; vitamin A, nil; vitamin B, nil; vitamin B_2, nil; niacin, nil; vitamin E, 5.1mg.

PEANUT OIL

Peanut oil is also known as *Arachis* oil or groundnut oil. It has a bland taste and stores well in cool conditions. The method of extraction is, as always, important, however. At present, manufacturers are not obliged to state which methods are used, and the cheaper brands of peanut oil generally use chemical solvents. The oil is then refined, heated and treated with antioxidents. (See also NUTS—PEANUTS).

Food Content of Peanut Oil (per 100g): calories, 885; protein, trace; fat, 10g (saturated), 78.7g (unsaturated); cholesterol, trace; carbohydrates, trace; fiber, nil; calcium, trace; phosphorus, nil; sodium, trace; potassium, nil; iron, nil; copper, 0.07mg; zinc, 0.18mg; vitamin A, nil; vitamin B_1, nil; vitamin B_2, nil; niacin, nil; vitamin C, nil; vitamin E, 12.8mg

SAFFLOWER OIL

Safflower and sunflower oils are often regarded as interchangeable but are, in fact, quite different, even though both plants are members of the same composital family. The tall thistlelike safflower was cultivated by ancient civilizations along the Nile, and the Arabs have adopted its cultivation. Each safflower seed contains half its weight in oil, which is richer in linoleic acid (up to 80 percent) than any other oil. Sunflower oil is the second richest. The extraction of the safflower oil is difficult, however, because of the hard, shining husk which has to be pressed with powerful hydraulic machines and sometimes chemical solvents are used. It is not always possible to know which method of pressing is applied, as by law this does not have to be stipulated on the label. Safflower oil contains up to 75mg of vitamin E per 100 grams of oil.

Food Content of Safflower Oil (per 100g): calories, 886; protein, nil; fat, 7.9g (saturated), 84.3g (unsaturated); cholesterol, trace; carbohydrates, nil; fiber, nil; calcium, trace; phosphorus, nil; sodium, trace; potassium, nil; iron, trace; copper, nil; zinc, 0.18mg; vitamin A, trace; vitamin B_1, trace; vitamin B_2, trace; niacin, trace; vitamin C, trace; vitamin E, 75mg.

SESAME OIL

Sesame oil is also known as *gingelly oil* or *benne oil*. It has been used for cooking in Africa and the Far East for centuries. It is probably, with cold-pressed corn oil, the best quality oil for general cooking and for baking. It is the principal vegetable oil of Mexico and is used as a flavoring in Chinese cooking. As there are no husks to be removed, the extraction of sesame oil can be achieved in a single cold pressing, producing a clear, pale-yellow colored liquid with the advantage that in hot and tropical climates it is not turned rancid by heat. For this reason it is popular in countries such as Africa, Australia and the US. Analysis shows that its stability is due to a substance called *sesamol*, which is now by law added to margarine in Sweden. Sesame oil contains around 16mg per 100 grams of vitamin E, around 40 percent linoleic acid and 50 percent oleic acid. Dark or "toasted" sesame oil is obtained by further pressing of the seeds under hydraulic pressure and is not considered "top grade" oil. It has a heavier, distinctive flavor which can at times enhance the cooking of certain vegetables. Snowpeas (mangetout) are delicious sautéed in a little toasted sesame oil with ginger (see also SEEDS—SESAME).

Food Content of Sesame Oil (per 100g): calories, 857; protein, trace; fat, 13.6g (saturated), 77.9 (unsaturated), cholesterol, trace; carbohydrates, trace; fiber, nil; calcium, trace; phosphorus, nil; sodium, trace; potassium; nil; iron, nil; zinc, 0.18mg; vitamin A, nil; vitamin B_1, nil; vitamin B_2, nil; niacin, nil; vitamin C, nil; vitamin E, 56.4mg.

SUNFLOWER OIL

The sunflower seed is generally second only to the safflower in linoleic acid content. Seeds grown in hot climates contain a lesser proportion than those grown in more moderate areas. Seeds from African plants, for instance, have as little as 20 percent, while certain Russian species can produce up to 70 percent. This linoleic content is considered of medicinal value and is thought to limit the risk of cholesterol deposits in the blood vessels. As with other oils, the less it is processed the better, and it needs to be used in moderation (see also SEEDS—SUNFLOWER).

Food Content of Sunflower Oil (per 100g): calories, 885; protein, trace; fat, 12.8g (saturated), 85.7g (unsaturated), cholesterol, trace; carbohydrates, trace; fiber, nil; calcium, trace; phosphorus, nil; sodium, trace; potassium, nil; iron, nil; vitamin A, nil; vitamin B_1, nil; vitamin B_2, nil; niacin, nil; vitamin C, nil; vitamin E, 9.3mg.

OKARA

This coarse soybean pulp, left over from making *tofu*, can be cooked with vegetables.

RICE (See GRAINS.)

RICE CAKES (See RICE.)

RICE SYRUP

Made from barley malt and rice, it is used as a sweetener. Also sold as "Yinnie syrup," rice honey and rice malt.

RICE VINEGAR (See BROWN RICE VINEGAR.)

SASHIMI

This is the Japanese name for raw fish that has been cut into thin strips. It is generally served with a dip made with tamari soy sauce, water, grated ginger and daikon or horseradish. The fish can be placed on a finger of soft, pressed rice and decorated with boiled or steamed vegetables and grated daikon. The arrangement, when serving, is very important. Fish to use are boned filet of red snapper, striped bass, tuna, sole, etc. Slice diagonally, with a sharp knife, no more than ¼" thick. Eating sashimi is a good way to eat raw fish, though animal food can be more yin than some root vegetables. (See also SUSHI.)

SALT—SEA SALT and ROCK SALT

Neither sea salt nor rock salt should be confused with refined table salt, which is practically pure sodium chloride with sugar, starch, phosphate of lime, potassium iodide and other substances often added. To the ancient Egyptians and Chinese it was a "giver of life" because it preserved food for hard times. Salt fish was a standard food for the Greeks; the Romans were skilled at mining it and extracting it from the sea. Salt has become synonymous with worthiness and good faith: The Arab will still say "There is salt between us" when an agreement is made. In the Bible, Jesus says, "Ye are the salt of the earth," and a worthy person is still referred to as such, but Jesus also said, "If the salt have lost his savor wherewith shall it be salted?" Even in those times, because of taxes levied on salt, it was often adulterated with clay and chalk. There are two types of natural salt: rock salt (or land salt), which occurs in veins below the ground, and sea salt, which is obtained by evaporating sea water. Sea salt has a high iodine content, but rock salt tends to contain less lead and phosphorus because it was formed before man began to pollute the oceans of the world. Crystal salt is mined rock salt or sea salt in large crystal form and generally contains no additives. Salt is yang and can be used in a solution as a disinfectant or gargle. A sea salt compress can be made by roasting salt in a dry skillet for several minutes, placing it in a cotton sack, wrapping it in a towel and applying it to relieve intestinal or menstrual cramps and muscle stiffness. When using it for cooking, add it only to bring out the flavor of the food, not to make it taste salty. The average diet contains far too much sodium (see THE BODY—A LABORATORY? MINERALS, SODIUM).

SEA VEGETABLES

Archeological sites of 10,000 years ago indicate that sea vegetables have been part of man's diet since ancient times and are possibly the oldest crop known to man. The ancient Greeks and Romans, however, paid little attention to them as food or medicine. In fact, European use of sea vegetables has been limited. The French have used their *kelp* supplies mainly as fertilizer and, in times of war, the potassium from it was used to make gunpowder. However, sea vegetables or seaweeds are still eaten in parts of Scotland, Wales, Ireland, Iceland, Norway and the Mediterranean. Today you can buy *laver* from the market stalls in Cardiff. *Carrageen*, known as Irish Moss, was boiled with milk in Ireland during times of famine; *dulse* (or dillisk) is still eaten there and in Scotland. In parts of Alaska dried seaweed is rolled and used as a substitute for chewing tobacco! The Australian coastal Aborigines and the New Zealand Maoris used sea plants for food. Seaweeds are an important part of the diet in China, Korea, South-east Asia, Polynesia, Hawaii and particularly Japan, where *nori*, *kombu* and *wakame* are cultivated. Along the Pacific coast of the US people eat ulva, and the Japanese and Chinese there collect great amounts of laver. In South America, ulva and kelp seaweeds are known as "goiter sticks", a prevention against goiter, which is a common disease in some areas. Sea vegetables are, in fact, a remarkable source of nourishment, and with recent research they are becoming appreciated for their supply of minerals. According to the Norwegian Institute of Seaweed Research, they can contain some thirteen vitamins, twenty amino acids and sixty trace elements. They are particularly rich in iodine, iron and calcium, in vitamin A, the B vitamins and even vitamins C and D. For macrobiotics they are an essential part of cooking.

Seaweeds are *not* a source of calories and are low in fat. They assist in the digestion of beans when cooked with them, help make superb soups and soup stocks, and they can be roasted and ground to make condiments or used in salads and vegetable dishes. They are said to have antibiotic qualities, to relieve constipation and intestinal and respiratory irritation, to aid mucous membrane, promote weight loss and relieve gout and rheumatism.

Here are some of the chief cooking varieties:

AGAR-AGAR/KANTEN (the *gelidiales*)

Kanten is generally referred to as agar-agar in the West. It is a gelatinlike substance made from various kinds of red algae known as *agarophytes*. For 1,200 years the Japanese have eaten a dish called *tokorotem* made from the *gelidium* species. The slightly reddish branched ribbons and fronds are gathered under water to a depth of 30 meters by women divers. These fronds are dried and cleaned before being boiled in huge iron kettles over a wood fire. The liquid is allowed to set, and is then cut into strips and laid out on bamboo mats in the rice fields during the winter weeks to dry and bleach. The kanten takes about ten days to dry—weather permitting! At night the moisture freezes and by day it melts and runs away, taking cloudy impurities with it. The flaky, brittle celluloidlike gelatin is then collected and packaged.

To use kanten place it first in water, apply heat and simmer for several minutes. Kanten does not actually dissolve in water but absorbs it; it becomes soft and swells. When heated to 80°C or more it melts; the liquid becomes viscous and coagulates as it cools and sets at 25°C to 35°C. It does not melt as readily as gelatin, which, by the way, is made by boiling parts of animals, e.g., calves' feet. Kanten also sets much firmer.

Agar-agar flakes are a more modern product made from another variety of seaweed called *gracilaria*, which grows horizontally along the ocean bed in shallow waters and is harvested at low tide. *Ogogusa*, as it is called, is used more generally for kanten because it is easier to process and has more concentrated bonding properties. Because of industrial pollution in the Bay of Tokyo, however, it now has to be imported from Argentina and Chile.

Food Content of Agar-Agar (per 100g): calories, nil; protein, 2.3g; fat, 0.1g; carbohydrates, 74.6g, fiber, nil; calcium, 400mg; phosphorus, 8mg; iron, 5mg; sodium, (–); potassium (–); vitamin A, nil: vitamin B_1, nil; vitamin B^2, nil; niacin, nil; vitamin C, nil.

ARAME (*Eisenia bicyclis*)

Arame is harvested wild and is wind dried; it may be parboiled, then preserved in its original form or shredded. *Eisenia bicyclis*, which is produced in Japan on the Pacific northeast coast, is eaten when the fronds are young. Another variety grows on the Pacific Coast of the US. Cooked arame may be eaten with a marinade of umeboshi vinegar, tamari soy sauce and barley malt. It is generally used in soups with rice or with other vegetables. Wash arame quickly under cold water, then soak in fresh water for 3 to 5 minutes (keep the soaking water).

To cook arame and vegetables:

2 cups arame
1 medium, sliced onion
1 carrot, sliced into matchsticks
1 teaspoon sesame oil
2 cups soaking water plus ½ cup water
3-4 tablespoons tamari soy sauce

1. After soaking arame strain off soaking water (and keep). If arame is not already shredded, slice finely.
2. Heat skillet and add oil. Layer on onions, carrots and then arame. (Do not mix until they are cooked.) Add soaking water plus ½ cup more. Reduce heat and cover. Simmer for 10 minutes.
3. Remove cover, add tamari soy sauce, cover and cook another 10 minutes.
4. Remove cover, increase heat and boil off excess liquid.
5. Mix vegetables and arame and serve.
6. Delicious served with fried tofu.

Food Content of Arame (per 100g): calories, nil; protein, 7.5g; fat, 0.1g; carbohydrates, 60.6g; fiber, 9.8g; calcium, 1,170mg; phosphorus, 150mg; iron, 12mg; sodium, (–); potassium, (–); iodine, 98-564mg; vitamin A, 50 IU; vitamin B_1, 0.20mg; vitamin B_2, 0.2mg; niacin, 2.6mg.

CARRAGEEN or IRISH MOSS (*Chondrus crispus*)

Dried seaweed called *carrageen* has long been a food in Ireland. The name is said to have originated from a village called Carragheen on the coast of Waterford in the south, where Irish moss is gathered and distributed. It is used in folk medicine to treat respiratory disease and as a clarifying agent in wine and beer processing. Carrageen is a red algae. It is harvested, washed in sea water and spread on the shore to dry and bleach until it is white or light yellow. Although when packaged carrageen appears to be an unappetizing tangle, the fronds are pretty when washed and soaked. It has a high viscosity in dilute solutions and mixes with various liquids. Consequently it is used commercially as a stabilizer and emulsifier for food processing in ice creams, fruit syrups, sherberts, cheeses and instant soups. It is also used in the glue, textile and cosmetic industries. In cooking, carrageen can help thicken soups, stews, puddings or can be used in jellies and aspics. It can be deep-fried and sautéed with vegetables.

To make a basic jelly:

1 cup soaked carrageen
5 cups water or vegetable water

1. Soak the carrageen, wash and clean thoroughly. Strain off water and rinse. Discard soaking water.
2. Bring water or vegetable stock (for savory jelly) to a boil. Add carrageen.
3. Simmer for half an hour.
4. Strain off carrageen liquid.

This liquid can be used as a base for jellied soups or jelly for fish dishes. The rest of the carrageen can be added to soups or stews.

DULSE (*Palmaria palmatta*)

In Scotland a hundred years ago *dulse tangle* and other sea plants were sold on the streets of Edinburgh. In Ireland, where it is still popular, dulse is called *dillisk* or *crannogh*. It is reddish-purple in color and can be eaten raw in salads, or can be steamed or fried. It becomes sticky when boiled and is useful in soups. Because dulse is harvested in the wild and has undergone very little prelimary processing, it is necessary to wash it thoroughly and to remove any tiny shells that may be attached to the surface. If using it for salad, dip in boiling water after washing. Dulse also makes a delicious soup.

Food Content of Dulse (per 100g): protein, (–); fat, 30g; carbohydrates, (–); fiber, 6.7g; calcium, 567mg; phosphorus, 22mg; iron, 6.3mg; sodium, 2,088mg; potassium, 8,071mg; vitamin A, (–); vitamin B_1, (–); vitamin B_2, (–); niacin, (–); vitamin C, (–).

HIJIKI (*Hizikia*)

This plant is another of the brown algae that preserves well because the alginic acids and fuciodan protect the cell walls from bacteria and fungi. After harvesting it is wind dried and preboiled, which turns it a blackish-brown color. The leaflike parts of *hizikia* fall away when it is dried, producing dark, wiry, tangled pieces. Although a native of Japan and Hong Kong, *hizikia* is grown along the coast of China and in other parts of the world. Hijiki is especially rich in iodine, iron and calcium.

To prepare hijiki:

1 cup hijiki
4 cups water
1 sliced onion
2 tablespoons toasted sesame oil
4 tablespoons tamari soy sauce
½ cup roasted cashews or pine nuts

1. Before cooking, hijiki needs to be soaked for some ten minutes, which will increase its bulk two or three times. Use 3 cups of water to 1 cup hijiki. Strain off and keep the water.
2. Sauté the onion in the oil, then add the hijiki, stir and simmer for ten minutes.
3. Add the soaking water plus another cup and bring to a boil. Simmer for 30 to 40 minutes.
4. Add tamari soy sauce and stir.
5. Serve sprinkled with roasted nuts (see Recipes 98-100).

Food Content of Hijiki (per 100g): protein, 10.1g; fat, 0.8g; carbohydrates, 30.6g; fiber, 16.7g; calcium, 1,400mg; phosphorus, 59mg; iron, 29mg; iodine, 40mg; potassium, 14,800mg; sodium (–), vitamin A, 150 IU; vitamin B_1, 0.01mg; vitamin B_2, 0.2mg; vitamin B_{12}, 0.87mcg; niacin, 4.6mg; vitamin C, 0mg.

KELP (*Laminaria sinclairii*)

The history of kelp—as a fertilizer—in Europe goes back to the twelfth century. In the seventeenth century on the west coast of France certain species of kelp meal from brown algae *Laminarie* and *Fucus* were used to make ash, a source of soda for preparing glass; other uses were found for kelp ash, too. Potassium from it was needed for chemical fertilizers; iodine for photography was needed in 1811. Kelp, in fact, was an important product during the growth of the western chemical industry and during World Wars I and II kelp ash potassium was in demand to make gunpowder. Kelp (*Laminaria sinclairii*) is endemic to the Pacific coasts of North America. In Europe *Fucus disticus* is known as bladder wrack or popping wrack, as the ends of the branches often expand to form air bladders. Like other sea plants, kelp is remarkably rich in calcium. It can be roasted and ground into a powder for use as a condiment but is not usually eaten as a vegetable.

Food Content of Kelp (per 100g): fat, 1.6g; carbohydrates, 49.1g; fiber, 5.4g; calcium, 1,093mg; phosphorus, 240mg; iron, 100mg; sodium, 3,007mg; potassium, 5,273mg; vitamin A, (−); vitamin B_1, (−); vitamin B_2, (−); niacin, (−); vitamin C, (−).

KOMBU (*Laminaria Japonica*)

Eating this sea vegetable went out of fashion in the West years ago, but it is still very popular in Japanese and Chinese cooking. It is a brown algae, and there are more than ten species. It grows in deep waters, and the fronds can be as long as fifteen feet. Its popular flavor is due to the amino acid, *glutamic acid*, it contains, which has subsequently been isolated from other sources to make the artificial chemical seasoning *monosodium glutamate*. Kombu is rich in iodine and has long been a curative for goiter in the East. It is popularly used to make soup stocks and broths, and a strip of kombu added to beans will help cook them faster, will give them flavor and will make them easier to digest (see LEGUMES). Before using kombu soak and clean it in a little water for a few moments until soft.

To make soup stock:

5 cups water (a little more than you will require for the soup)
1 piece of kombu 3"×1½"

1. Place the kombu in the cold water and heat gently.
2. Just before the water boils remove the kombu, as high temperatures dissolve polysaccharides, which will make the soup rather sticky. This may not always matter.

The same piece of kombu can be used several times, or chop it finely and cook it with vegetables, legumes or soups.

Food Content of Kombu (per 100g): protein, 7.3g; fat, 1.1g; carbohydrates, 51.9g; fiber, 3.0g; calcium, 800mg; phosphorus, 150mg; sodium, 2,500mg; potassium, 5,800mg; iodine, 193mg; vitamin A, 430 IU; vitamin B_1, 0.08mg; vitamin B_2, 0.32mg; vitamin B_3, 1.8mg; vitamin B_{12}, 0.3mg; vitamin C, 11mg.

LAVER (*Porphyre laciniata*)
NORI (*Porphyre tenera*)

Welsh housewives in Pembrokeshire still collect laver at low tide and send it to town to be boiled and processed into "black butter". This can be mixed with oatmeal to make laver bread croquettes or spread on whole-wheat bread or toast and a squeeze of lemon added. Laver is of the red algae family and a species of it is so popular in Japan that it has to be cultivated. It is called nori (*porphyre tenera, tenera* meaning soft), and in 1973 the consumption of dried *aakusa nori* amounted to 9.6 billion sheets! The California Pacific Coast also yields large quantities of laver, which is popular with the local Oriental population—and the macrobiotics! Nori has a multitude of uses and is a fine food. It is as rich in protein as eggs and meat—with only a tiny proportion of fat— and practically all vitamins also, especially vitamin A (the same amount weight for weight as carrots). It is generally stored in airtight containers to keep it crisp, which helps preserve its considerable vitamin C content. It is also rich in minerals. Dried nori sheets can be roasted, cut or crumbled to garnish noodles and salads or added to soups and stews. Rice can be wrapped in it or rolled to make sushi rolls (see SUSHI). Nori sheets can also be used to make a laver "black butter".

Food Content of Nori (per 100g): protein, 35.6g; fat, 0.7g; carbohydrates, 44.3g; fiber, 4.7g; calcium, 260mg; phosphorus, 510mg; iron, 12mg; sodium, 60mg; potassium, 3,800mg; iodine, 0.5mg; vitamin A, 11,000 IU; vitamin B$_1$, 0.25mg; vitamin B$_2$, 1.24mg; niacin, 10mg; vitamin B$_{12}$, 13-29 mcgs; vitamin C, 20mg.

WAKAME (*Undaria pinnatifida*)

Wakame has been a popular sea plant in cooking for thousands of years, and in Japan in 1970 to 1971 the per capita consumption of it was about 2½ pounds—more than any other sea vegetable, including nori. Wakame is one of the brown algae cultivated in all parts of Japan today. It also grows on the coasts of Korea and China. After the harvest the *Undaria* blades are hung out to dry, much like laundry, on clotheslines. The midribs (*kuki-wakame*) are prized delicacies. Use in soups, bouillabaisse, marinated dishes or salad. Like kombu it has the property of softening the tough fibers of certain foods and can be cooked with beans. Wakame is an important source of calcium, and the laminine it contains is said to prevent ageing of the arteries and to be effective in preventing hypertension.

Wakame is easy to prepare and the grayish dried-up and wrinkled pieces are quickly restored to a tender and handsome green color by brief washing and then soaking for 3 to 5 minutes. Slice the "leaves" carefully into 1″ pieces and make sure that the "midribs" are sliced small and are cooked well.

To cook wakame:

2 cups soaked wakame
Soaking water
1 medium, sliced onion
1 tablespoon tamari soy sauce

1. After soaking wakame 3 to 5 minutes, drain off water (keep it) and slice wakame into 1″ pieces.
2. Place onions in a pot and cover with wakame. Add enough soaking water to almost cover the sea weed. Bring to a boil.
3. Reduce heat and simmer for 30 minutes, or until wakame is soft.
4. Add tamari soy sauce and simmer another 10 minutes.

Other vegetables—such as carrots, green peas, etc., or cashew nuts—can be added. If used for salad, wash, soak and dip briefly in boiling water.

Food Content of Wakame (per 100g): protein, 1.2g; fat, 1.5g; carbohydrates, 51.4g; fiber, 3.6g; calcium, 1,300mg; phosphorus, 260mg; iron, 13mg; sodium, 2,500mg; potassium, 2,700mg; vitamin A, 140mg; vitamin B$_1$, 0.11mg; vitamin B$_2$, 0.14mg; niacin, 10mg; vitamin C, 15mg; iodine, 18mg.

SEEDS

Seeds are the ripened ovules of plants and are rich in vitamins, minerals, protein and oil supply. The oil each contains is the chief energy store for the new plant life it will nourish. This oil is often extracted by pressure (cold pressed) or other methods and is then used for cooking (see also OILS). Seeds and the oil from them need to be stored carefully and used sparingly, as both will turn rancid in a short space of time. As with nuts, keep them in an airtight container and in a cool, dark place. Before using, roast them to release some of the oil and to increase the flavor. They make delicious condiments. Of the oils from seeds, sesame oil is probably the most suitable for daily cooking. Sunflower and safflower oils are also recommended.

The condiment or "spice" seeds from the East and the eastern Mediterranean are used occasionally for seasoning in small quantities.

CARAWAY SEEDS (Carum carvi)
These sickle-shaped seeds are native to Asia, but they are well known in Europe and are used in baking, cheese making, savory dishes and to flavor liqueurs! Related to anise, their pungent, characteristic taste can add "spice" to your cooking.

Food Content of Caraway Seeds (per 100g): calories, 333; protein, 20g; fat, 14.8g; carbohydrates, 50g; fiber, 12.9g; calcium, 662mg; phosphorus, 572mg; iron, 16.2mg; sodium, trace; potassium, 1,333mg; magnesium, 238mg; selenium, 22.9mg; zinc, 5.7mg; vitamin A, 380mg; vitamin B_1, 0.38mg; vitamin B_2, 0.38mg; niacin, 3.7mg; vitamin C, (–).

CORIANDER SEEDS (Coriandrum sativam)
This is an annual plant related to parsley from southern Europe and the Middle East. The seeds are dried and roasted and can be used ground or whole. Coriander is one of the main ingredients of curry pastes and powder. It is also used in pickles.

Food Content of Coriander Seeds (per 100g): calories, 277; protein, 12.2g; fat, 28.9g; carbohydrates, 55g; fiber, 32.2g; calcium, 722mg; phosphorus, 388mg; iron, 16.1mg; sodium, 55.6mg; potassium, 1,278mg; magnesium, 333mg; zinc, 4.4mg; vitamin A, (–); vitamin B_1, 0.22mg; vitamin B_2, 0.28 IU; niacin, 2.1mg; vitamin C, (–).

FENUGREEK SEEDS (Trigonella foenum-graceum)
The name *fenugreek* means "Greek hay," but this seed, native to the Middle East, is featured more in Indian cooking than in Greek cooking. It is recommended by one doctor as a source of choline—which helps digestion of fats.

Food Content of Fenugreek Seeds (per 100g): calories, 329, protein, 23g; fat, 6.5g; carbohydrates, 58.4g; fiber, 10g; calcium, 162mg; phosphorus, 297mg; iron, 33.6mg; sodium, 54mg; potassium, 757mg; magnesium, 189mg; zinc, 2.4mg; vitamin A, (–); vitamin B_1, 0.32mg; vitamin B_2, 0.38; niacin, 1.6mg; folic acid, 57mg; vitamin C, 2.97mg.

POPPY SEEDS (Papaver somniferum)
These are seeds of the opium poppy that is native to the Middle East. Some are yellow and some are bluish-black, but they contain no habit-forming alkaloid! They feature in Indian and Jewish cooking and are used to decorate bread and confectionery and to make cakes and bun fillings such as the Jewish *hamentaschen*.

Food Content of Poppy Seeds (per 100g): calories, 535; protein, 17.8g; fat, 17.8g; carbohydrates, 23.5g; fiber, 6.5g; calcium, 146mg; phosphorus, 85.7mg; iron, 9.3mg; sodium, 35.7mg; potassium, 714mg; magnesium, 321mg; zinc, 10.3mg; vitamin A, (–); vitamin B_1, 0.14mg; vitamin B_2, 0.18mg; vitamin B_6; 0.43mg; niacin, 0.96mg; vitamin C, (–).

PUMPKIN SEEDS (Curcurbita maxima)
In China the pumpkin is called the "Emperor of the Garden" and is the symbol of fruitfulness. The word is from *pepon*, the Greek for "cooked in the sun." A native of Asia, the pumpkin is a member of the gourd family. Its seeds, with those of the squash, are one of the most

popular types for eating. Roasted with perhaps some tamari they can be sprinkled over land or sea vegetables with delicious results! They are reputed to be rich in zinc by some nutritionists, but I can find no figures confirming this. They are richer in iron than any other seed and are high in phosphorus.

The pumpkin seed is an old herbalist treatment for prostate disorders, and modern tests by Dr. W. Devrient in Berlin and Dr. G. Klein in Vienna seem to be confirming its effect on "hormone production, the prostate and bladder" and "its regenerative, invigorative and vitalizing influences." It does, though, have a 46.7 percent fat content.

Food Content of Pumpkin Seeds (per 100g): calories, 553; protein, 29.0g; fat, 46.7g; carbohydrates, 15.0g; fiber, 1.9g; calcium, 51mg; phosphorus, 1,144mg; iron, 11.2mg; vitamin A, 190 IU; vitamin B_1, 0.24mg; niacin, 2.4mg; vitamin C, (–).

SAFFLOWER SEEDS (Carthamus tinctoria)
The oils of the safflower seeds and sunflower seeds are quite different, but they are frequently thought of as interchangeable (see also OILS). Safflower seed oil is one of the richest in linoleic acid (80 percent); sunflower seed oil contains 65 percent.

SESAME SEEDS (Sesamium indicum)
The sesame is an annual plant native to India and, through mythology, it has come to be regarded in the East as the symbol of immortality. It is one of the world's oldest spices and easiest source of oil (see OILS—SESAME) and grows plentifully. Until fairly recently, however, it was difficult to harvest because the plant literally throws its seeds to the winds when they are ripe; a new, nonscattering variety has now been produced. The oil can be removed in a single cold pressing and is good for cooking.

Sesame is harvested the world over. The seeds are a particularly rich source of calcium, iron, protein, vitamins and minerals. In the West they are baked in bread or are used in cakes and cookies. In the Middle East they are ground into a paste to make tahini.

Sesame Butter and Tahini Paste
These are made from roasted or unroasted seeds. Tahini or tahina is popular in the Middle East and is the principal ingredient of *halva* and *hummus*. Tahini is prepared from ground, hulled, white seeds. Sesame butter, on the other hand, is made from the unhulled roasted seeds. The butter is therefore a more complete food. Both are high in oil but can be used for salad dressings, as spreads for breads or rice cakes, as sauces, and as flavoring for soups or in cakes. A spoonful added to rice while cooking gives a delicious nutty flavor to the grain.

Sesame Salt (Gomasio)
Gomasio is a popular condiment made from sesame seeds and sea salt. Prepare it as follows:

15 to 20 teaspoons sesame seeds
1 teaspoon sea salt or rock salt

1. Dry roast the seeds to a golden brown. Stir well to prevent burning.
2. Place seeds with salt in your suribachi and grind well to make a fragrant-smelling condiment. You can use the coffee grinder to blend, but you might end up with butter instead!

Gomasio, or sesame salt, sprinkled over your rice and vegetables, salads or cereal in the morning gives them a delicate nutty flavor. Use it sparingly, and don't make too much at a time. Renew your supply every few days and keep it stored in an airtight container in a cool, dark place. Although the salt helps preserve the crushed seeds, they still deteriorate and the flavor is better if made fresh. Ohsawa claimed that children who are fretful and cry too much are helped by a teaspoon of this condiment sprinkled over their food each day. It is also said to help certain types of headache.

Food Content of Sesame Seeds (per 100g): calories, 563; protein, 18.6g; fat, 49.1g; carbohydrates, 21.6g; fiber, 6.3g; calcium, 1,160mg; phosphorus, 616mg; iron, 10.5mg; sodium, 60mg; potassium, 725mg; magnesium, 180mg; copper, 1.6mg; vitamin A, 30 IU; vitamin B_1, 0.98mg; vitamin B_2, 0.24mg; niacin, 5.4mg; vitamin C (−).

SUNFLOWER SEEDS (*Helianthus annuus*)

The sunflower in Spain is called *girasol*—it turns on its stem to follow the sun with its golden, petaled face. It has been the mystic symbol of many sunlit, primitive people, notably the Incas, who worshipped the sun itself. The North American Indians grew crops of them for medicinal purposes and used the petals for animal food and dyes. Today even the leaves are being used to treat malaria, and the stalks are burned for use as a fertilizer. The Russians have multimillion-rouble crops of sunflowers.

Sunflower seeds are unusually rich in B complex vitamins and are useful for decorating desserts or vegetables (see also OILS).

Food Content of Sunflower Seeds (per 100g): calories, 560; protein, 24g; fat, 47.5g; carbohydrates, 19.9g; fiber, 3.8g; calcium, 120mg; phosphorus, 837mg; iron, 7.1mg; sodium, 30mg; potassium, 920mg; manganese, 33.3mg; copper, 1.97mg; vitamin A, 50 IU; vitamin B_1; 1.96mg; vitamin B^2, 0.23mg; niacin, 5.4mg; vitamin B_6, 1.25mg; vitamin C, (−).

SEITAN

Seitan is a wheat gluten cooked in tamari soy sauce, best made from hard spring whole-wheat flour. It is very high in protein, calcium and niacin. This traditional food has a meatlike texture and is eaten in many parts of the world. It can be used in soups and stews, cooked with vegetables, in sukiyaki, for sandwiches or stuffing made with breadcrumbs.

Seitan can be made quite quickly as follows:

5 cups whole-wheat flour
6 cups water
1 kombu strip
⅓ cup tamari soy sauce
1 tablespoon ginger juice

1. Mix 4 cups flour with enough water to make a dough as for bread. Save an extra cup of flour to add in case dough is too wet. Knead for 5 minutes.
2. Place dough in a bowl and cover with cold water. Leave for 10 minutes.
3. Replace cold with warm water and knead for 5 minutes *in the water* to remove the bran and starch. This water can be saved and used as a thickening agent for soups and stews or soured for 3 or 4 days and used as a starter for making bread.
4. Place the sticky gluten in a large strainer and run cold water over it while you knead it for 2 minutes. Change water to

hot and knead another 2 minutes.

5. Repeat this, alternating hot and cold water until all the bran and starch are washed out (four or five times). The last rinse is with cold water, after which the gluten is contracted into a sticky ball.

6. Cut the gluten into two or three chunks. Drop these into 3 cups boiling water and boil until they float to the top (10 minutes).

7. Remove and slice into strips (for sautéing) or cubes (for soup).

8. Place a strip of kombu with tamari soy sauce and ginger juice in a pan half filled with water. Bring to a boil.

9. Add cubes or slices of gluten, reduce heat and simmer, uncovered, for 25 to 40 minutes. If the pan is covered, the gluten is lighter and more expanded and not such a solid texture.

SESAME BUTTER (See SEEDS—SESAME.)

SESAME SALT (See SEEDS—SESAME.)

SHIITAKE MUSHROOMS

Referred to as "medicinal mushroom" shiitake are imported dry from Japan and need to be soaked for 15 to 30 minutes before cooking (keep soaking water for soups or stews). They can be obtained fresh in the US, where they are known as Black Forest mushrooms. The thick, fleshy cap has a smooth, firm texture. The ends of the stalks may need to be trimmed as they can be tough, but the delicate flavor of shiitake is a delicious addition to soups, rice dishes or sauces. They are a high-protein vegetable. Shiitake tea is made by boiling 2 or 3 mushrooms in water for 15 to 20 minutes. Remove the mushrooms and drink the "tea." It is used to help the discharge of yang from eating too much animal food, fish, buckwheat or salt but should be taken only every few days.

Food Content of Shiitake Mushrooms (per 100g): calories, N.A.; protein, 12.5g; fat, 1.6g; carbohydrates, 65.5g; fiber, 5.5g; calcium, 30mg; phosphorus, 80mg; iron, 5.5mg; sodium, 30mg; vitamin A, 0; vitamin B_1, 0.05mg; vitamin B_2, 0.03mg; niacin, 0.5mg; vitamin C, 20mg. They are also reputed to contain 2,639 IU of vitamin D.

SHISO (*Perilla frotescens*)

This plant is a member of the mint family. *Shi* means purple and *so* means leaf. Because of its color it is known also as the beefsteak plant. The *shiso* leaves provide the color and flavor in pickling umeboshi plums and also contain *perilla aldehyde*, which is a strong preservative. A condiment sold commercially can be made by roasting the leaves from umeboshi production (see also UMEBOSHI). After roasting the leaves are ground and can be sprinkled on grains and soups or can be used to flavor rice balls, etc. If obtainable fresh, the purple (yin) *shiso* leaves are useful in salads and as a garnish for soups, etc.

Michio Kushi in *Macrobiotic Home Remedies* says that *shiso* leaves contain chlorophyll, vitamins A, B_2 and C, calcium, iron and phosphorus. They are traditionally used to help the treatment of colds and to calm the nervous system.

SHOYU SAUCE (See TAMARI.)

SOBA (See NOODLES.)

SOYBEANS (See LEGUMES.)

SOY SAUCE (See TAMARI.)

SUKIYAKI

Sukiyaki is a popular dish in Japanese restaurants and is traditionally cooked at the table, but it can as easily be prepared in the kitchen and served at the table! You can use your cast-iron skillet and the ingredients can consist of vegetables with noodles, seitan, fish or tofu products (see Recipe 175).

SURIBACHI

This is a glazed clay bowl with many uses in the preparation of food. The inside surface of the suribachi is serrated to give a texture rough enough to purée and grind against with a wooden pestle called a *surikogi*. Miso, for example, can be mixed thoroughly in water and sesame seeds can be easily ground, and the process is gentler and quieter than using a noisy electric blender. Less washing up too!

SUSHI

There are, in fact, several types of sushi, and if you have ever watched the delicate precision and artistry of a good Japanese chef at a sushi bar you have probably tasted *nigirizushi*—a variety of different fish strips, raw or cooked, pressed onto small oval beds of sushi rice with a flavor of horseradish. It is served with fresh, shredded daikon radish.

Most people's introduction to sushi in a Japanese restaurant are *tekkamaki*—raw tuna fish and sushi rice rolled in a sheet of nori seaweed, and served with *wasabi* added to a soy sauce dip. *Tekka* means "gambling place" and just as the Earl of Sandwich invented that quick "snack" named after him so that he could gamble without interruption, so apparently the Japanese invented *tekkamaki*!

The sushi nori rolls, or *nakizushi* referred to in macrobiotic cookbooks, can have various ingredients wrapped in them—fish, vegetables, etc.—rolled in the rice and the sheet of nori.

Sushi nori rolls are bite-sized, the roll 1″ in diameter and the slices ½″ or so thick. If you make them too large, eating them can be a messy business. Be sure you use roasted nori sheets so that they stay crisp (see Recipe 121).

SUSHI MAT

This is a small, flexible mat made from fine strips of bamboo that are strung together. It is so called because it is used to make sushi rolls (see SUSHI), but it has a number of other functions in the kitchen. It can cover food while it cools, it can keep it warm or it can even be used as a table mat to protect table surfaces from hot pans.

TAHINI (See SEEDS—SESAME.)

TAMARI SOY SAUCE or SHOYU SAUCE

The word *tamari* is found in Japanese documents as early as 776 AD. It was the liquid which rose to the surface of soybean *hishio miso* during fermentation. The Japanese characters used for writing the world *tamari* meant "soybean filtering." The liquid from soybean miso kegs was ladled off and heated to stop fermentation. It became popular as a savory seasoning and still is today.

In 1560 a product known as *tamari-shoyu* became popular. It was made from a koji containing soybeans and roasted barley, with sea salt and water. A hundred years later shoyu was being produced commercially from equal parts of soybeans and roasted, cracked wheat. By 1670 early traders discovered it and were taking it back to Europe. Dutch traders exported it to France at the request of Louis XIV, who used it at his banquets. From early in the nineteenth century up to and during World War II, the rapid westernization of Japan led to the use of more and more commercial, short-cut methods in the shoyu industry. Stainless steel and concrete tanks began to replace the traditional cedar vats. Today most brands of "soy sauce" are cheap, quick, synthetic products, manufactured in a few days and sold under Chinese brand names. No fermentation time is required, and they are usually prepared with defatted soybean meal and hydrolyzed vegetable protein—even hydrochloric acid is sometimes used! They can be flavored with additives, such as monosodium glutamate, corn syrup or caramel, and some varieties may contain sodium benzoate or alcohol preservatives. So read your labels!

Tamari is the name recently given to soy or shoyu sauce prepared by reputable makers using natural traditional fermentation of soybeans, or soybeans and wheat with sea salt and spring water. It is brewed for up to three years in wooden barrels that have been used and reused over the centuries. Tamari is a rich dark brown and is of a fairly thick consistency. It is obtainable in any good wholefood shop. The name tamari is given to distinguish it from the quick, commercial and chemically processed "soy" sauces.

Tamari soy or shoyu sauce is used mainly as a condiment to flavor soups, vegetables, sea vegetables, cereal and rice dishes, sauces, or is served with noodles and broths; it is also used for basting, grilling, sautéeing and boiling. It mixes with brown rice vinegar, umeboshi plums (on fish), wasabi or with lemon juice for dips. Don't swamp them with it, though. It is very yang. Use a little in the right place!

Food Content of Tamari Soy Sauce (per 100g): calories, 68; protein, 5.6g; fat, 1.3g; carbohydrates, 9.5g; fiber, 0; calcium, 82mg; phosphorus, 104mg; iron, 4.8mg; sodium, 8,367mg; potassium, 457mg; vitamin A, nil; vitamin B_1, 0.02mg; vitamin B_2, 0.25mg; niacin, 0.4mg; vitamin C, nil.

TEKKA MISO

The word *tekka* is made from the Chinese characters for metal and fire. This condiment was cooked in a heavy iron pot over low heat. The ingredients used to make tekka are *hatcho miso*, sesame oil and various roots. They are sautéed over low heat for several hours. It is a popular flavoring sprinkled over rice, deep-fried tofu, etc. Tekka is a blackish-brown powder said to have medicinal properties. It is rich in iron, is very yang and is to be used sparingly.

To make fine-textured crumbly tekka miso:

2 tablespoons unrefined sesame oil
¼ cup grated carrot
¼ cup grated lotus root
¼ cup grated burdock root
2½ teaspoons grated ginger root
¼ cup black sesame seeds, ground to a
  paste (or sesame butter)
¼ cup bonito flakes
1 cup hatcho miso

1. Heat an iron skillet and coat it with oil.
2. Add the roots, sesame and bonito flakes. Sauté for 5 minutes.
3. Add the miso, stirring well, until the ingredients are mixed evenly.
4. Reduce heat to low and cook gently for 3 to 4 hours. Stir from time to time until the tekka miso is dry, black and as crumbly as possible.

Makes 2 cups

Food Content of Tekka Miso (per 100g): calories, 249; protein, 9g; fat, 5.2g; carbohydrates, 42.8g; fiber, 2.0g; calcium, 1.5mg; phosphorus, 250mg; iron, 60mg; sodium, (–); potassium, (–); vitamin A, nil; vitamin B_1, 0.10mg; vitamin B_2, 0.15mg; niacin, 1.5mg; vitamin C, nil.

TEMPEH

Tempeh is a food popular in Indonesia. It is produced by a natural culture of soybeans and sometimes other legumes, seeds or grains. The process is very similar to that by which cheese or yoghurt are made. Tempeh has a full-bodied, meaty texture and can be used as a main course and substitute for animal foods—in stews, soups, spreads, sauces, sushis or sandwiches. It is readily available in the US. There are even tempeh "burgers" on the market, which are seasoned with tamari, ginger, etc.

The flavor of raw tempeh has been variously described as "nutty," "mushroomy" and "yeasty," but the taste may, in fact, take some acquiring. Tempeh, like most raw food, needs seasoning. The protein content of tempeh is a high 19.5 percent, which compares favourably with animal products but another important nutrient contribution is vitamin B_{12}, which is often lacking in a vegetarian diet. The *rhizopus* mold used in tempeh fermentation produces natural antibiotic agents which are thought to increase the body's resistance to intestinal infection.

Food Content of Tempeh (per 100g): calories, 157; protein, 19.5g; fat, 7.5g; carbohydrates, 9.9g; fiber, 1.4g; calcium, 142mg; phosphorus, 240mg; sodium, (–); potassium, (–); iron, 5.0mg; vitamin A, 42 IU; vitamin B_1, 0.28mg; vitamin B_2, 0.65mg; niacin, 2.5mg; vitamin B_6, 830mcg; vitamin B_{12}, 3.9mcg vitamin C, nil.

TEMPURA

The fish of the famous English favorite "fish and chips" are tempuraed! Sliced vegetables and noodles look quite beautiful after the same treatment. Small pieces of fish, prawns, vegetables, grain patties, tofu and even fruit slices make a delightful and decorative dish served with rice. The best quality oil to use for tempura is sesame oil. Corn oil is too yin for deep-frying and will tend to bubble over onto the stove. It is possible to make tempura by shallow-frying, but the results can be untidy!

To make tempura batter:

¾ cup whole-wheat pastry flour
¼ cup cornmeal or sweet rice flour
1 tablespoon kuzu in ½ cup water
1 cup cold water
¼ teaspoon salt
Various vegetables, noodles, fish or
*   prawns (peeled)*

1. Mix the dry ingredients and water gradually, stirring until the batter is smooth and creamy. Add kuzu and water. The mixture shouldn't be too runny.
2. Leave the batter to stand in a cool place for an hour before using.
3. Place 2 or 3 inches of oil in a pan and heat to 350°F—just before it begins to smoke. Never have the oil too hot. It is ready when a drop of batter placed in it sinks to the bottom and immediately rises to the top.
4. Dip vegetable pieces into the batter and drop into the hot oil. Suitable vegetables for tempura are: carrots sliced diagonally or grated, cauliflower or broccoli florets broken off by hand, Brussel sprouts, sliced or whole mushrooms, pieces of kale, dandelion leaves, parsley, carrot tops, squash, celery in 1½" pieces, green beans, onion rings or slices and burdock root. Dry them before dipping them into the batter. Cut them into a variety of shapes. Sliced tofu, small fish pieces or prawns are also delicious.
5. As the tempura pieces become golden brown, remove them from the oil and drain on paper towels to remove excess oil.
6. Serve with fresh, grated daikon or with grated ginger, tamari soy sauce and water to help the digestion of the oil.

Do not re-use the oil for cooking more than three or four times. Before storing (in a cool, dark place), cook an umebashi plum in the oil for ten minutes, then strain off any pieces of batter or food. This will help preserve it.

TOFU

Tofu is a white curd made from soybeans, *nigari* (magnesium salts extracted from raw salt and water). Tofu is as much part of Oriental culture and cooking as is dairy food in the West. There are some seven different types of tofu in Japan and even more in China. The subtle and gentle flavor of tofu is very adaptable in the kitchen. It can be used for toppings, spreads, dressings and sauces or is delicious added to soups and stews. It can be pan-fried or deep-fried to a golden color, or broiled or grilled. It will make pie fillings, "tofutti" ices and dessert toppings, and is, of course, a protein booster for grains. It is generally sold in small blocks, water-packed in plastic containers. Tofu can be made at home by using a special tofu box. The white cakes should be kept in water and refrigerated. Change the water every day or so.

Food Content of Tofu (per 100g): calories, 72; protein, 7.8g; fat, 4.2g; carbohydrates, 2.4g; fiber, 0.1g; calcium, 128mg; phosphorus, 126mg; iron, 1.9mg; sodium, 7mg; potassium, 42mg; magnesium, 111mg; vitamin B_1, 0.06mg; vitamin B_2, 0.03mg; niacin, 0.5mg.

UDON (See NOODLES.)

UMEBOSHI PLUMS

Umeboshi means "dried plum." The plant was introduced to Japan some thousand years ago and became more popular there than it was in its native China. Its sharp, tart taste is the result of combining yin, green, sour plums with yang raw salt. The Japanese plum is now a rounder and fatter variety than the original Chinese fruit, which would seem to have a protruding navel as well! The umeboshi blossom, appearing in the cold of late February, rivals the famous cherry for beauty in Japan. The fruit is gathered while it is still green and is packed in vats with raw salt, which draws out a liquid called plum vinegar. The purple *shiso*, or beefsteak, leaves are placed over the plums and the color dyes them a deep red and helps to preserve them. By mid-July, when the rains end and the sun shines, the plums can be spread out, dried and returned to the umeboshi vinegar.

Umeboshi's flavor is somewhat similar to that of anchovies—without the fishy taste! They are eaten daily in the Orient and are attributed the medicinal properties of helping digestion, settling the stomach and maintaining the slightly alkaline condition of the blood. They are certainly an invaluable condiment: Their sharp, sour, tangy taste helps to flavor salads. Try slicing one into apple juice, sesame oil and tamari soy for a dressing. It is good spread on sweet corn cobs or placed in the center of a rice ball to preserve it. This preservative factor is due to *perilla aldehyde*, which when ingested also helps clear the intestinal tract (see also SHISO). Umeboshi and kuzu sauce is a good combination with vegetables, too.

Here are some traditional umeboshi remedies:

UME-SHO-KUZU-DRINK
To neutralize acidity

1 teaspoon kuzu
1 cup cold water
1 umeboshi plum
1 teaspoon tamari soy sauce

1. Mix kuzu well in the water.
2. Heat the kuzu and water with the umeboshi plum. Bring to a boil.
3. Reduce heat and simmer until transparent. Stir to avoid lumps.
4. Add tamari.
5. Serve hot.

UME-SHO-KUZU AND GINGER
Useful against colds.

½ teaspoon grated ginger or
  1 tablespoon fresh ginger juice
1 teaspoon kuzu
1½ pints of water
1 umeboshi plum

1. Disperse ginger and kuzu separately in a little cold water.
2. Add these mixtures to the rest of the water, add the umeboshi plum and bring to a boil.
3. Stir until the liquid becomes transparent.

UME-SHO-BANCHA
Good for headaches caused by too much yin food. Relieves tiredness.

1 pitted umeboshi plum
1 cup bancha tea or twig tea
4 drops tamari soy sauce

1. Place plum in a cup and pour tea over it.
2. Add soy sauce.
3. Drink while hot.

Food Content of Umeboshi Plums (per 100g): calories, 17; protein, 0.3g; fat, 0.8g; carbohydrates, 3.4g; fiber; 0.3g; calcium, 6.1mg; phosphorus, 26mg; iron, 2.0mg; sodium, 9,400mg; potassium, (−); vitamin A, nil; vitamin B_1, 0.06mg; vitamin B_2, 0.09mg; niacin, 0.6mg; vitamin C, nil.

UMEBOSHI VINEGAR
Plum vinegar is the juice extracted by osmosis from the still green *ume* fruits when they are packed in raw salt for pickling. Its red color is due to the *shiso* leaves placed over the plums (see UMEBOSHI). This highly saline, yet citric solution becomes more and more alkaline with age, and its original, sharp acidity turns increasingly sour. It is sold commercially as umeboshi vinegar or red plum "seasoning" and can make a sharp contribution to salad dressings or sweet and sour sauces. It can be sprinkled over boiled land or sea vegetables and salads or blended with tofu for a sauce.

WAKAME (see SEA VEGETABLES).

WASABI
Wasabi is a pale green and fiery horseradish, which is often eaten with Japanese fish dishes (see SUSHI).

YANNOH
Yannoh is a grain coffee substitute. The recipe is from Georges Ohsawa and it is made from five different grains and beans which are roasted and ground.

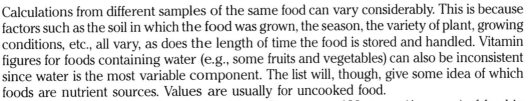

About the food content lists

Calculations from different samples of the same food can vary considerably. This is because factors such as the soil in which the food was grown, the season, the variety of plant, growing conditions, etc., all vary, as does the length of time the food is stored and handled. Vitamin figures for foods containing water (e.g., some fruits and vegetables) can also be inconsistent since water is the most variable component. The list will, though, give some idea of which foods are nutrient sources. Values are usually for uncooked food.

The quantities are usually measured in milligrams per 100 grams (4 ounces) of food in micrograms, or in the case of vitamins A and D in International Units. To give an idea of how small these weights are, 1 milligram is 1/1000th part of a gram (or 0.000035 of an ounce!). A microgram is 1/1000th of that!

References
Macrobiotic Home Remedies by Michio Kushi; *Nutrition Almanac* by John D. Kirschmann, Nutrition Search Inc., *Nutrition for a Better Life* by Nan Bronfen; *Introducing Macrobiotic Cooking* by Wendy Esko; *Macrobiotic Cooking for Everyone* by Edward and Wendy Esko; *The Natural Food Catalogue* by Vicki Peterson; *The Book of Tofu* by Shurtleff and Aoyagi; *The Book of Miso* by Shurtleff and Aoyagi; *The Book of Tempeh* by Shurtleff and Aoyagi; *Vegetables from the Sea* by S and T Arasaki; *Cooks Ingredients* by Davell and Bailey; *Composition and Facts About Food* by Ford Heritage; *Sushi* by Mi Detrick; *Whole Meals* by Marcea Weber; *The Truth About Bancha Tea* by Leonard Jocobs, East West Journal; *Standard Tables of Food Composition in Japan*, 1982, Ridal Press testing facilities; *The Structure of Everyday Life* by Fernard Brandel.

Recipes

The recommended balance

Soups, approximately 5 percent

Grains and Grain Products (breads, pastries, and pancake mixes),
50 percent or more

Vegetables/Sea Vegetables/Salads/Seeds, about 25 percent

Legumes, more or less 10 percent

Sauces, Spreads and Dips

Animal Food, 5 percent or no more than 10 percent

Desserts, Fruit and Nuts, a moderate 5 percent

Most of the good cooks I know, when asked for precise recipes, make remarks like, "I used what was left of this ingredient with some from a new packet and enough of the other and a handful of that." Not much help when you have a publisher to please! But it is the way of cooks and seems to produce the best results.

These recipes simply give an idea of some dishes to cook and the proportions to use. The invention and improvisation is part of the joy of preparing macrobiotic meals.

Approximate oven temperatures for the recipes are indicated in Fahrenheit. Oven temperatures vary with different stoves but the following is a general guide to Regulo, Fahrenheit and Celsius readings:

LOW OVEN	MEDIUM OVEN	HIGH OVEN
Regulo 0–2	Regulo 2–4	Regulo 4–9
225°F–300°F	300°F–375°F	375°F–500°F
107°C–150°C	150°C–200°C	200°C–250°C

Cup measures are ⅓ pint or about 7 fluid ounces.

Wendy Esko, in *Introducing Macrobiotic Cooking* says, "Learn to rely on your cookbook as little as possible. The sooner you learn common sense and intuition in cooking the better and more efficient your cooking will become. Once you know the proportions, begin experimenting with different combinations of food. Be creative and artistic . . . instead of using a measuring cup or spoon use the amount that looks right. Trust your senses instead of utensils."

Soup

5% of your meal might consist of **SOUP** WHICH CAN CONTAIN ONE OR ALL OF THE DIFFERENT TYPES OF FOOD: grains, legumes, land & sea vegetables, fish etc. **MISO SOUP** can make a complete meal in itself.

Soups

1. BARLEY BROTH
Serves 4 to 6

5 cups vegetable water, or water with
 strip of kombu
1 cup cooked barley (see GRAINS)
1 onion, sliced
1 diced carrot
1 stalk sliced celery
1 cup chopped parsley
1 tablespoon soy sauce

1. Bring vegetable water (or kombu and water) to a boil (remove kombu and keep).
2. Add barley, onion, carrot, celery and half the parsley. Simmer an hour.
3. Add soy sauce and stir.
4. Garnish with rest of the parsley and serve.

2. BARLEY, SQUASH AND VEGETABLE SOUP
Serves 4 to 6

2 cups barley
3 to 4 cups water (to cover)
10 cups vegetable or kombu stock
4 to 6 cups diced squash (marrow)
3 medium carrots, sliced
3 medium parsnips, sliced
1 tablespoon corn oil
1 tablespoon sesame oil
2 tablespoons yellow miso
2 cups hot water
1 tablespoon chopped chives or sliced
 scallion

1. Cover barley with water and soak for 2 days. Strain off water.
2. Place barley in saucepan with vegetable/kombu stock, bring to a boil, and simmer for 4 hours.
3. Sauté squash and carrots, turnips and parsnips in oil mixture until soft. Let stand until barley is cooked.
4. Add vegetables to barley. Purée two-thirds of the mixture. Mix in the rest of the vegetables.
5. Mix miso in hot water. Add to the pot or to each bowl of soup separately.
6. Decorate with chopped chives or scallion and serve.

3. BEET SOUP (BORSCH) AND MISO
Serves 4

2 cups water or vegetable water
1 slice of kombu
1 finely chopped carrot
1 finely chopped medium onion
2 cups finely diced beet
1 cup finely shredded cabbage
1 tablespoon rice vinegar or umeboshi
 vinegar
1 tablespoon shiso miso in 1 cup hot
 water

1. Bring water to a boil with kombu slice.
2. Add carrots, onion and beet: cover and simmer gently for 15 minutes.
3. Remove kombu and slice into fine, small squares. Return to soup and add cabbage. Simmer another 5 minutes.
4. Mix miso smoothly in water: add vinegar and miso. Bring almost to a boil. Remove heat.
5. Serve hot or cold.

½ cup goat's yoghurt
½ cup grated cucumber
½ teaspoon shiso condiment or sesame
  salt

6. Mix the yoghurt, grated cucumber and shiso and add a teaspoon to each bowl of borsch. Sprinkle with condiment.

4. BONITO, ONION AND CAULIFLOWER SOUP
Serves 4

2 tablespoons bonito flakes
4 cups water or vegetable stock
1 large onion, sliced
1 tablespoon sesame or corn oil
2 cups cauliflower
1 tablespoon soy sauce
½ cup chopped parsley

1. Boil bonito flakes in water for 5 minutes.
2. Sauté onion in oil until golden brown and soft.
3. Add onions and cauliflower to the bonito water. Simmer 10 minutes.
4. Add soy sauce.
5. Garnish with parsley and serve.

5. CARRAGEEN, MISO AND PUMPKIN SOUP
Serves 4

½ cup soaked and washed carrageen
4 cups water or vegetable water
1 sliced onion
1 cup finely diced pumpkin or squash
  (without skin)
Juice from 1 tablespoon fresh, grated
  ·ginger
½ cup warm water
2 teaspoons mugi miso
½ cup chopped parsley

1. Wash and clean carrageen well.
2. Add to vegetable water and bring to a boil. Simmer for ½ hour.
3. Add the onion and pumpkin or squash and ginger juice. Simmer another 10 minutes.
4. Mix mugi miso in water and pour into soup.
5. Bring to a boil and remove from heat.
6. Garnish with parsley and serve.

(Wakame or dulse can be used instead of carrageen.)

6. CARRAGEEN JELLIED CONSOMMÉ
Serves 4

1 cup soaked and cleaned carrageen
4½ cups vegetable water
4 tablespoons tamari soy sauce
2 tablespoons umeboshi vinegar
Juice of 1 lemon
½ cup chopped parsley or chives

1. Bring carrageen to a boil in vegetable water. Simmer for ½ hour.
2. Strain off carrageen (keep to use in soups or stews).
3. Add tamari soy sauce and umeboshi vinegar to the carrageen water.
4. Let set in a bowl or in separate containers. Refrigerate if necessary.
5. Squeeze lemon juice over and garnish with parsley or chives. Serve cold.

(A finely chopped onion may be cooked with the carrageen.)

7. CARROT SOUP OR CARROT AND ORANGE SOUP
Serves 4

4 cups water
½ cup soaked wakame, sliced fine
3 medium carrots, grated
1 finely chopped onion
2 bay leaves or juice and grated peel of
    one small fresh orange
2 teaspoons kuzu
½ cup cold water
1 tablespoon yellow miso
½ cup warm water
Chopped parsley or scallions (spring
    onions) to garnish

1. Bring water to a boil with wakame slices.
2. Add grated carrot, onions and bay leaves. Simmer 20 minutes.
3. Remove bay leaves. Blend the soup and put back in pan.
4. Dissolve kuzu in cold water and stir into the soup while bringing it gently to a boil. Remove from heat.
5. Take ½ cup of the soup and purée the miso.
6. Garnish with parsley or scallions (spring onions).

(Instead of bay leaves, try using juice and grated peel of one small orange when adding the kuzu water.)

8. CARROT (OR ZUCCHINI) AND OAT SOUP
Serves 4 to 6

6 cups water
6 medium carrots sliced in 4 pieces
    or 5 zucchini sliced in 4 pieces
1 cup oat flakes
1 tablespoon white miso
1 cup boiling water
Parsley to garnish

1. Bring water to a boil and add carrots. Simmer for an hour.
2. Add oak flakes stir and cook 45 minutes.
3. Blend and reheat.
4. Mix white miso in boiling water.
5. Serve soup with parsley and miso on the side to be added to taste.

9. CHICK PEA SOUP WITH SCALLION (SPRING ONION) GARNISH
Serves 4

¼ cup chick peas
4 cups water
1 large onion
4 strips kombu, each 2"×3"
2 cups vegetable water stock
2 teaspoons miso
1 cup hot water
1 cup finely sliced scallion (spring
    onion)

1. Soak chick peas overnight in 2 cups water. (Discard soaking water.)
2. Slice onion in crescent shapes, and pressure cook with chick peas and kombu strips in soaking water plus 2 cups water for 1½ hours (or simmer for 2½ hours).
3. Take out and chop kombu strips finely.
4. Mix miso thoroughly in cup of hot water.
5. Add 2 cups vegetable water, kombu and miso to chick peas. Heat for a minute or two.
6. Garnish with scallions (spring onion) and serve.

10. GINGER AND TAMARI SOY BROTH WITH TEMPURAED PARSLEY
Serves 4

4 cups vegetable water
1 teaspoon bonito flakes
1 medium onion, sliced in crescent
  shapes
2 teaspoons grated ginger juice
1 tablespoon tamari soy sauce
1 cup parsley sprigs, tempuraed

1. Bring vegetable water to a boil. Add bonito flakes. Simmer for 2 minutes.
2. Add onion and cook for 10 minutes.
3. Squeeze in ginger juice and add tamari soy sauce.
4. Serve with tempuraed parsley. (See Recipe 111.)

11. HIZIKI AND ADUKI SOUP
Serves 4

1 cup aduki beans
3 cups water
1 strip kombu, 6"×2"
1 cup soaked hiziki
1 teaspoon caraway seeds
1 clove garlic, sliced
1 tablespoon kuzu
½ cup cold water
1 tablespoon tamari soy sauce
1 scallion (spring onion), chopped
1 lemon, sliced

1. Soak aduki beans overnight. Discard water.
2. Bring aduki and kombu to a boil in the water and simmer for 1 hour.
3. Soak the hiziki in water for 10 minutes. Keep the water (about 1 cup). Slice hiziki finely.
4. Place hiziki and water in the aduki beans with caraway seeds and garlic slices. Bring to a boil and simmer another ¾ hour.
5. Puree ¾ cup of mixture and return to the pan.
6. Dissolve kuzu in water and add to the soup with tamari soy sauce, stir well and bring to a boil. Turn off heat. Soup should be creamy thick. Add more water if necessary.
7. Garnish with scallion (spring onion) and serve with lemon slices.

12. LEEK SOUP WITH CARROT FLOWERS
Serves 4

4 cups water
1 strip kombu, 6"×2"
4 leaves Chinese cabbage
1 very finely sliced leek
1 carrot, sliced in flowers

1. Add kombu to water. Bring to a boil and remove kombu (keep for future use).
2. Add cabbage and boil 5 minutes, or until soft. Take out. Roll each leaf and slice each roll in half. Place them in the soup bowls.
3. Add leeks and carrots to the water and boil 4 minutes.
4. Serve over the cabbage rolls. Garnish with pan-fried mochi squares (as for Onion Miso Soup, Recipe 17).

13. LENTIL SOUP
Serves 4 to 6

1 large onion, sliced fine
1 tablespoon toasted or plain sesame oil
6 cups water
2 cups lentils
¾ cup soaked wakame, sliced
1 tablespoon genmai (rice) miso, to taste
1 sprig parsley or 1 scallion (spring onion) chopped, to garnish

1. Sauté onions in sesame oil for 3 minutes, or until transparent.
2. Add water, lentils, wakame and soaking water to pot. Bring to a boil and simmer for 45 minutes to an hour, or until lentils are soft.
3. Mix miso in ½ cup of the soup and stir into the soup to season it.
4. Garnish with parsley or scallion (spring onion) and serve.

14. MISO, CARROT, SCALLION (SPRING ONION), CELERY AND CABBAGE WITH WAKAME AND TOFU
Serves 4

Miso soup can be made from many different recipes, depending on the season and what ingredients are available at the time. There are various types of miso to choose from, each with a distinctive flavor (see INGREDIENTS—MISO).

4 cups vegetable water
½ cup soaked and sliced wakame
½ cup sliced carrots
½ cup finely sliced celery
½ cup sliced savoy cabbage
4 sliced scallions (spring onions)
1 teaspoon grated, fresh ginger
1 tablespoon yellow miso
½ cup hot water
1 cup tofu, sliced in ½" squares

1. Bring vegetable water to a boil with wakame pieces and soaking water.
2. Add vegetables, carrots first, three of the scallions (spring onions), celery and cabbage. Simmer for 10 minutes.
3. Mix yellow miso (made from koji rice and soybeans) in the ½ cup hot water. Add to the soup with the tofu squares. If yellow miso is not available, another type will do.

4. Bring soup almost to a boil and turn off heat.
5. Sprinkle the rest of the scallions (spring onions) on top when serving.

(The above soup can be made as a meal or a snack by adding 2 ounces of whole wheat (udon) noodles or ¾ cup of cooked, whole grain rice, barley or oats.)

15. MISO, DULSE AND ONION SOUP WITH TOFU
Serves 4

2 medium onions
3 cups boiling water
1 cup washed and chopped dulse
½ cup ½" squares tofu
2 teaspoons brown rice miso
2 scallions (spring onions)

1. Slice the onion into thin, even crescent shapes from root to crown.
2. Place in boiling water and simmer, uncovered, until the strong, acid vapors have escaped and the steam begins to smell sweet. The onions will turn translucent in 3 or 4 minutes.
3. Add the chopped dulse and the tofu squares and allow to simmer for 10 minutes.
4. Dissolve the miso thoroughly in some of the soup liquid, be sure there are no lumps (use your suribachi). Add to the soup. Bring to a boil and turn off heat.
5. Just before serving, sprinkle with the finely chopped scallions (spring onions). Use the whole of the onions, green and all.

16. MISO, ONION, PUMPKIN, WATERCRESS, DULSE AND SOBA NOODLE SOUP
Serves 4

4 cups water
1 strip kombu, 6"×2"
1 medium, sliced onion
1 cup diced pumpkin
½ cup watercress pieces
½ cup washed and finely sliced dulse
2 ounces soba noodles
1 tablespoon buckwheat or mugi (barley) miso
½ cup boiling water or the soup liquid

1. Heat kombu in water. Remove kombu just before water boils and save for future use.
2. Drop in onions and allow to boil (uncovered) for 2 minutes.
3. Add pumpkin, watercress, dulse and noodles. Simmer for 10 minutes.
4. Puree miso well in boiling water and add to the soup.
5. Garnish with chopped parsley or small nori squares.

103

17.MISO-ONION SOUP WITH PAN-FRIED MOCHI
Serves 4

4 cups water
1 kombu strip
3 medium, sliced onions
1 tablespoon mugi miso
½ cup hot water or the soup liquid
12 ½" squares of brown rich mochi
1 tablespoon sesame oil
2 tablespoons umeboshi vinegar

1. Place kombu in the water and bring to a boil. Remove kombu and keep for future use.
2. Add onions and simmer until very soft (25 to 30 minutes).
3. Purée miso in hot water and add to the onions.
4. Place mochi squares in skillet with a little oil and pan-fry until puffed up and golden brown. Sprinkle with umeboshi vinegar before placing a few in each bowl of soup.
5. Garnish with parsley and serve.

18. MOCK TURTLE SOUP WITH BATTER CROÛTONS
Serves 4

4 cups water or vegetable stock
1 tablespoon bonito flakes
1 medium, finely diced carrot
1 bay leaf
1 tablespoon tamari soy sauce
½ sheet nori in 1" squares

1. Place bonito flakes, carrot and bay leaf in water. Simmer for 15 minutes.
2. Add the tamari soy sauce and nori squares. Simmer 1 minute.
3. Remove bay leaf and serve with batter croûtons and chopped parsley.

BATTER CROÛTONS
Serves 4

1 tablespoon 85 percent whole-wheat
    pastry flour
1 tablespoon corn flour
1 teaspoon of kuzu
Pinch salt
1 cup water
1 tablespoon umeboshi vinegar
Corn oil
½ cup finely chopped parsley

1. Mix flour, kuzu and salt with water. Stir to make a smooth batter.
2. Let stand for 20 minutes in refrigerator (overnight if necessary).
3. Add umeboshi vinegar.
4. Brush pan with a little oil, drop "buttons" of batter in and sauté until golden brown.
5. Dry on paper towels before serving with soup.

19. MUSHROOM-NOODLE BROTH
Serves 4

6 cups water or vegetable water
1 strip kombu, 6"×2"
1 tablespoon bonito flakes
6 dried shiitake mushrooms, soaked 10
    minutes and sliced or 6 fresh
    mushrooms, sliced
¼ cup tamari soy sauce
1 tablespoon mirin or sake (optional) or
    1 teaspoon barley malt

1. Place kombu in vegetable water and bring to a boil, then remove.
2. Add bonito flakes and shiitake (with soaking water) or fresh mushrooms. Simmer for 15 minutes.
3. Add tamari soy sauce and sake, mirin or barley malt.
4. Serve as a broth for noodles or with noodles and sukiyaki.

20. MUSHROOM AND LOTUS ROOT CREAM SOUP
Serves 4

¾ cup finely chopped lotus root
4 cups vegetable stock or water
1 strip kombu, 6"×2"
1 small, chopped onion
6 medium mushrooms, sliced
½ cup soy milk
2 tablespoons tamari soy sauce
2 teaspoons kuzu in 1 cup cold water
2 tablespoons chopped chives or
    parsley

1. If using dried lotus root, soak in 1 cup water for an hour or until soft enough to chop fine. Add the soaking water to stock.
2. Bring water or stock to a boil with kombu. Remove kombu and keep for re-use.
3. Add onion and lotus root. Simmer for half an hour.
4. Add mushrooms and boil gently for 10 minutes.
5. Add soy milk and tamari soy sauce and blend.
6. Dissolve kuzu in the cold water and stir into the soup. Heat until creamy.
7. Sprinkle with chives or parsley and serve.

21. ONION AND DULSE SOUP WITH TAMARI SOY SAUCE
Serves 4

1 cup soaked dulse
4 cups vegetable water or kombu stock
4 medium onions, finely sliced
2 tablespoons tamari soy sauce or 1
*   tablespoon genmai miso, dissolved in*
*   ½ cup hot water*

1. Wash the dulse and clean off any tiny shells or sand. Chop fine.
2. Bring water to a boil. Put in the onion and let boil, uncovered, for 2 to 3 minutes.
3. Turn down heat to medium-low. Add the dulse and cover.
4. Simmer for 30 minutes.
5. Add the tamari soy sauce (or miso in water) and stir.
6. Serve with whole-wheat croûtons. (See Recipe 28.)

(Onions can be sautéed first in 2 teaspoons toasted sesame or nut oil.)

22. PUMPKIN SOUP
Serves 4 to 6

3 cups diced pumpkin
1 strip kombu, 6"×1"
2 cups water
2 cups vegetable water
1 cup whole-wheat bread cubes for
*   croûtons*
2 tablespoon chopped scallions (spring
*   onions)*

1. Peel the pumpkin carefully if the skin is hard. Dice fine.
2. Bring 2 cups water to a boil with kombu strip in it, then remove kombu.
3. Add pumpkin to kombu water and cook ½ hour. Blend well.
4. Serve with croûtons (see Recipe 28) or sprinkle with chopped scallions (spring onions).

23. PUMPKIN AND MISO SOUP
Serves 4

1 pound pumpkin
3 cups water
1 teaspoon sunflower oil
1 small chopped onion
1 clove crushed garlic
1 tablespoon ginger juice
1 tablespoon light shiro miso
½ cup cold water
2 teaspoons kuzu
2 tablespoons chopped scallions (spring
*   onions)*

1. Dice pumpkin.
2. Bring 3 cups of water to a boil and add pumpkin pieces. Simmer for ½ hour, or until tender. Allow to cool and remove skin.
3. Brush oil in skillet. Sauté onion and garlic for 5 minutes.
4. Add onion, garlic and ginger juice to pumpkin. Stir.
5. Mix miso in ½ cup pumpkin water. Add to cooked pumpkin. Blend mixture.
6. Mix kuzu in cold water and add to the

soup. Stir and reheat. Remove from heat
before soup boils.
7. Serve with finely chopped scallions
(spring onions) on top.

24. ROLLED OATS AND CELERY SOUP
Serves 4

4 cups water
Pinch salt
2 cups chopped celery
1 cup rolled oats
Pinch black pepper

1. Bring water to a boil. Add salt and
celery. Cook 10 minutes.
2. Add the oats and cook for another 45
minutes (add more water if necessary).
3. Add the pinch of pepper.
4. Serve as soup or, if creamed soup is
preferred, purée and reheat before
serving.

25. SEA VEGETABLE SOUP
Serves 4

This soup was made by using water in which prawns fresh from the Mediterranean had been
cooked. When prawn stock isn't available, proceed as follows.

4 cups water
1 tablespoon bonito flakes
1 medium, sliced onion
½ cup soaked wakame, sliced in ¼"
  squares
1 slice 6"×2" cooked kombu sliced in
  very small squares
1 sheet nori, cut into 1" squares
½ cup dulse, sliced fine
1 tablespoon tamari soy sauce
2 slices whole-wheat bread
1 tablespoon toasted sesame oil

1. Bring water to a boil and add bonito
flakes and onion. Simmer for 5 minutes.
2. Add wakame, kombu and nori. Simmer
gently for 10 to 15 minutes.
3. Cut bread into croûtons (¼" squares) and
shallow-fry in very little oil.
4. Serve croutons in separate bowl to
garnish soup.

26. SHIITAKE MUSHROOM AND KOMBU BROTH
Serves 4

4 or 5 sliced shiitake mushrooms (fresh,
*   or if dried, soaked for 15 minutes)*
1 onion, sliced finely
1 teaspoon toasted sesame oil
5 cups water
2 pieces kombu, 2"×6"
2 tablespoons tamari soy sauce

1. If the mushrooms are dried, soak in a cup of water for 15 minutes and use the water for the soup. Remove stalk ends.
2. Sauté mushrooms and onion gently in the toasted sesame oil for 5 minutes.
3. Add soaking water plus 5 cups of water and kombu. Simmer for 30 minutes.
4. Remove kombu and slice into small pieces. Return to soup.
5. Season with the tamari soy sauce.
6. Decorate with parsley and serve.

27. SEITAN AND BARLEY SOUP
Serves 4

½ cup barley
4 cups water
1 medium onion, sliced
2 carrots, sliced
½ cup mushrooms, sliced
¼ cup celery, sliced
½ cup cooked seitan cubes (see
*   SEITAN)*
2 tablespoons tamari soy sauce
Watercress or scallions (spring onions),
*   to garnish*

1. Wash barley, and soak in water overnight.
2. Add 1 cup water and boil for ¾ hour.
3. Add onion, carrots, mushrooms and celery. Cook 15 minutes.
4. Add seitan cubes (See INGREDIENTS— SEITAN). Bring to a boil and simmer for 15 minutes.
5. Add tamari soy sauce and simmer for 10 minutes.
6. Garnish with watercress or scallions (spring onions) and serve.

28. WATERCRESS SOUP
Serves 4

4 cups water
½ cup soaked wakame, sliced
1 small, sliced onion
2 bunches chopped watercress stalks
*   and leaves (washed well)*
Pinch salt
2 teaspoons kuzu
½ cup cold water
Watercress or parsley, chopped to
*   garnish*

1. Bring water and wakame with soaking water to a boil.
2. Add onion. Simmer gently for 5 minutes.
3. Add watercress and salt and simmer 5 minutes.
4. Blend the soup and return to pan.
5. Mix kuzu in cold water, add to the soup and bring gently to a boil; stir carefully.
6. Decorate with watercress or parsley.

BREAD CROÛTONS

1 cup whole-wheat bread cubes for croûtons
1 teaspoon toasted sesame oil
1 teaspoon tamari soy sauce

1. Serve with bread croûtons. Brush a skillet with sesame oil and toast the bread cubes gently until golden brown. Sprinkle with tamari soy sauce but *not* in the skillet as tamari soy sauce will burn.

Grains

50% or more, the principal food of the meal, should ideally be GRAINS & GRAIN PRODUCTS. They can be PREPARED WITH LEGUMES, VEGETABLES, FRUITS ETC., USED IN SAUCES & SOUPS, AS the MAIN COURSE or in DESSERTS (cakes pastry etc.) — & BREAD. Use chiefly WHOLE GRAINS: the more they are processed the more their VITALITY & NOURISHMENT is lost

Grains

29. BARLEY AND BURDOCK STEW
Serves 4

1 cup barley
4 cups water
4 pieces of kombu, each 1"×2"
1 cup water
1 cup diced rutabaga (swede)
1 cup diced celeriac
½ cup sliced burdock root (Soak for 10
  minutes and discard water.)
Pinch salt
Chopped parsley to garnish

1. Soak barley in 3 cups water overnight.
2. Add kombu slices and 1 cup water, bring to a boil and simmer for ¾ hour.
3. Add one cup water, rutabaga (swede) celeriac, burdock and salt. Stew for 45 minutes.
4. Garnish with parsley and serve.

30. BARLEY AND VEGETABLE STEW
Serves 4

6 shiitake dried mushrooms
1 cup water
2 cups cooked barley (see
  INGREDIENTS—GRAINS)
1 chopped leek
1 carrot, sliced in large pieces
1 onion, sliced
1 cup water
½ cup cooked lentils
1 tablespoon miso
½ cup hot water

1. Soak mushrooms in water for 10 minutes and remove stalk ends. Use water for your stew.
2. Place cooked barley in pot and over it the mushrooms, leek, carrot, onion and cooked lentils and mushroom water, plus 1 extra cup of water.
3. Cook for half an hour over gentle heat until vegetables are tender.
4. Mix miso well in hot water, stir into the stew and just bring to a simmer before serving.

   (Barley can be roasted before cooking for a change of flavor.)

31. BREAKFAST MUESLI CRUNCH
Serves 8 to 10

2 cups oat flakes
1 cup wheat flakes or puffed wheat
1 cup barley flakes
1 cup rye flakes
¾ cup raisins
½ cup pumpkin seeds
½ cup sunflower seeds
½ cup chopped, mixed nuts
1 tablespoon sesame salt
½ cup apple juice (optional)
2 tablespoons rice malt or maple syrup
1 teaspoon vanilla (optional)

1. Mix dry ingredients in oiled ovenproof pan.
2. Heat apple juice, rice malt or maple syrup and vanilla in separate pan to blend. Pour over the cereal mixture, stirring well to avoid lumps.
3. Place in 350°F oven for 20 minutes. Take out and stir.
4. Bake another 20 minutes, then stir and bake 20 minutes more, or until it *begins* to turn golden brown. Allow to cool.
5. Serve with stewed apples and raisins or with fruit in season, apple juice and a dash of soy milk.

32. BREAKFAST WHOLE-OAT PORRIDGE

Whole oats make by far the most nourishing and satisfying morning porridge. Steel-cut oats are quicker to prepare (they cook in 40 minutes). Avoid refined, precooked oat flakes.

For cooking oats see INGREDIENTS—GRAINS. Whole oats will also cook overnight if placed in a very low (250°F) oven before you go to bed. Use 1 cup of oats to 4 cups boiling water. If the mixture is too watery in the morning, place over medium heat, stirring well or add a little soy milk until creamy. Add raisins or cinnamon if desired. Oats can be served for breakfast, as a dessert or savory.

Summer recipe:
Serves 1

1 bowl cooked, whole oats
¼ teaspoon cinnamon
½ tablespoon barley malt
½ tablespoon raisins
1 tablespoon Muesli Crunch
¼ cup soy milk
Stewed apples

1. Stir cinnamon and raisins into the cooked oats and heat.
2. Pour barley malt over the top or sprinkle on some Muesli Crunch (see Recipe 31).
3. Add soy milk and stewed apples to taste.

Winter recipe:
Serves 1

1 tablespoon sauerkraut (in sea salt) or
   1 sliced, salt-pickled gherkin
   (optional)
1 bowl hot, cooked oats
½ teaspoon soy sauce
½ teaspoon sesame salt or tekka

1. If using sauerkraut or sliced pickles place in bottom of the bowl. Add cooked oats and stir.
2. Sprinkle soy sauce and sesame salt or tekka over.
3. Serve with toast or oat cakes and Tahini Spread (see Recipe 152).

33. BROWN RICE, ADUKI BEANS AND VEGETABLES

A good meal and easily prepared.

*2 cups cooked short grained brown
    rice*
1 cup cooked aduki beans

1. For cooking of rice and aduki see
   INGREDIENTS—GRAINS and LEGUMES.
   Serving them together boosts the protein
   available (see PROTEINS).
2. Serve vegetables over the rice and
   beans.

THE VEGETABLES:
The slicing of vegetables is important to the decoration and appearance of the meal. The
onions are sliced fine and vertically, the carrots and roots are cut diagonally or sharpened
as you would a pencil or are cut in matchsticks or even flowers. The greens can also be sliced
fine. Use any vegetables in season, except potatoes, tomatoes or eggplant.

1 tablespoon safflower oil
1 small burdock root, pencil sliced
1 onion, sliced vertically
1 carrot, sliced in matchsticks
1 small parsnip, sliced
1 cabbage leaf, sliced fine or
    1 cup bamboo shoots or
    3 string beans, sliced
4 fresh mushrooms, sliced
1 tablespoon kuzu in ½ cup cold water
*1 tablespoon white miso in ½ cup hot
    water*

1. Soak burdock root slices for 10 minutes
   before cooking. (Discard water).
2. Heat oil in pan and add burdock root
   and onion. Sauté gently for 10 minutes,
   stirring to prevent sticking.
3. Add carrot and parsnip and stir for
   another 3 minutes.
4. Add cabbage or bamboo shoots or string
   beans and mushrooms. Stir continually
   for 5 minutes.
5. Mix kuzu in ½ cup cold water and miso
   in ½ cup hot water and pour over
   vegetables. Bring to a boil and serve
   over hot rice and aduki beans. Aduki
   beans may be served as a side dish
   instead of with the rice.

34. BROWN RICE CROQUETTES (RICE BALLS)
Serves 6 to 8

These are a delicious and practical standby—and they won't stand by all that long! They are made from leftover rice, which needs to be well cooked and soft. They are good for traveling and when proper food is likely to be scarce.

*3 cups soft cooked, short grained
  brown rice*
1 tablespoon sesame paste (optional)
2 umeboshi plums
*½ cup sesame seeds or 1 cup whole-
  wheat breadcrumbs*
1 tablespoon sesame or corn oil

1. If the rice is not soft and sticky you will need to stir in ½ cup water, stir and cook gently for 5 minutes, or until the grains hold together. Leave to cool.
2. Add the sesame paste if a nutty flavor is desired.
3. Remove the pits from the plums and slice each into quarters.
4. Wet hands and shape rice into croquettes. Dig a hole in each and place a piece of plum inside—this adds flavor and helps preserve the rice ball when traveling.
5. The surface should be wet. Roll in sesame seeds or breadcrumbs or flour.
6. Rice balls are recommended deep-fried, but you will consume less oil if you wipe the skillet with a little sesame or corn oil and gently pan-fry until golden brown. When cooked, place on paper towels to drain. Serve with salad, parsley sauce or eat them on their own.

(1 cup of soft-cooked aduki beans or lentils, chopped parsley or onion may be mixed with the rice for variety.)

These rice balls can also be wrapped in nori sheets instead of frying them. This will keep them fresh when traveling.

6-8 rice balls
3-4 sheets nori

1. Roast the nori sheets gently over a flame. They should turn a green-grey color and be crisp.
2. Fold each sheet into quarters and tear neatly into four squares.
3. Wrap each rice ball in one of the squares. Wet edges to stick the nori to the rice ball.
4. Turn rice ball over and place on a second square, dampen and cover the rice ball with the nori.

35. BROWN RICE AND BULGHUR CROQUETTES
Serves 4

1 cup bulghur wheat
1 cup water
2 cups soft, cooked brown rice (see
  INGREDIENTS—GRAINS)
2 teaspoons chopped basil
Pinch salt
½ cup chopped parsley
½ cup flour or 1 cup whole-wheat
  breadcrumbs
1 teaspoon corn oil

1. Soak bulghur for an hour in a cup of water and steam for 20 minutes.
2. Mix with soft, cooked rice.
3. Add basil, salt and parsley. Wet hands and shape into croquettes.
4. Roll in flour or breadcrumbs.
5. Brush pan with corn oil and sauté gently.
6. Serve with steamed vegetables and Umeboshi Kuzu Sauce (see Recipe 159).

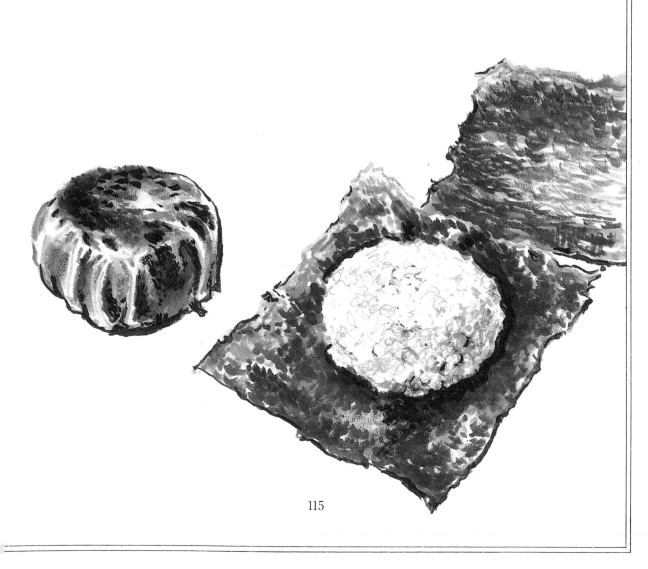

36. BROWN RICE AND CHINESE-STYLE VEGETABLES
Serves 4

*3 cups cooked short grained brown
    rice*
*(For cooking rice see
    INGREDIENTS—GRAINS.)*
4 shiitake mushrooms
1 large onion, sliced thin
1 large matchstick-sliced carrot
3 cups shredded cabbage
3 cups vegetable water
2 cups diced squash (without skin)
1 cup snow peas (mangetout peas)
½ cup sliced green or red pepper
1 tablespoon kuzu
½ cup apple juice
1 teaspoon mirin
2 tablespoons tamari soy sauce
1 tablespoon roasted sesame seeds
*Chopped parsley or scallions (spring
    onions), to garnish*

1. If shiitake mushrooms are dried, soak for 10 minutes and boil for 15 minutes. Slice fine, removing stalk ends.
2. Layer onions, carrots, cabbage, pepper and mushrooms in pot. Add vegetable water (plus mushroom water). Cover and boil for 5 minutes.
3. Add squash and snow peas (mangetout). Cover and simmer 5 minutes.
4. Dissolve kuzu in apple juice, add mirin and tamari soy sauce. Mix vegetables and stir until mixture thickens.
5. Serve over rice (or noodles) and garnish with sesame seeds and parsley or scallions (spring onions).

37. BROWN RICE AND VEGETABLE PIE
Serves 4 to 6

1 medium onion, chopped fine
4 carrots, sliced fine
1 tablespoon corn oil
2 medium leeks, sliced fine
½ cup water
4 cups cooked brown rice
*1 cup cooked aduki beans (see
    INGREDIENTS: ADUKI)*
½ cup water
1 clove garlic, crushed
½ cup chopped parsley
1 dessertspoon tamari soy sauce
*1 teaspoon light miso in ½ cup
    hot water*
2 teaspoons kuzu in ½ cup cold water
2 tablespoons tahini
1 teaspoon roasted sesame seeds

1. Sauté onion and carrots in oil for 5 minutes. Add leeks and sauté, stirring well, for 3 minutes. Add water and bring to a boil.
2. Add vegetables to rice and aduki beans with garlic and parsley. Sprinkle soy sauce over mixture.
3. Brush a little oil inside pie dish and line dish with pastry (see Recipes 74, 75). Place rice and vegetables in pastry.
4. Mix miso in hot water and kuzu in cold water, pour them into a pan, add tahini, stir and bring to a boil. Pour this sauce over the vegetables.
5. Cover with pastry, decorate with sesame seeds—press them on top—and bake in a preheated 450°F oven for 35 minutes.

38. BROWN RICE SUMMER SALAD
Serves 4 to 6

For taking to the beach in the summer.

*3 cups cooked brown rice (see
   INGREDIENTS—GRAINS)*
¾ cup diced apple
*½ cup diced, pickled daikon radish
   (optional)*
1 cup diced tofu
1 cup grated carrot
½ cup seeded raisins
½ cup chopped watercress or parsley
½ cup roasted Brazil nuts or pine nuts
*¾ cup diced melon or ½ cup seedless
   grapes*
1 tablespoon umeboshi vinegar

1. Mix the ingredients with the rice in a container that can be sealed.
2. Sprinkle with umeboshi vinegar and keep in a cool place.

Serve with the following dressing:

½ cup apple juice
2 tablespoons sesame oil
2 umeboshi plums (pitted & sliced)
½ teaspoon sesame salt
½ teaspoon tamari soy sauce

1. Mix dressing in a screw-top bottle. Keep salad and dressing cool. Pour dressing over salad immediately before serving.
2. Add more rice if preferred.

39. BUCKWHEAT BURGERS
Serves 4

These are made from kasha (see INGREDIENTS—GRAINS).

1 large onion
1 tablespoon toasted sesame oil
1 cup buckwheat, roasted (see GRAINS)
3 cups water
2 teaspoons genmai miso
1 teaspoon light tahini
3 teaspoons umeboshi vinegar
2 teaspoons water
½ cup chopped parsley
1 cup whole wheat breadcrumbs
1 tablespoon corn or sesame oil

1. Sauté onion in oil for 3 minutes.
2. Add buckwheat and sauté for 5 to 10 minutes, or until golden brown.
3. Add water, bring to a boil and simmer gently for 20 minutes.
4. Turn off heat and let stand, covered, for 10 minutes.
5. Mix miso, tahini, and umeboshi vinegar with 2 teaspoons of water. Pour into the buckwheat, add parsley and stir well. Cover and let cool. The mixture should be soft and sticky.
6. Wet your hands and shape kasha into croquettes—about 4 to 6.
7. Wet the surface and roll in breadcrumbs.
8. Brush skillet with oil and gently sauté "burgers" until brown.
9. Serve with Mochi Onion Sauce (see Recipe 142) or Onion and Squash Sauce (see Recipe 146).

40. BUCKWHEAT KASHA WITH CABBAGE AND CARAWAY-TOFU SAUCE

Serves 4 to 6

2 cups roasted buckwheat
4 cups water
2 tablespoons light tahini
2 tablespoons umeboshi vinegar
2 teaspoons tamari soy sauce
1 cup finely chopped scallions (spring onions)

1. Simmer buckwheat gently in water for 20 minutes. Turn off heat and allow to steam 5 minutes. It should be fluffy and soft. Add water if necessary.
2. Mix in tahini, vinegar, soy sauce and chopped scallions (spring onions). Put lid back on and allow to cook for ten more minutes.
3. Serve with Cabbage and Caraway-Tofu Sauce (see Recipe 136).

(These can be made into "burgers" if preferred.)

41. BUCKWHEAT-STUFFED SQUASH (MARROW)
Serves 4

1 small squash (marrow)
3 dried shiitake mushrooms, soaked in
*   1 cup of water (save water) and*
*   sliced*
1 chopped onion
1 tablespoon sunflower oil
1 cup roasted buckwheat
1 carrot, grated
1 parsnip, grated
¼ cup chopped parsley
½ teaspoon caraway seeds
1 clove garlic, chopped fine
2 tablespoons tahini

1. Slice squash (marrow) lengthwise or in 2½″ slices and remove seeds. Pour boiling water over and simmer 5 minutes. Drain off water and save.
2. Gently sauté onion for 5 minutes in the oil.
3. Add buckwheat and stir till golden brown (10 minutes).
4. Add carrot, parsnip, shiitake, parsley, caraway seeds and garlic. Add squash (marrow) water and shiitake water to make up 3 cups, bring to a boil, stir and simmer for 10 minutes.
5. Add tahini and stir to make soft stuffing "paste."
6. Fill the squash (marrow) with stuffing.
7. Bake in a 350°F oven for an hour.
8. Serve with Bechamel sauce (see Recipe 134).

42. CABBAGE STUFFED WITH BUCKWHEAT WITH OATMEAL SAUCE
Serves 4

4 cabbage leaves
2 cups water
Pinch salt
½ cup chopped onion
½ cup diced carrot
¼ cup diced mushrooms
¼ cup chopped celery
1 tablespoon toasted sesame oil
1 cup roasted buckwheat
1 teaspoon tahini
3 cups water
2 teaspoons genmai miso
½ cup hot water
½ cup roast, whole-wheat breadcrumbs

1. Boil cabbage leaves in 2 cups water and salt for 5 or 10 minutes, or until soft. Save water for sauce.
2. Sauté onions, carrots, mushrooms and celery in oil for 5 to 10 minutes.
3. Add buckwheat, tahini and cabbage water. Bring to a boil, cover and simmer for 20 to 30 minutes. Remove from heat.
4. Mix miso in hot water and add to mixture. Allow to cool.
5. Cut the hard stem from bottom of cabbage leaves.
6. Shape buckwheat into croquettes with wet hands. Place one on each leaf and wrap leaf around it, folding the outer sides toward the center. Roll and fasten with a toothpick. Place in oven.
7. Serve with Oatmeal Sauce (see Recipe 145) and sprinkle with breadcrumbs.

43. CORN ON THE COB WITH UMEBOSHI
Serves 4

Delicious served with Long Island Lobster.

4 ears of corn
2 cups water
3 umeboshi plums
1 tablespoon olive oil
1 tablespoon tamari soy sauce

1. Bring water to a boil in a large pot or steamer.
2. Steam or boil corn for half an hour, or until soft.
3. Pit plums and mash with oil and tamari soy sauce.
4. Spread this mixture smoothly around each ear of corn and serve.

44. COUS COUS

There are traditional and elaborate ways to prepare cous cous which involve a lot of time and trouble. This way is quick and the cous cous is still delicious.

2 cups cous cous
4 cups water
1 tablespoon safflower or sunflower oil
2 tablespoons raisins
½ teaspoon nutmeg (optional)

1. Soak the cous cous in water for half an hour, or until the water is absorbed.
2. Add the oil and mix in with a fork. Sprinkle in the raisins and nutmeg. Stir. Place in a covered casserole in a 350°F oven for ½ hour.

THE VEGETABLES:
Serves 4

2 cups water
2 large onions, sliced in quarters
½ cup cooked chick peas (see
*   INGREDIENTS—LEGUMES)*
4 slices squash (marrow), diced
3 carrots, sliced in large pieces
1 leek, sliced in large pieces
1 clove garlic, crushed
1 tablespoon miso
½ cup hot water
½ teaspoon turmeric or saffron
*   (optional)*

1. Bring water to a boil, add the onion and simmer for 3 minutes. Add the chick peas, squash (marrow), carrots, leek and garlic. Cook for 10 minutes.
2. Mix miso in hot water and add to the sauce with turmeric or saffron.
3. Serve vegetables and sauce over the cous cous. Decorate with parsley.

Pieces of lamb are traditionally cooked with the cous cous stew. Serve with chili pepper sauce (tabasco), sprinkled to taste as an option.

45. COUS COUS OR BULGHUR WHEAT TABOOLI SALAD
Serves 4

*3 cups cooked cous cous or bulghur
   wheat (see Recipe 44)*
1 cup finely chopped peeled cucumber
1 cup parsley, finely chopped
*½ cup fresh dill, chopped (or fresh
   mint)*
½ cup raisins
Pinch of ground coriander (or cumin)
1 tablespoon soy sauce
2 tablespoons brown rice vinegar
1 tablespoon roasted sunflower seeds

1. Mix the cucumber, parsley and dill (or mint) with the cous cous (or bulghur wheat) and add raisins.
2. Add coriander (or cumin), soy sauce and rice vinegar and mix well.
3. Sprinkle with the sunflower seeds.
4. Serve as a cold salad.

46. FIVE-COLORED RICE
Serves 4 to 6

(Or five shades of beige!)

2 cups short grained brown rice
½ cup kombu
½ cup water
6 dried shiitake mushrooms
1 cup water
½ cup dried lotus root
½ cup water
*1 cup finely diced fresh burdock root
   (soaked for 10 minutes)*
¾ cup diced tofu
1 cup finely diced carrots
¾ cup dried, shredded daikon
½ cup water

1. Roast rice in a dry skillet until deep golden brown. Stir continually to prevent sticking. When roasted, remove from pan or rice will burn.
2. Soak the shiitake and lotus for 10 minutes in water (kombu needs soaking for only 2 minutes). Keep soaking water (except burdock water).
3. Place ingredients in pressure cooker in this order: kombu on the bottom, shiitake, tofu, carrots, daikon, burdock and then lotus. Cover with the rice.
4. Add the soaking water (about 2½ cups) plus 3 more cups.
5. Pressure cook for 45 minutes.
6. Serve with green vegetables or carrots, or mixed vegetables.

47. "FIVE ELEMENT" VEGETABLE-MILLET PIE AND MUSTARD SAUCE IN WHEATLESS CRUST

1 cup millet
3 cups water
1 teaspoon salt
1 cup cauliflower pieces
2 teaspoons olive oil
2 cups daikon soaked (10 minutes) and sliced in matchsticks
1 cup carrots, sliced diagonally
2 cups broccoli (stems and leaves) sliced diagonally
2 medium onions in half moon shapes
2 cups chopped kale
2 large scallions (spring onions) diagonally sliced
½ tablespoon tarragon
2 tablespoons fresh, chopped dill
½ cup fresh, chopped parsley
2 cooked ears of corn
1 cup broccoli tops, broken small

1. Bring water to a boil in a pan; add millet, salt and cauliflower.
2. Simmer for 30 minutes. While it is cooking:
3. Heat oil in an iron skillet. Add daikon, carrots, broccoli stems, onions, kale, scallions, tarragon, dill and parsley.
4. Stir well over high heat for 20 minutes.
5. Remove corn from the cobs.
6. Remove millet and cauliflower from heat and mash the mixture.
7. Add millet and cauliflower, corn kernels and broccoli tops to vegetable mixture.

MUSTARD SAUCE:
Serves 4

1¾ cups vegetable water
1 teaspoon kuzu
2 tablespoons arrowroot
2 tablespoons natural (Dijon) mustard
1 tablespoon umeboshi paste or 3 umeboshi plums, pitted and mashed
2 tablespoons tamari soy sauce (wheat free if necessary)

1. Mix kuzu and arrowroot in cold vegetable water.
2. Add mustard, umeboshi and tamari soy sauce.
3. Heat, stirring well, until the mixture thickens (boil for 3 minutes).
4. Pour the sauce over the vegetable and millet mixture and mix in well.
5. Press Wheatless Pastry (see recipe 80) into a 9″ pie dish and spread vegetable-millet and sauce mixture in it.
6. Bake in preheated 375°F oven for 35 minutes

48. FRIED RICE AND SHIITAKE WITH LEEKS, CHINESE CABBAGE AND PARSLEY

1 tablespoon corn or sesame oil
1 cup cooked shiitake mushrooms, sliced or fresh mushrooms, sliced
3 cups boiled brown rice
1 tablespoon tamari soy sauce

1. Oil pan and sauté mushrooms.
2. Add rice and stir-fry.
3. Sprinkle in tamari soy sauce.
4. Stir and serve.

THE VEGETABLES:
Serves 4

1 leek, sliced diagonally
1 medium carrot sliced in matchsticks
¼ Chinese cabbage, cut lengthwise then finely sliced
1 teaspoon toasted sesame oil
Pinch salt
1 teaspoon kuzu
1 cup water
½ cup chopped parsley

1. Sauté leek, carrot and cabbage in oil and salt until soft, 5 to 10 minutes.
2. Mix kuzu in water and pour over vegetables. Bring to a boil.
3. Sprinkle with parsley and serve with rice.

49. MILLET-ADUKI CROQUETTES
Serves 4

2 cups soft, cooked millet (see INGREDIENTS—GRAINS)
2 cups cooked aduki beans (see INGREDIENTS—LEGUMES)
1 diced carrot
1 cup diced scallions (spring onions)
Pinch salt
2½ cups whole-wheat breadcrumbs
1 teaspoon sesame oil

1. Millet should be well cooked, moist and soft. Beans should also be cooked very soft but not too wet. Mix well together.
2. Sauté carrots and onions in a little water with salt, for 10 minutes.
3. Mix ingredients, wet hands and shape croquettes.
4. Roll in whole-wheat breadcrumbs.
5. Sauté gently in a pan brushed with oil.
6. Serve with Fresh Dill Sauce (see Recipe 137) or Onion and Squash Sauce (see Recipe 146).

50. MILLET-ARAME CROQUETTES
Makes 4 to 6

1 medium, chopped onion
2 teaspoons sesame oil
2 cups soft, cooked millet (see INGREDIENTS—GRAINS)
1 cup cooked arame, chopped fine (see INGREDIENTS—SEA VEGETABLES)
½ cup raisins
1 tablespoon soy sauce
1½ cups breadcrumbs
1 tablespoon corn oil

1. Heat oil in pan. Add onion. Stir for 3 to 4 minutes.
2. Add millet, arame, raisins and soy sauce. The millet should be soft. Stir well. Allow to cool.
3. Wet hands and shape into 4 to 6 croquettes.
4. Roll in breadcrumbs and sauté in a little corn oil.
5. Garnish with parsley and serve with Lemon Sauce (see Recipe 140).

51. MILLET AND CAULIFLOWER MASH
Serves 4

1 teaspoon sesame oil
1 cup millet
1½ cups cauliflower florets
¼ teaspoon salt
3½ cups water

1. Heat oil in a pan with a lid. Add millet and sauté 3 to 4 minutes.
2. Add cauliflower, salt and water. Bring to a boil.
3. Simmer, covered, for 30 minutes. Let stand 15 minutes.
4. Mash with a wooden spoon and serve with vegetables (see Recipe 53).

52. MILLET AND VEGETABLES
Serves 4 to 6

1 diced onion
1 tablespoon toasted sesame oil
1 cup fresh green peas
1 small, diced carrot
2 cups millet (washed)
6-8 cups boiling water
Pinch sea salt
½ cup chopped parsley

1. Brush sesame oil over the bottom of a pan. Sauté onion for 2 to 3 minutes.
2. Add carrot. Sauté another 5 minutes.
3. Add millet and sauté 2 or 3 minutes, stir to avoid burning.
4. Add boiling water and sea salt and bring to a boil. Cover and reduce heat. Simmer for 30 minutes. The more water you add, the softer the millet will be. If you prefer it dry, add only 6 cups water.
5. Add the peas and cook another 10 minutes.
6. Stir in parsley and serve with vegetables (see Recipe 53).

(This mixture can also be used to make croquettes: roll in breadcrumbs.)

53. MILLET AND BAKED PARSNIPS WITH VEGETABLES
Serves 4

1 finely sliced onion
Pinch salt
2 cups millet
4 cups water
½ cup chopped parsley

1. Sauté onion in ½ cup water and salt for 10 minutes.
2. Add millet and stir for 5 minutes.
3. Add the rest of the water and salt and bring to a boil. Simmer for 30 minutes, or until water has evaporated.
4. Sprinkle with parsley and serve.

THE VEGETABLES:

2 parsnips, sliced lengthwise
½ teaspoon sesame oil
Pinch salt
¼ small cabbage, shredded
2 cups diced pumpkin
½ cup washed ulva, sliced
2 cups sliced cauliflower
1 tablespoon roasted pumpkin seeds

1. Sprinkle parsnips with salt and brush with oil. Bake at 350°F for ½ hour.
2. Steam cabbage, pumpkin, ulva and cauliflower for 10 minutes.
3. Serve vegetables, garnished with pumpkin seeds, around millet.

54. MOCHI AND VEGETABLE CASSEROLE
Serves 4 to 6

6 shiitake mushrooms, sliced
1 onion, sliced
Pinch salt
1 tablespoon sesame oil
½ head cabbage, chopped fine
2 carrots, sliced diagonally
2 cups mochi in 1" squares (see INGREDIENTS—MOCHI)
2 tablespoons tamari soy sauce

1. If shiitake mushrooms are dried, soak for 10 minutes (save water) and then slice. Remove stalk ends.
2. Sauté onions shiitake and salt in oil for 5 minutes.
3. Add cabbage and carrots, cover, and simmer for 10 minutes.
4. Pan-fry mochi squares for 5 minutes, until they puff up and are golden brown.
5. Place mochi on top of vegetables, sprinkle with tamari soy sauce and serve with rice.

55. NOODLES WITH RADISH AND SCALLIONS (SPRING ONIONS)
Serves 4

¼ pound green tea soba noodles
2 cups (vegetable) water
1 cup chopped scallions (spring onions)
1 cup grated daikon radish
1 teaspoon sesame oil
2 teaspoons kuzu
1 cup cold water
1 tablespoon umeboshi vinegar
2 teaspoons tamari soy sauce

1. Cook the noodles in water (see INGREDIENTS—NOODLES).
2. Sauté onions and radish in teaspoon of oil (3 minutes).
3. Mix kuzu in cold water and add to vegetables. Gently stir and bring to a boil.
4. Add umeboshi vinegar and tamari soy sauce. Serve over noodles.

56. OAT AND RICE PATTIES WITH PARSLEY AND ONION
Serves 4 to 6

Use boiled whole oats left over from breakfast.

1 medium, chopped onion
½ cup water
Pinch salt
2 cups soft, cooked short grained
   brown rice
2 cups soft, cooked whole oats (see
   INGREDIENTS—GRAINS)
½ cup chopped parsley
1 cup whole-wheat flour

1. Braise the onion in water and salt for a few minutes.
2. Add onion to rice and oats and mix in parsley. Mixture should be soft enough to roll into patties. You need to wet your hands to do this.
3. Roll in flour or breadcrumbs.
4. Brush pan with oil and place over moderate heat. Gently sauté the patties until golden brown.
5. Serve with Umeboshi-Kuzu Vegetables (see Recipe 124) or Mochi and Onion Sauce (see Recipe 142).

57. RICE, AVOCADO AND CORN SALAD
Serves 4

For a hot day.

3 cups cooked brown rice (see
   INGREDIENTS—GRAINS)
1 avocado
2 ears of corn, cooked
2 diced salt-pickled cucumbers
½ cup cashew nuts, roasted
1 onion, finely chopped
1 teaspoon lemon juice
1 teaspoon olive oil
1 teaspoon brown rice vinegar
1 teaspoon tamari soy sauce
4 young lettuce leaves, washed

1. Peel and pit avocado, then slice and mash in with the rice.
2. Remove corn from the cob and add to the mixture.
3. Add cucumber, cashews and chopped onion.
4. Mix juice, oil, vinegar and tamari and dress the salad.
5. Serve chilled over a bed of lettuce.

58. RICE AND BEAN CROQUETTES WITH MOCHI SAUCE
Serves 4

1 cup water
Pinch salt
1 small, finely chopped onion
1 small, finely diced carrot
2 cups cooked, short grained brown
   rice
1 cup cooked black turtle beans (or
   aduki)

1. Bring water to a boil and add salt, onion and carrot. Simmer for 10 minutes, or until carrot and onion are soft.
2. Rice and beans need to be well cooked and soft (see INGREDIENTS—GRAINS and LEGUMES). Add these to the mixture and stir. Let cool.
3. Wet your hands and from the mixture

*1 large umeboshi plum, sliced into six
   sections*
3 cups whole wheat breadcrumbs
2 teaspoons unrefined sesame oil

make six croquettes. Place a piece of umeboshi plum in each. Roll in breadcrumbs.
4. Brush oil onto a heavy pan over moderate heat. Add the croquettes. Cook golden brown, turning occasionally.
5. Serve with Mochi and Onion or Pesto Sauce (Recipes 142 and 148).

59. RICE AND OAT CAKES WITH ONION AND CELERY
Serves 3 to 4

1 cup soft, cooked whole oats
*2 cups soft, cooked short grained rice
   (see INGREDIENTS—GRAINS)*
½ cup water
1 large, chopped onion
1 chopped clove garlic
*2 stalks of stringed and finely chopped
   celery*
1 cup chopped parsley
½ sheet finely cut nori pieces
*1 heaped tablespoon light miso mixed
   in ½ cup water*
2 cups breadcrumbs
2 tablespoons sesame oil

1. Mix the oats and rice in a bowl.
2. Heat water in pan and add onions and garlic. Stir and braise for 3 minutes.
3. Add celery or parsley and the nori pieces. Stir and cook for 3 minutes. Stir in miso.
4. Mix vegetables with rice and oats. Add 2 tablespoons breadcrumbs.
5. Wet hands and make rice cakes—6 to 8—from the mixture.
6. Roll them in breadcrumbs and pan-fry until golden brown.

60. SEITAN PARCELS
Serves 4

Seitan is a very useful wheat protein food, similar to meat in texture (for making it see INGREDIENTS—SEITAN). It can be bought ready-made, marinated in tamari soy sauce and ginger, in good whole food stores.

*6 slices of seitain, each about 1½ "
   square*
¾ cup pencil-shaved burdock
1 tablespoon toasted sesame oil
1 cup diagonally cut celery
1 teaspoon, fresh, dry, brown mustard
2 teaspoons rice vinegar or apple juice
½ cup water
1 tablespoon tamari soy sauce
1 teaspoon grated ginger
1 tablespoon sesame or safflower oil

1. Slice a "pocket" in each seitan piece.
2. Soak burdock for 10 minutes before cooking. Discard water.
3. Heat oil in pan. Add burdock and sauté for 10 minutes.
4. Add celery and cook another 5 minutes.
5. Mix mustard in rice vinegar or apple juice and add to the vegetables with tamari soy sauce and ginger.
6. Place stuffing into seitan pieces.
7. Sauté parcels gently (add a little more oil to pan if needed) and serve with grains and vegetables.

61. SEITAN AND VEGETABLE CASSEROLE
Serves 4

1 teaspoon sesame oil
1 teaspoon corn oil
1 cup sliced and soaked (10 minutes)
  burdock root
1 cup sliced daikon radish
1 large carrot, sliced
1 small leek, chopped
1 cup sliced fresh mushrooms
1½ cups marinated seitan pieces (see
  INGREDIENTS: SEITAN)
¾ cup bancha (or kukicha) tea
2 teaspoons tamari soy sauce
2 teaspoons kuzu
½ cup cold water

1. Heat oils in pan. Add burdock and sauté gently for 5 minutes.
2. Add daikon and sauté another 4 minutes.
3. Add carrots and leeks and simmer for 10 minutes.
4. Add mushrooms, seitan, tea and tamari.
5. Dissolve kuzu in cold water and add to thicken the stew.
6. Serve with noodles or rice.

62. SOBA NOODLES WITH TOFU "ALFREDO" SAUCE

3 cups tofu
4 cups boiling water
1 tablespoon yellow or white miso
1 teaspoon basil
2 teaspoons olive oil
1 medium, finely chopped leek
2 medium, finely chopped onions
4 mushrooms, sliced fine

1. Place tofu in boiling water to blanch it.
2. Remove tofu (keep water), and place in blender with miso, basil and enough of the blanching water and blend to a creamy texture.
3. Heat the olive oil in a pan, add leeks, onions and mushrooms and sauté for 15 minutes, or until soft.
4. Add tofu cream to the vegetables, heat and stir well. Serve as a sauce for hot soba noodles (see INGREDIENTS—NOODLES) and steamed green vegetables.

63. STUFFED VINE LEAVES (DOLMADES)
Makes 12

12 fresh vine leaves
1½ cups water
1 teaspoon salt

1. Bring water to a boil and add salt. Cook vine leaves in it for 4 minutes and keep the water to make the stuffing.
2. Cut out the lower, hard portion of each center stem.

THE STUFFING:

1 tablespoon olive oil
1 medium, chopped onion
2 cups soft, cooked, short grained
  brown rice (see INGREDIENTS—
  GRAINS)
1 tablespoon currants
1 tablespoon roasted pine nuts
1 clove garlic, crushed
2 tablespoons fresh, chopped parsley
½ teaspoon ground cinnamon
1 teaspoon grated lemon peel
1 cup water
3 sliced umeboshi plums
Juice of ½ lemon
1 tablespoon umeboshi vinegar

1. Heat oil in pan, add onions and sauté until transparent (3 minutes).
2. Add rice and stir in currants, pine nuts, garlic, parsley, cinnamon and lemon peel.
3. Add water from vine leaves. Bring to a boil, stir and simmer for 10 minutes. Add a little more water if necessary.
4. Lay out the vine leaves and place a teaspoon or so of filling in the center of each. Push in a piece of umeboshi plum. Roll the leaf from the bottom over the filling and tuck in the sides as you do so.
5. Arrange the rolled leaves in a steamer with about 3 cups water in the pan. Cover pot and steam gently for 45 minutes over low heat. Be sure leaves are tender.
6. When dolmades are cold, sprinkle with lemon juice and serve. (Keep your steam water for stock.)

64. SUSHI WITH CARROT, SPINACH AND OMELET
Serves 4 to 6

*4 cups soft, short grained, cooked
   brown rice (see INGREDIENTS—
   GRAINS)*
4 tablespoons umeboshi vinegar
1 carrot, sliced in ¼" wide strips
1 tablespoon toasted sesame oil
2 dozen spinach leaves
2 cups water
1 tablespoon tamari soy sauce
2 eggs
2 tablespoons tamari soy sauce
¼ cup vegetable water (from spinach)
4 sheets nori
*1 teaspoon fresh lemon juice or ginger
   juice*

1. Mix soft rice with umeboshi vinegar.
2. Sauté carrot strips in oil over low heat until soft (10 minutes). Let cool.
3. Boil or steam spinach until soft. Strain and keep water. Cool and squeeze into a long, flat shape. Slice into long strips. Sprinkle with tamari soy sauce.
4. Mix eggs, tamari soy sauce and spinach water. Cook omelet over medium heat. Fold omelet four times to make a long shape. Cool and slice into strips.
5. Roast the nori sheet over low flame. It will become a greenish color. Place the sheet on a sushi mat, and spread the rice over the nori sheets. The rice should be spread to about ½" from the side edges of the nori sheet and 1" from the top and bottom edges.
6. About 1½" from the bottom edge make a "trench", and place strips of carrot, spinach and omelet across it.
7. Roll the sushi in the mat as though making a large cigarette. Keep it firm, even and smooth. Wet the edge with lemon juice or ginger juice to stick the nori together.
8. Use a sharp knife to slice the roll across to make smaller "sushi" rolls.

(Tofu strips may be used instead of omelet. The tofu is fried and garnished with ginger juice and tamari soy sauce.)
(See also INGREDIENTS—SUSHI.)

65. UDON (WHEAT) NOODLES AND VEGETABLE SALAD
Serves 4

8 ounces udon noodles
1 cup sliced cauliflower
1 cup diced celeriac
1 cup diced rutabaga (swede)
1 cup broccoli florets
1 cup red radish, sliced
1 cup water
½ cup rice vinegar
1 tablespoon soy sauce
2 teaspoons kuzu
¾ cup water
*½ cup pan- or oven-roasted pumpkin
  seeds*

1. Boil noodles in water. (For cooking noodles see INGREDIENTS—NOODLES.)
2. Strain and rinse in cold water.
3. Boil cauliflower, celeriac, rutabaga (swede), broccoli and radish in 1 cup water for 2 to 3 minutes.
4. Add rice vinegar and soy sauce.
5. Mix kuzu in cold water. Add to vegetables and bring to a boil. Pour vegetable mixture over the noodles. Decorate with pumpkin seeds and serve.

This recipe can be made with soba (buckwheat) or chasoba (green tea and buckwheat) noodles.

66. WHOLE-WHEAT SPAGHETTI AND TOFU-PARSLEY SAUCE
Serves 4

*8 ounces whole-wheat spaghetti or
  Udon noodles*
2 cups boiling water
1 teaspoon olive oil
Pinch salt

1. Add spaghetti or noodles to boiling water, salt and oil. Stir well.
2. Boil for 10 minutes, by which time water should be absorbed.
3. Stand (covered) to steam in 250°F oven for 10 minutes before serving with:

TOFU-PARSLEY SAUCE:

½ cup chopped parsley
1 teaspoon basil, chopped fine
1 teaspoon sunflower oil
1 tablespoon rice vinegar
1 teaspoon ground pine nuts
½ teaspoon kuzu
2 cups water
1½ cups diced tofu

1. Sauté parsley and basil in oil for 2 minutes.
2. Add rice vinegar and pine nuts.
3. Mix kuzu in water, add tofu and blend.
4. Mix ingredients in a pan and, stirring well, bring to a boil.
5. Serve over the noodles.

Breads, Pastries and Pancake Mixes

67. BREAD WITH BUCKWHEAT, CHESTNUT, WHOLE-WHEAT AND RYE FLOURS
Serves 4

Bread can be made by using various combinations of grain flours. Experiment! Instead of using only whole-wheat flour, try this combination:

2 cups whole-wheat flour
2 cups rye flour
2 cups buckwheat flour
2 cups chestnut flour
1 tablespoon sea salt
3 cups corn and sesame oil mix
3¼ cups water

1. Mix flours.
2. Distribute salt and add oil carefully. Rub oil in well.
3. Add water gradually and work the mixture thoroughly with your hands, breaking up any lumps.
4. Knead for 10 minutes.
5. Cover dough with a damp cloth and leave in a warm, dry place such as a 95°F oven.
   Allow to rise for 24 hours.
6. Knead again for about 10 minutes and place in oiled bread pans to rise for another 4 hours in oven or warm cabinet.
7. Cut a simple crisscross design on the top surface and bake in a 325°F oven for 45 minutes. For even cooking, place a pan of water in the oven while baking the bread. (If making whole-wheat bread, use 8 cups whole-wheat flour.)

68. BREAD WITH CORN, RYE AND WHOLE-WHEAT FLOURS
Makes 1 loaf

2 cups whole-wheat pastry flour
1½ cups corn flour
1 cup rye flour
1 teaspoon baking powder
½ teaspoon salt
4 tablespoons oil (sesame and corn mix)
2 cups soy milk
⅓ cup maple syrup

1. Mix flours, baking soda and salt and drop in the oil.
2. Add soy milk and maple syrup and stir thoroughly.
3. Wipe a bread pan with oil, and sprinkle with a little corn flour before placing dough in it.
4. Bake in a preheated 350°F oven for 45 minutes.

69. BREAD OF FIVE GRAINS
Makes 1 loaf

4 cups whole wheat flour
2 cups rye flour
2 cups oat flour
1 cup millet flour
⅔ cup mixed sesame and corn oil
1 tablespoon sea salt
3 cups water

1. Mix flours.
2. Distribute salt and pour in oil carefully. Rub oil in well.
3. Gradually add water, working mixture thoroughly with your hands. Do not allow dough to become too wet.
4. Knead dough for 10 to 15 minutes.
5. Cover dough with a damp cloth and leave in a warm, dry place such as a 95°F oven for 24 hours.
6. Knead another 10 minutes. Place in oiled pans to rise for 4 more hours.
7. Cut crisscross pattern on top and bake in 325°F oven for 45 minutes.

BREAD made with buckwheat chestnut, wholewheat. & rye flours.

70. BREAD USING SOURDOUGH AND ONION
Serves 4

You will need to make a sourdough starter first:

STARTER:

1 tablespoon dry yeast
2½ cups warm water
2½ cups whole wheat pastry flour
2 tablespoons barley malt or rice syrup

1. Mix ingredients in a jar, and cover with a mesh cloth (several layers of cheesecloth), then seal with a rubber band and leave for 5 days in a warm, dry place.
2. Uncover daily and stir the mixture.
3. After 5 days the starter begins to ferment and will need to be refrigerated.
4. Each time you use some of your starter to make bread, add flour and water. Stir it each day and keep refrigerated.

BREAD:

1 cup rye flour
1 cup whole-wheat pastry flour
1 cup millet flour
1 teaspoon sea salt
⅔ cup sourdough starter
2 cups water
3 medium onions, sliced in crescents
2 teaspoons corn and sesame oil mix
1 teaspoon roasted sesame (or caraway) seeds

1. Combine flours and salt and stir well with hands. To make dough, add starter and water. If mixture is too wet, add more whole wheat flour.
2. Cover with a damp cloth and leave in a warm, dry place such as a 95°F oven for 24 hours to rise.
3. Sauté onions in corn-sesame oil for 5 to 6 minutes and pan-fry sesame (or caraway) seeds until golden brown.
4. Add onions and most of the seeds to dough and shape into a loaf. Leave in oven another 2½ hours to rise.
5. Sprinkle and press in the rest of the seeds on top of loaf. Bake in preheated 325°F oven for 55 minutes.

71. BUCKWHEAT PANCAKE MIX

½ cup buckwheat flour
½ cup whole-wheat pastry flour
Pinch salt
½ cup soy milk
½ cup cold mineral water (or iced
* water)*
1 free-range egg (optional)
2 teaspoons safflower/sunflower oil

1. Pour flours in mixing bowl with salt, add milk, water and egg. Mix with a fork. Refrigerate for half an hour.
2. Wipe a cast iron skillet with oil, pour some of the mixture into the center of the hot pan, spreading it to make a *thin* layer of pancake. Turn and serve.

(These pancakes can be filled with sweet (see Recipe 192), or savoury filling. If sweet filling is to be used, add ½ teaspoon cinnamon to the mixture.)

72. FRUIT PIE CRUST

2 cups cooked millet
1 cup roasted rolled oats
½ cup maple syrup
1½ tablespoons miso mixed in
¼ cup water
2 tablespoons seeded raisins
1 teaspoon soya oil

1. Mix millet and rolled oats.
2. Add maple syrup and miso mixed in water and raisins. Stir well.
3. Wipe pie pan with oil, press pastry in and place fruit on top (see Recipe 187).

73. OATMEAL CRUST

3 cups rolled oats
1½ cups whole wheat pastry flour
½ teaspoon sea salt
2 to 3 tablespoons corn oil
2 cups water

1. Mix oats, flour and salt.
2. Add oil and mix.
3. Add water to form a thick batter.
4. Spread batter on an oiled baking sheet or pie pan and bake in a preheated 375°F oven for 10 minutes.
5. Remove from oven and place fruit or filling on crust and bake again at 375°F for 25 to 30 minutes (see recipes 187, 191, 217).

74. PASTRY PIE CRUST

Always use cold utensils and keep your hands cold when making pastry.

3 cups whole-wheat flour
Pinch sea salt
½ teaspoon cinnamon for sweet pastry
¾ cup safflower oil
1 cup water (more or less as needed)

1. Mix flour and salt in a bowl. Add cinnamon if making a sweet pastry.
2. Gently pour in oil and mix quickly with your hands or a spoon.
3. Add water, gradually stirring to make dough. Be sure it is *not too wet*; if it is, add more flour.
4. Let stand ½ hour before baking.

(It can be kept in the refrigerator if you wish to use it later.)

75. PASTRY PIE CRUST 2

1 cup corn flour
2 cups whole-wheat flour
Pinch sea salt
¼ cup corn oil and toasted sesame oil
1 cup water (more or less as needed)

1. Mix flours and salt in a bowl.
2. Gently pour in oil, and mix quickly with your hands or a spoon.
3. Add water gradually, using enough to make a dough that's not too wet. Knead well.

76. PIZZA PASTRY PIE CRUST 3

2 cups whole-wheat flour
Pinch salt
½ teaspoon curry powder
2 tablespoons sesame or corn oil
1 cup cold water (more or less as needed)

1. Mix flour, salt and curry powder.
2. Rub in the oil quickly, and gradually add water to make a dough that's not too wet. Let stand ½ hour.
3. Sprinkle board with flour and roll out dough.
4. Oil a pie pan and press the pastry in it.
5. Place in a preheated 350°F oven for 15 minutes to precook the pastry. Use lower oven tray to avoid scorching the top edge.
6. Cover with Aduki Pizza mixture (see Recipe 127) and top with sauce (see Recipes 134 and 143).

77. PANCAKES FOR BECHAMEL VEGETABLE SAUCE
Serves 4

Pancake mix:

1 cup whole-wheat pastry flour
Pinch salt
1 cup cold soy milk
1 cup cold water
1 free-range egg
1 tablespoon sesame oil

1. Mix the ingredients quickly to a thin creamy consistency and let stand in a cool place for at least 1 hour.
2. Brush a little corn oil on skillet. Heat gently but it should not be too hot. To test the heat of your skillet, let a few drops of water fall on it. If the water stays and boils the surface is not hot enough: if it vanishes quickly it is too hot. The water should bounce and sputter.
3. Drop in the pancake mixture. Pancakes should not be too thick. (See Recipe 109 for sauce.)

(When making dessert pancakes add 1 tablespoon rice malt or maple syrup.)

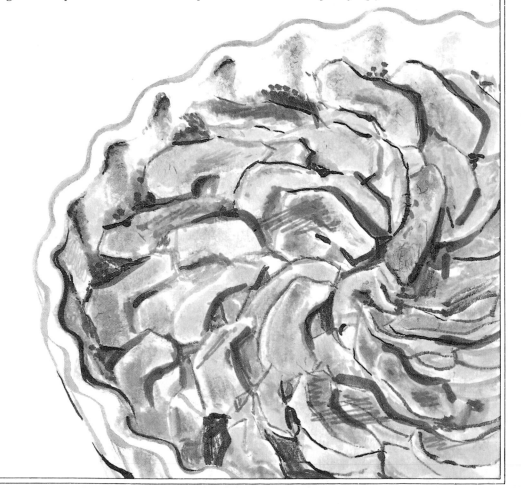

78. PANCAKES FOR ROAST "CRISPY" DUCK
Makes 16 pancakes

1 cup whole-wheat flour
Pinch salt
¾ cup boiling water
½ tablespoon sesame or corn oil

1. Sift flour into a bowl. Add salt.
2. Pour boiling water onto flour, gently stirring with a wooden spoon. Use less water if necessary.
3. Add oil, continuing to stir. The mixture will make a soft light dough. Knead for 4 to 5 minutes.
4. Divide dough into four — make rolls ¾" in diameter by 3" long. Slice each roll to make four cubes of dough. Roll these into balls.
5. On a well-floured surface, roll out each ball to make a 6" pancake. They should be paper-thin circles. Trim with a sharp knife if necessary.
6. Oil a skillet and cook each side of the pancakes for 30 seconds, or until they are dry. They can then be wrapped in plastic wrap and refrigerated.
7. If you need to heat the pancakes, place in a steamer or wrap in foil and place in shallow pan of boiling water, taking care they don't get wet and soggy.
8. Serve with Roast "Crispy" Duck (see Recipe 172) and Bechamel Vegetable Sauce (see Recipe 109). Any pancakes that are left can be sliced fine and added to soups.

79. TOFU PIE CRUST

3 cups whole-wheat pastry flour
1 cup cornmeal
Pinch salt
¼ teaspoon cinnamon
3 tablespoons corn oil and sesame oil
1½ cups water (more or less as needed)

1. Mix flour, meal, salt and cinnamon in a bowl.
2. Gently pour in oil mixture.
3. Add water gradually to make a dough.
4. Knead for 8 minutes.
5. Roll out and place on the bottom of a shallow ovenproof dish.
6. Bake in a 350°F oven for 30 minutes.
7. Add Tofu Filling (see Recipe 217).

80. WHEATLESS PASTRY

1 cup rye flour
1 cup brown rice flour
1 cup cornmeal
⅓ teaspoon salt
¼ cup mixed corn and sesame oil
⅔ cup water

1. Mix dry ingredients.
2. Sprinkle in oil and stir well.
3. Mix in water to make dough.
4. Roll out and press into pie pan.
5. Spread with Vegetable-Millet and Sauce (see Recipe 47).

81. WHOLE-WHEAT UNLEAVENED BREAD
Makes 1 loaf

6 cups whole-wheat flour
1 teaspoon sea salt
½ cup sesame seeds
3 cups water
½ cup goat yoghurt (optional)

1. Mix flour, salt and sesame seeds.
2. Add water gradually then yoghurt to make a smooth, not too wet, dough.
3. Knead this 200 times. Sprinkle flour on kneading surface if necessary.
4. Wrap dough in a damp cloth and let stand in a warm, dry place, such as a 95°F oven, for 10 to 12 hours.
5. Knead another 100 times.
6. Oil your bread pan and place dough in it. Sprinkle a teaspoon of sesame seeds on top and press in gently. Slice lines across the top with a sharp knife.
7. Bake in preheated 450°F oven for ½ hour and 350°F oven for 45 minutes, use lower tray of oven. This bread can be made without being kneaded. It is delicious served with Tahini, Ginger and Scallion (Spring Onion) Spread (see Recipe 152) or tahini and raisins.

Wheat

Vegetables

25% of the meal can contain **VEGETABLES**
THEY CAN BE USED IN SOUPS, AS SIDE DISHES, COOKED WITH
THE MAIN GRAIN OR SERVED AS SALADS. They are usually cooked:
sauted in a **LITTLE** oil or water, boiled, baked or steamed.
5% can be salad   **5%** SEA VEGETABLES

Vegetables

82. ARAME AND CARAWAY SEEDS
Side dish for 4

1 cup dried arame
2 cups water
1 tablespoon safflower oil
1 sliced onion
1 teaspoon caraway seeds
½ cup water
2 tablespoons tamari soy sauce
1 tablespoon roasted pumpkin seeds

1. Soak arame in water for 1 or 2 minutes. Remove and keep water.
2. Heat oil in a pan. Sauté onion for 2 minutes. Add arame and caraway seeds and stir for 5 minutes. Pour in soaking water with ½ cup more water and bring to a boil.
3. Simmer for 30 minutes over low heat.
4. Add tamari soy sauce, remove cover and steam off rest of water.
5. Decorate with pumpkin seeds and serve as a side dish.

83. ARAME WITH ONIONS, PUMPKIN AND ROASTED SESAME SEEDS
Side dish for 4

1 cup arame
1½ cups water
1 tablespoon toasted sesame oil
2 small, sliced onions
1 cup diced pumpkin (peeled)
1 tablespoon tamari soy sauce
1 cup water
1 tablespoon roasted sesame seeds

1. Soak the arame in water for 2 minutes and strain (keep water).
2. Heat sesame oil in a pan. Sauté onions until golden brown.
3. Add arame and stir. Sauté for 5 minutes.
4. Add soaking water plus 1 cup water, tamari, soy sauce, bring to the boil and simmer for 15 minutes.
5. Add pumpkin, uncover and boil to remove excess water (10 minutes).
6. Garnish with sesame seeds and serve.

84. AVOCADO WITH SAUERKRAUT DRESSING
Serves 2

1 avocado
1 tablespoons sauerkraut (see Recipe 113)
1 tablespoon sesame oil
2 tablespoons apple juice
Juice of half a lemon
1 teaspoon chopped parsley

1. Cut avocado in half, remove pit and fill each half with sauerkraut.
2. Mix sesame oil, apple juice, and lemon juice and pour over the sauerkraut.
3. Decorate with parsley and serve.

One sliced umeboshi plum can be used instead of sauerkraut.

85. BROCCOLI, CARROT, CORN AND SHIITAKE KANTEN
Serves 4

4 cups vegetable cooking water
2 slices kombu, each 2"×6"
3 sliced shiitake mushrooms (soak 10 minutes if dried and use water)
2 tablespoons kuzu
1 cup cold water
½ cup brown rice vinegar
1 tablespoon tamari soy sauce
1 teaspoon fresh, grated ginger juice
2 tablespoons agar-agar flakes
Kernels from 1 cooked ear of corn
2 cups cooked broccoli heads, cut small
1 medium, cooked carrot, sliced in flowers

1. Add kombu and mushrooms to water. Bring to a boil. Simmer 20 minutes.
2. Remove kombu, slice into fine ½" squares and return to pot. Simmer 10 minutes.
3. Mix kuzu in water and stir into mixture.
4. Add rice vinegar, tamari soy sauce and ginger juice. Bring to a boil.
5. Add agar-agar flakes and stir well. Turn off heat.
6. Wet inside surface of a clean pyrex dish or mold and pour in mixture.
7. Arrange corn, broccoli and carrot flowers decoratively in the kanten and allow to cool, then refrigerate for an hour.

86. BROCCOLI WITH ROASTED PUMPKIN SEEDS

2 tablespoons pumpkin seeds
2 cups broccoli florets (remove large stems and use for soups or stews)
1½ cups water
Pinch salt

1. Place pumpkin seeds in iron skillet and roast over medium heat for 3 minutes.
2. Bring water to a boil. Add salt and broccoli. Do not cover. Simmer for 5 minutes.
3. Strain off water and use it for soup stock.
4. Sprinkle broccoli with seeds and serve. Lower stems can be boiled in the vegetable water for 10 to 15 minutes and used as a vegetable or for soup.

87. CARRAGEEN VEGETABLE ASPIC
Serves 4

3 cups water
1 cup soaked and washed carrageen
1 cup water
½ cup green peas
1 cup diced, peeled pumpkin
½ cup beansprouts
½ cup sliced daikon radish (mooli)
1 teaspoon grated lemon peel
1 tablespoon sauerkraut
Juice of half a lemon
*1 tablespoon chopped parsley, to
    decorate*

1. Bring water to a boil and add carrageen. Simmer for half an hour.
2. Meanwhile, in another pan, steam peas and pumpkin for 10 minutes (keep the steaming water).
3. Place the vegetables in a flat dish and arrange beansprouts, daikon, lemon peel and sauerkraut over them.
4. Strain off water from carrageen (keep the carrageen and use for soups, aspics, etc.).
5. Mix hot carrageen water with ½ cup vegetable water and pour over the vegetables in dish. Let set. Refrigerate.
6. Squeeze lemon juice over aspic, decorate with parsley and serve as salad with hot or cold rice or noodles.

88. CARROT, APPLE AND ONION SALAD WITH RAISINS
Serves 4

A summer salad.

1 grated carrot
1 finely diced onion
1 diced apple
¾ cup diced melon
½ cup diced tofu
½ cup apple juice
1 tablespoon umeboshi vinegar
1 teaspoon olive oil
1 teaspoon tamari soy sauce
½ cup chopped parsley

1. Mix carrots, onion, apple and tofu.
2. Mix apple juice, vinegar, oils and soy sauce.
3. Garnish with parsley and serve with cold brown rice.

89. CARROT, DULSE AND CELERY BOILED SALAD WITH BROWN RICE VINEGAR
Side dish for 4

1 cup soaked and cleaned dulse
2 carrots, sliced in strips
3 stalks sliced celery
2 cups boiling water
1 tablespoon brown rice vinegar
2 teaspoons roasted pine nuts

1. Slice soaked dulse.
2. Place dulse, carrots and celery in pan.
3. Pour boiling water over vegetables and blanch for 30 seconds.
4. Remove vegetables (use water for soup).
5. Sprinkle with brown rice vinegar and roasted pine nuts. Serve.

90. CARROT AND SCALLION (SPRING ONION) SALAD
Side dish for 4

4 finely grated carrots
5 finely chopped scallions (spring onions)
1 tablespoon rice vinegar
2 tablespoons olive oil
Pinch salt

1. Mix carrots and scallions (spring onions).
2. Mix vinegar, oil and salt.
3. Pour dressing over and mix well. Let stand for 10 minutes in refrigerator.

Serve as a salad or decorate with Mangetout and Ginger Salad (see Recipe 106).

91. CARROT AND TURNIP COOKED "SALAD" IN UMEBOSHI VINEGAR
Side dish for 4

2 carrots, sliced
2 turnips, sliced
2 cups water
½ tablespoon umeboshi vinegar
1 teaspoon sesame salt

1. Boil carrots and turnips in water for 5 to 6 minutes, or until tender.
2. Strain off water (keep for soup stock).
3. Sprinkle with umeboshi vinegar and sesame salt.

92. BOILED CAULIFLOWER AND KUZU SALAD
Side dish for 4

1 small cauliflower head
1 cup water
2 tablespoons umeboshi vinegar
1 cup vegetable stock
2 teaspoons kuzu
1 cup cold water

1. Break up the cauliflower into small florets.
2. Bring water to a boil and place heads in it. Simmer for 3 minutes, until tender. Use this water for sauce.
3. Place the cooked cauliflower in a dish to cool.
4. Using cauliflower water, add umeboshi vinegar and heat.
5. Dissolve kuzu in 1 cup water and add to the umeboshi water. Just bring to a boil, stirring all the time, and remove from heat.
6. Pour sauce over the cauliflower florets.

93. CAULIFLOWER IN UMEBOSHI VINEGAR
Side dish for 4

3 cups cauliflower florets
1 cup water
¼ cup umeboshi vinegar
¼ cup water

1. Break the cauliflower into florets rather than cut them.
2. Place in the boiling salted water for about 2 minutes (until tender).
3. Take out and allow to cool (keep water for soup stock).
4. Mix the umeboshi vinegar with an equal amount of water, place the cauliflower florets in the mixture and allow to stand for 20 to 30 minutes. Stir.
5. Take out of the vinegar solution and serve.

94. CAULIFLOWER, YELLOW SQUASH AND LEEKS WITH CHICK PEAS
Serves 4

1 cup chick peas
½ cup sliced dulse
4 cups water
pinch of salt
1 tablespoon olive oil
1 cup parsnip, roll cut
1 cup chopped leek
1 clove garlic, chopped
1" ginger, grated fine
3 cups cauliflower florets
1 tablespoon fresh, chopped dill
1 teaspoon fresh tarragon, chopped fine
1 small, yellow summer squash, sliced
*   in rounds*
3 sliced leaves spinach (or kale)
1 tablespoon tamari soy sauce
½ cup chopped, roasted walnuts

1. Soak chick peas overnight, and cook with dulse for 3 hours (see INGREDIENTS—LEGUMES).
2. Place oil in a pan and heat gently. Add parsnip, leek, garlic and ginger. Sauté, stirring well, for 10 minutes.
3. Add cauliflower, dill and tarragon and sauté for 5 minutes with lid covering pot.
4. Add squash and spinach (or kale), replace lid and simmer for 10 minutes.
5. Stir in tamari soy sauce, sprinkle on walnuts and serve on a bed of brown rice or millet.

95. CHINESE HAND-PRESSED CABBAGE SALAD
Side dish for 4

This salad can be made quickly.

¼ Chinese cabbage
1 teaspoon salt
2 tablespoon umeboshi vinegar
1 sprig chopped parsley

1. Slice the cabbage lengthwise, then very finely across.
2. Sprinkle with the salt and press by hand, squeezing out water.
3. When it is well pressed, strain off the cabbage water and rinse cabbage with fresh, running water.
4. Place in bowl and mix in umeboshi vinegar.
5. Decorate with chopped parsley and serve.

96. CHINESE PRESSED CABBAGE SALAD
Side dish for 4

You will need a salad press for this recipe.

½ Chinese cabbage, finely sliced
1 tablespoon tamari soy sauce
2 teaspoons grated ginger juice

1. Press lettuce by hand into press.
2. Pour over soy sauce and ginger juice.
3. Leave pressed for 1 hour. (The pressure also helps to "yangize" the lettuce.)
4. Drain off water, rinse if preferred and serve.

97. DAIKON AND UMEBOSHI VINEGAR
Side dish for 4

2 cups grated daikon
2 tablespoons umeboshi vinegar

1. Sprinkle the umeboshi vinegar over the grated daikon. It will turn a delicate, pink color.
2. Makes a clean-tasting side dish, to be served with a grain meal or with meat.

98. HIJIKE-SHIITAKE SIDE DISH
Serves 4 to 6

1 cup hijike
3 cups water
1 medium, sliced onion
1 carrot, matchstick sliced
1 tablespoon toasted sesame oil
4 sliced shiitake mushrooms (If dried soak 10 minutes and remove stalk ends. Use water.)
1 cup apple juice
2 tablespoons tamari soy sauce
1 teaspoon fresh, grated ginger juice
Parsley, to garnish

1. Soak hijiki for 10 minutes in water. Strain off (keep water).
2. Sauté onions and carrots in sesame oil until onions are transparent (5 minutes).
3. Add hijiki, shiitake and soaking water plus 1 cup apple juice to cover surface. Bring to a boil, cover and simmer gently for 45 minutes.
4. Stir in tamari soy sauce and ginger juice. Simmer another 15 minutes to evaporate most of the liquid.
5. Garnish with parsley and serve hot as a side dish or chilled over a bed of lettuce.

99. HIJIKI WITH ONIONS, CARROTS AND NUTS
Serves 4 to 6

1 cup hijiki
4 cups water
1 tablespoon sunflower oil
1 sliced onion
1 grated carrot or 1 cup diced pumpkin
   (peeled)
½ cup cashew nuts
1 tablespoon pine nuts
1 tablespoon miso
½ cup boiling water

1. Soak hijiki in 2 cups water, until soft (10 minutes).
2. Strain off water and keep it.
3. Place oil in a deep pan, heat gently and put in onion; stir until golden brown. Add the hijiki and stir well for 5 minutes.
4. Add the hijiki soaking water and the two extra cups of water and bring to a boil. Simmer for 40 minutes, or until most of the water has boiled away.
5. Add the grated carrot or pumpkin, water and nuts. Mix gently. Let simmer for 10 minutes, or until carrot or pumpkin is soft.
6. Mix miso well in ½ cup water and add to the hijiki, stirring well.
7. Serve as a side dish or use as a stuffing for cabbage.

100. HIJIKI AND GINGER
Serves 4 to 6

1 cup hijiki
4 cups water
1 tablespoon safflower oil
2 tablespoons tamari soy sauce
1 tablespoon fresh, grated ginger
½ cup goat yoghurt (optional)

1. Rinse hijiki; then soak in 2 cups water for 10 minutes.
2. Strain off and keep the water.
3. Sauté hijiki in the oil for 10 minutes.
4. Add tamari soy sauce, ginger and the straining water and bring to a boil; turn down heat and simmer for 40 minutes, or until water has evaporated.
5. Sprinkle each serving with parsley and a squeeze of lemon juice. Decorate with a teaspoon of goat yoghurt (optional). (If served cold, sautéed (or raw) grated carrot may be added for variety.)

101. KALE AND MUSHROOMS BOILED
Serves 4

6 kale leaves
1 cup water
6 shiitake dried mushrooms or fresh
  mushrooms
2 teaspoons soy sauce
½ cup water
1 tablespoon freshly roasted sesame
  seeds

1. Steam or boil the kale leaves whole for 3 to 4 minutes in water until tender. Then slice fine. (Save the water for soup.)
2. If shiitake dried mushrooms are used, soak them for 10 minutes. Place mushrooms in ½ cup water and tamari soy sauce. Allow to simmer without cover for 15 minutes. Slice. Remove stems if tough.
3. Mix sliced kale with mushrooms and sesame seeds and serve.

102. KALE WATER-SAUTÉED
Serves 4

Vegetables are delicious if sautéed vigorously for a couple of minutes in a *little* boiling water.

12 leaves curly kale, sliced
½ cup water
Pinch salt
1 tablespoon roasted pumpkin seeds

1. Bring water to a boil and keep heat at medium.
2. Add kale and stir. Keep it moving for 3 minutes, or until the color suddenly becomes intensely green. It should then be tender.
3. Sprinkle with pumpkin seeds and serve immediately.

103. KAMPYO-KALE BUNDLES
Serves 4

Kampyo is made from dried strips of gourd skin. It looks very much like a grain or pasta but is, in fact, a vegetable.

8 ounces gourd strips (kampyo)
3 cups boiling water
1 tablespoon tamari soy sauce
8 ounces kale leaves, with stem
Pinch salt
2 cups water

1. Soak kampyo for 10 minutes.
2. Boil the gourd strips gently for 45 minutes in water and tamari.
3. Place kale leaves in salted boiling water for 3 to 4 minutes. Remove (keep water for soup stock).
4. Tie the leaves by the stems with the gourd strips in a tidy bow.
5. Serve the bundles with a main grain dish and vegetables.

104. KOMBU AND CARROTS
Serves 4 to 6

1½ cups water
¾ cup soaked kombu, cut into 1"
  squares
Pinch salt
2 teaspoons tamari soy sauce
2 carrots
2 teaspoons safflower oil

1. Bring water to a boil, add kombu and simmer over low heat for 30 minutes. Add more water if necessary.
2. Add soy sauce and boil another 10 minutes, or until most of the liquid has evaporated.
3. Meanwhile slice carrots into rounds and sauté in 1 teaspoon oil for 5 minutes. Add kombu and sauté with carrots until they are soft.
   Wakame can be used instead of kombu. It will take less time to cook — 10 minutes instead of 30.

105. LENTIL PÂTÉ
Serves 4

Great for a party!

3 cups water
1 strip kombu
2 cups lentils
1 bay leaf
2½ cups sourdough bread (see Recipe 70)
2 cups water
2 large onions, sliced
2 tablespoons olive oil
¾ cup fresh, chopped parsley
1 tablespoon sage
2 tablespoons thyme
¼ cup tahini
1 tablespoon genmai miso

1. Bring water and kombu to a boil, add lentils and bay leaf and simmer for 40 minutes, or until lentils are soft..
2. Remove bay leaf and blend.
3. Soak bread for 20 minutes in water. Drain off (keep water) and blend the bread and lentils.
4. Sauté onions for 5 minutes in the olive oil
5. Add parsley and herbs. Sauté 5 minutes.
6. Meanwhile mix tahini and miso with ½ cup of the bread water.
7. Mix the onions, herbs, tahini and miso with the bread and lentils and stir well.
8. Place in an oiled pan and bake for 40 minutes in a 350°F oven.

106. MANGETOUT (SNOW PEA) AND GINGER SALAD
Serves 4

1 tablespoon toasted sesame oil
½ pound snow (mangetout) peas
1 tablespoon fresh, grated ginger juice
1 teaspoon tamari soy sauce

1. Gently heat oil in a pan.
2. Sauté snow peas (mangetout) for 5 minutes.
3. Add ginger juice. Stir for 2 minutes.
4. Turn off heat. Add 1 tablespoon tamari soy sauce.
5. Serve as a salad or use to decorate other vegetable salads (see Recipe 90).

107. MUSTARD GREENS WITH PUMPKIN SEED SALAD
Serves 4

3 cups sliced mustard greens
1 cup water
½ cup toasted pumpkin seeds
3 tablespoons sweet rice vinegar

1. Place water in a pot and the greens in a steamer. Cover and steam vegetables for 10 to 15 minutes.
2. Place cooked greens in a bowl. Save the water for soup.
3. Sprinkle the pumpkin seeds over greens and garnish with the rice vinegar. Serve hot or cold.

108. NORI "BLACK BUTTER" AND MUSHROOMS ON TOAST
Serves 2 to 3

2 sheets nori
1 teaspoon sesame oil
1 small onion, sliced
2 medium mushrooms sliced (optional)
1 cup water
1 teaspoon kuzu
1 tablespoon tamari soy sauce
2-3 slices whole-wheat bread, toasted
2-3 slices of lemon
Sprig of parsley

1. Break up the nori sheets into small pieces.
2. Heat oil in pan, place onion and mushroom in and sauté gently.
3. Add nori and stir for a minute.
4. Pour in ½ cup water and stir well. Boil for 5 minutes.
5. Mix kuzu in ½ cup water. Add kuzu and tamari to the nori. Stir. Bring almost to a boil.
6. Serve on slices of whole-wheat toast with a slice of lemon and a sprinkling of tamari soy sauce. Garnish with parsley.

109. PANCAKES WITH BECHAMEL VEGETABLE SAUCE
Serves 4

1 cup chopped white cabbage
1 small, finely diced carrot
½ cup chopped scallions (spring onions)
½ cup beansprouts
1 cup water
1 cup soy milk
1 tablespoon kuzu
Pinch salt
1 tablespoon rice vinegar
½ cup chopped parsley

1. Boil cabbage, carrot, scallions (spring onions) and beansprouts gently in water for 5 minutes.
2. Mix kuzu in soy milk with salt and rice vinegar and add to the vegetables to thicken. Bring to a boil, stirring until sauce thickens. Turn off heat.
3. Make pancakes (see Recipe 77). Place one pancake on a plate and cover with sauce. Add next pancake on top of this, cover with sauce and repeat until last pancake is used. Garnish with any remaining sauce, decorate with parsley and serve. Slice as you would a cake.

110. PARSNIPS AND ONION BAKED WITH PARSLEY AND MOCHI SAUCE
Side dish for 4

2 medium parsnips, sliced diagonally
1 large, sliced onion
2 teaspoons sesame oil
Pinch salt
½ cup grated mochi
1 cup water
1 teaspoon tahini
1 tablespoon tamari soy sauce
1 tablespoon rice vinegar
2 tablespoons chopped parsley

1. Gently sauté onions and parsnips in oil for 5 minutes. Ensure that they are lightly and evenly covered and slightly cooked.
2. Sprinkle on salt and place in a shallow dish in a 350°F oven for ½ hour.
3. Make sauce by adding mochi to 1 cup boiling water over heat.
4. Add tahini and tamari soy sauce to the mixture, stirring well.
5. Simmer and stir in rice vinegar and parsley.
6. Cover parsnips and onion, with the sauce and serve as a side dish.

111. PARSLEY IN TEMPURA BATTER

6 sprigs fresh parsley
2 tablespoons 80 percent whole-wheat
  pastry flour
1 tablespoon yellow cornmeal (maize
  flour)
Pinch salt
1 tablespoon kuzu in 1 cup cold water
1½ cups cold water
½ cup sesame oil

1. Wash parsley. Dry it in a cloth.
2. Mix whole-wheat flour, cornmeal (maize flour) and salt
3. Dissolve kuzu in cup of cold water.
4. Add kuzu and water and extra water to flour to make batter. Stand in a cool place for an hour before using.
5. Dip parsley into batter and fry quickly in hot oil. Oil should not be too hot. (See INGREDIENTS—TEMPURA).

(Other vegetables can also be cooked in this way. Serve with grains or soup.)

112. PICKLED DILL CUCUMBER

Pickling is, of course, an ancient method of preserving food naturally. It also helps digestion, and there are many recipes for preparing pickles. Sea salt, pressure and time yangize the food. Salted pickles can be purchased in most whole food shops, but here is a recipe for making them.

10 cups water
⅓ cup sea salt
2 pounds cucumbers
1 large, sliced onion
2 sprigs fresh or dry dill

1. Gently boil salt and water for 2 minutes, until salt dissolves. Allow to cool.
2. Wash cucumbers and place in pickling jars with onion and dill. Pour cooled salt water over them.
3. Leave uncovered in a dark, cool place for 3 to 4 days.
4. Place in jars and refrigerate — they will keep for a month or so.

113. PICKLED SAUERKRAUT

2 large cabbages
⅓ cup sea salt

1. Wash cabbage well. Dry and slice very thin.
2. Place in a wooden keg or china crock and sprinkle salt over it.
3. Cover with a wooden dish or plate, slightly smaller than the container opening, so that when a weight is placed on it there is pressure on the cabbage. Cover with cheesecloth and leave in a cool, dark place.
4. After 10 hours or so, water should cover the cabbage. If not, increase weight.
5. Check daily. If mold forms, remove it — it is not harmful but can affect the flavor.
6. After two weeks, rinse the cabbage in cold water. It is now ready for use.

114. POTATO AND LEEK SALAD
Serves 4

Just for a change!

1 pound small, organic red potatoes
2 cups water
Pinch salt
2 finely sliced leek tops
Juice of ½ lemon
1 tablespoon olive oil

1. Boil potatoes in water and salt for 20 minutes, or until tender.
2. Cut potatoes in half. Allow to cool.
3. Add the very finely shredded leek tops.
4. Toss the vegetables in olive oil and lemon juice.

115. RADISHES, DULSE AND DAIKON SALAD
Serves 4

6 finely sliced radishes
1 cup finely sliced daikon
2 tablespoons umeboshi vinegar
1 cup boiling water
1 cup dulse (washed)
½ cup boiling water

1. Blanch radishes and daikon in boiling water. Strain (keep water for soups).
2. Sprinkle with umeboshi vinegar.
3. Pour boiling water over dulse. Stir and leave for a minute. Strain dulse (keep water for soup). Add dulse to radishes and mix together.
4. Serve as a side salad.

116. RADISH FLOWERS AND UMEBOSHI KANTEN

12 radishes
1 cup boiling water
3 cups vegetable water
½ cup umeboshi vinegar
3 tablespoons agar-agar flakes

1. Slice radishes into flowers. Cut bottom across (so they stand straight).
2. Blanch in boiling water. Flowers will then open up. Remove and stand in umeboshi vinegar (keep water).
3. Heat vegetable water stock with blanching water and umeboshi vinegar. Sprinkle agar-agar flakes over and stir well. Turn off heat just before boiling.
4. Rinse shallow pyrex dish in cold water and pour the vegetable water and agar-agar into it. It should be deep enough to cover the radishes.
5. When it has partly set, push radishes in to form a pattern. Let set.
6. Turn out of the dish, slice to serve.

117. RED CABBAGE, APPLE AND UMEBOSHI
Serves 4

1 tablespoon corn oil
1 small, red cabbage, sliced fine
2 cups apple juice
2 tablespoons umeboshi vinegar
1 diced apple
¾ cup sultanas or raisins

1. Heat oil in a skillet and add cabbage. Stir gently over medium-low heat for 2 minutes.
2. Add apple juice, umeboshi vinegar, apple and sultanas or raisins. Bring to a boil. Simmer slowly over low heat for 45 minutes.
3. Stir and serve. The umeboshi vinegar keeps the cabbage a bright red color.

118. SAUERKRAUT, AVOCADO, ADUKI AND ULVA KANTEN SALAD
Side dish for 4

1 cup sauerkraut (see Recipe 113)
1 umeboshi plum, chopped fine
½ sliced avocado
2 tablespoons cooked adzuki beans
½ cup soaked ulva (sea lettuce)
1 tablespoon agar-agar flakes
1 cup water (vegetable water preferred)
1 tablespoon tamari soy sauce
½ cup chopped parsley or sliced
*   scallions (spring onions), to garnish*

1. Mix sauerkraut and umeboshi and place in wet salad bowl.
2. Spread slices of avocado over sauerkraut.
3. Sprinkle aduki beans around this and place ulva on top.
4. Mix agar-agar flakes in hot water, stir and bring gently to boiling point. Turn off heat and add tamari soy sauce.
5. Allow agar-agar water to cool slightly and pour over the vegetables. Let set 10 to 15 minutes. Refrigerate.
6. Turn out kanten onto plate and garnish with parsley or sliced scallions (spring onions).

119. SAUERKRAUT AND RADISH KANTEN
Side dish for 4

2 cups boiling water
Pinch salt
1 heaping tablespoon agar-agar
2 tablespoons sauerkraut
6 or 8 large, sliced red radishes
1 chopped umeboshi plum
1 sprig parsley
Chopped parsley, to garnish

1. Let water simmer gently over low heat. Add salt and agar-agar. Stir until dissolved.
2. Turn off heat. Add sauerkraut, sliced radishes and umeboshi. Stir well.
3. Wet the inside of a shallow earthenware or pyrex dish with cold water to prevent the kanten sticking when it sets. Pour in the mixture.
4. Leave to set for 10 to 20 minutes at room temperature. Refrigerate.
5. Turn out onto a shallow plate, decorate with parsley and serve as a side dish.

120. SAUERKRAUT ON TOAST
Serves 4

4 slices bread
1 tablespoon tahini spread
1 cup sauerkraut

1. Toast bread and then spread with tahini. Heat under broiler (grill) for 1 minute.
2. Place sauerkraut in pan and simmer for 2 minutes. Spread on the bread.

121. SUSHI NORI ROLL WITH TEMPEH, GINGER, CARROT AND SCALLION (SPRING ONION)
Serves 4 to 6

4 slices cooked tempeh each ¼" square by 6" long
1 carrot, sliced lengthwise into ¼" square strips
½ cup water
½ tablespoon dark sesame oil
2 tablespoons ginger juice
3 cups soft, cooked brown rice
2 tablespoons rice vinegar
2 tablespoons lemon juice
4 sheets nori seaweed gently toasted over flame
1 scallion (spring onion) sliced into 6" lengths

1. Prepare tempeh in pan, as for recipe 129.
2. Bring the carrot to a boil in ½ cup water and simmer gently in covered pan until soft (15 minutes) and water has evaporated. Add dark sesame oil and ginger juice and sauté another 5 minutes.
3. Mix rice vinegar and lemon juice into the rice.
4. Toast sheets of nori gently over a low flame until a deep green color and crisp.
5. Place a sheet of nori on your sushi mat. The soft rice should be evenly spread about ½" from the edge of the sheet and 1" from the top and bottom. You are making four rolls, so use a quarter of each ingredient.
6. Wet your hands and make a groove across the rice, 1½" from the bottom, into which you can layer the tempeh and ginger, carrot and scallion (spring onion).
7. Roll the sushi in a mat as though making a long cigarette. Keep it firm, even and smooth.
8. Use a very sharp knife to slice each roll across into bite-sized pieces (about ¾ inch wide).

Serve with a dip of tamari soy sauce with a touch of wasabi horseradish, mixing the powder with a few drops of water. (See also INGREDIENTS—SUSHI.)

122. SWEET BOILED CARROTS

3 cups sliced, medium carrots
Water

1. Place carrots in enough water to almost cover them. Leave lid off pot.
2. Bring to a boil and cook gently for 20 minutes, or until the water has evaporated. Do not stir, but shake the pot to stop sticking if necessary.
3. Decorate with parsley or peas and serve.

123. ULVA, DULSE AND ORANGE SALAD
Serves 4

1 cup washed ulva and dulse
1 cup boiling water
1 orange, peeled
¾ cup apple juice
1 umeboshi plum, pitted and sliced
1 teaspoon white (shiro) miso
3 cups cooked and strained soba or udon noodles (see INGREDIENTS—NOODLES)
¾ cup watercress

1. Wash ulva and dulse thoroughly and slice into pieces. Pour a cup of boiling water over them. Let stand for a minute. Strain off water and keep for soups.
2. Remove most of the outside pith from the orange and slice finely.
3. Mix apple juice and umeboshi plum with miso.
4. Chop cooked noodles to 2 to 3″ lengths and place in bowl. Cover with ulva, dulse, orange and dressing. Mix together until evenly coated with dressing.
5. Garnish with watercress. This can stand for an hour before serving.

124. UMEBOSHI-KUZU VEGETABLES
Serves 2

6 sliced mushrooms
1 small, sliced zucchini
8 small, young spinach leaves
2 cups water
2 teaspoons kuzu
½ cup cold water
1 sliced umeboshi plum

1. Place vegetables in a steamer.
2. Bring water to a boil and steam vegetables for 5 minutes, until tender. Remove from pan.
3. Mix kuzu in ½ cup cold water. Add with umeboshi plum to the vegetable water. Bring gently to boiling point, stirring until liquid is clear. Add vegetables and serve with boiled rice or rice croquettes.

125. WATERCRESS AND ONION SALAD
Side dish for 4

3 cups watercress
1 large onion, sliced finely or diced
½ cup apple juice
¼ cup sesame oil
1 teaspoon tamari soy sauce
1 umeboshi plum
1 orange, peeled

1. Wash watercress thoroughly and drain. Place in salad bowl.
2. Add onion to watercress.
3. Mix apple juice, oil, tamari and umeboshi plums.
4. Remove skin and most of the outside white pith from the orange and slice finely.
5. Pour dressing over the salad and stir. Decorate with the oranges and serve.

Legumes

BEANS or LEGUMES can make up **10%** of a meal—in soups, as side dishes, eaten with GRAINS —as a PROTEIN supplement — even taken with desserts. BEANS blend with SEA VEGETABLES & cooking them together helps digestion. SOY BEAN products: TOFU, TEMPEH, SOY SAUCE & MISO may be used.

Legumes

126. ADUKI AND PUMPKIN
Side dish for 4 to 6

1 cup aduki beans
¾ cup soaked and chopped wakame or
  2 strips kombu, 6"×2"
4 cups water
2 cups diced 1" pumpkin squares
1 sliced onion
¼ cup tamari soy sauce
Chopped parsley, to garnish

1. Wash aduki and soak for 1 or 2 hours.
2. Wipe wakame strips (or kombu) with a damp cloth to remove excess salt as this will harden beans when cooking.
3. Place beans and wakame or kombu in pan, cover with water and bring to a boil. Lower heat and simmer for 45 minutes.
4. Place onion and pumpkin on top and cook another 30 minutes.
5. Add tamari soy sauce and turn up heat to boil off excess water.
6. Mix ingredients, garnish with parsley and serve.

127. ADUKI PIZZA
Serves 4 to 6

1 cup aduki beans soaked in 3 cups
  water
1 slice kombu, 6"×2"
4 cups water
1 teaspoon caraway seeds
1 onion, sliced
1 parsnip, diced
2 tablespoons tamari soy sauce
6 olives
2 rings sweet red pepper
1 cup mochi-umeboshi sauce

1. Soak aduki beans for 2 hours. Discard water.
2. Wipe excess salt from the kombu strip with a damp cloth.
3. Bring fresh water to a boil with aduki, kombu and caraway seeds. Cover and simmer for 45 minutes.
4. Place onion and parsnip on top of aduki, cover and continue to simmer for another 20 minutes. Add tamari soy sauce. Boil off excess water.
5. Beans and parsnip should be soft enough to mash to make topping for pizza.
6. Spread aduki mixture on pre-cooked pastry (see Recipe 76), cover with Mochi-Umeboshi Sauce (see recipe 143) or Bechamel Cheese Sauce (see recipe 134) and decorate with olives and pieces of red pepper.
7. Place in 350°F oven for another 15 minutes.

128. ADUKI RICE AND SWEET CORN CROQUETTES
Serves 4 to 6

1 cup water
1 small, finely chopped onion
1 small, finely diced carrot
2 teaspoons tamari soy sauce
2 cups soft, cooked brown rice (see INGREDIENTS—GRAINS)
½ cup sweet corn kernels
1 cup soft, cooked aduki (or black) beans
2 cups whole-wheat breadcrumbs
1 tablespoon sesame or corn oil

1. Bring water to a boil. Add onion and carrot. Simmer for 10 minutes, or until vegetables are soft. Add tamari soy sauce.
2. Mix rice, corn and beans together. Add vegetables and enough of the water to make mixture stick together. Allow to cool.
3. Wet your hands and roll mixture into croquettes (6 or 8).
4. Roll croquettes in breadcrumbs.
5. Brush skillet with oil and heat gently. Sauté croquettes until brown.
6. Serve with Mochi-Umeboshi Sauce (see Recipe 143) and garnish with parsley.

129. TEMPEH, GINGER AND TAMARI SLICES

4 ounces tempeh
1 strip kombu in 1" squares
2 tablespoons tamari soy sauce
1 tablespoon grated ginger
2 cups apple juice

1. Slice tempeh into strips 3"×1."
2. Place in pan with kombu, tamari soy sauce, ginger and apple juice.
3. Bring to a boil, lower heat, cover and simmer for 40 minutes, or until most of the liquid has evaporated.
4. Use this tempeh for stews, sandwiches or in Sushi rolls (see Recipe 121).

(Can also be rolled in sesame or caraway seeds and shallow-fried in 1 teaspoon of sesame oil. Drain and serve with a natural mustard and grated daikon.)

130. TEMPEH AND MOCHI LAYERED STEW
Serves 4 to 6

4 slices cooked tempeh in 1"×2" strips
6 slices mochi
1 tablespoon safflower oil
Pinch salt
¾ cup sliced burdock root (soaked)
1 cup water
1 cup sliced rutabaga (swedes)
½ Chinese cabbage, sliced
1 cup beansprouts
1 cup watercress (washed)
Pinch salt

1. Prepare tempeh as for recipe 129.
2. Gently sauté mochi in the oil with salt until pieces burst and are golden brown (about 10 minutes).
3. After soaking burdock root for 10 minutes, discard water and place slices in a pan with a cup of water, bring to a boil and simmer, uncovered, for 15 minutes.
4. Add rutabaga (swedes), and simmer for 15 minutes.
5. Add tempeh, cabbage, beansprouts, watercress and salt, cover and simmer for 5 minutes.
6. Add mochi and serve with grains.

131. TEMPEH WITH TAHINI AND MISO CREAM SAUCE

1 tablespoon light tahini
1 teaspoon kuzu in
1 cup cold water
1 tablespoon light shiro miso in ½ cup hot water
8 ounces tempeh, prepared as in Recipe 129 and sliced into ½" squares

1. Heat tahini in pan and stir until it begins to bubble.
2. Mix miso and kuzu in water and add to the tahini. Stir until sauce thickens.
3. Add tempeh and stir.
4. Serve over brown rice or grains with a side dish of vegetables or salad.

132. TOFU ON SAUTÉED ONION
Side dish for 4

8 slices of tofu, 2" squares ¼" thick
1 tablespoon safflower oil
2 medium onions, sliced
1 teaspoon tamari soy sauce
½ cup water
2 teaspoons grated, fresh ginger juice

1. Heat oil in skillet and gently sauté tofu until both sides are golden brown.
2. In another pan sauté onion in ½ cup water for 3 minutes or until golden brown.
3. Add tamari soy sauce and ginger.
4. Serve tofu on a bed of onions. (Fried tofu can also be used in soups, stews or on other vegetables.)

133. TOFU STICKS SAUTÉED WITH BURDOCK AND VEGETABLES

Serves 2 to 4

1 tablespoon sesame oil
8 slices of tofu, ½"×2"×1"
½ cup finely pencil-sliced fresh burdock
  root
1 teaspoon toasted sesame oil
1 sliced onion
1 small, sliced carrot
1 strip chopped sweet red pepper
1 cup water
1 teaspoon kuzu
½ cup water

1. Wipe skillet with oil and place in tofu slices. Sauté and turn gently over medium-low heat until golden brown.
2. Soak burdock root for 10 minutes in a little water. Discard water.
3. Sauté burdock in oil for 20 minutes. Add onion, carrots and pepper. Stir. Pour in 1 cup water. Simmer for 15 minutes.
4. Dissolve kuzu in water and add to vegetables. Sauce should not be too thick; add more water if necessary.
5. Serve vegetables with tofu and brown rice.

Sauces, Spreads and Dips

134. BECHAMEL SAUCE

1½ tablespoons whole-wheat flour
1 cup water
1 cup soy milk
1 tablespoon umeboshi vinegar or
1 tablespoon fresh, grated ginger juice
  or 1 tablespoon fresh lemon juice
1 tablespoon tamari soy sauce
2 teaspoons kuzu
½ cup water

1. Mix flour in the cold water and heat gently, stirring well.
2. Add half the soy milk and the umeboshi vinegar (or ginger juice or lemon juice) with tamari soy sauce. Bring to a boil. The flour should thicken slightly. Add rest soy milk.
3. Mix the kuzu in cold water and pour into the mixture, stirring well, until it thickens into a smooth sauce.
4. Serve over vegetables, rice, noodles or fish.

The above sauce can be used as a base for:
Cheese Sauce — Add 2 tablespoons of grated provolone or goat cheese with umeboshi vinegar.
Parsley Sauce — Add 2 tablespoons of chopped parsley with ginger juice.
Onion Sauce — Add a small chopped onion with umeboshi vinegar.
Mushroom Sauce — Add 1 small chopped onion and 1 cup sliced mushrooms with ginger juice.
Lemon Sauce — Add 1 teaspoon grated lemon rind with lemon juice.

135. BLACK BEAN AND CHICK PEA PATÉ
Serves 4 to 6

½ cup cooked chick peas with kombu
½ cup black turtle beans
1 strip kombu, 3"×1"
4 cups water
1 chopped clove garlic
2 tablespoons soy sauce
1 teaspoon caraway seeds
¼ green pepper, sliced
½ cup chopped parsley

1. Soak chick peas overnight. Soak beans for 1 hour. Discard water.
2. Add kombu to fresh water and bring to a boil. Add beans and chick peas.
3. Boil for 3 hours, or until chick peas are soft.
4. Add garlic, soy sauce and caraway seeds. Blend. Decorate with parsley and green pepper and serve with whole-wheat crackers or bread.

136. CABBAGE AND CARAWAY-TOFU SAUCE
Serves 6

½ *small, hard white cabbage*
½ *cup water*
1 teaspoon caraway seeds
1 cup tofu pieces
2 umeboshi plums, seeded
2 tablespoons kuzu, in ½ *cup water*

1. Slice cabbage fine and boil in water with caraway seeds for 5 minutes.
2. Blend tofu, umeboshi plums and kuzu (mixed in ½ cup cold water). Place in pan and bring gently to a boil. Stir well.
3. Pour over cabbage and serve.

137. FRESH DILL SAUCE
Serves 4

½ *cup fresh dill weed*
½ *cup soy milk (unsweetened)*
2 teaspoons kuzu
1 cup water
Pinch salt

1. Chop the dill weed fine.
2. Heat the soy milk and add the dill.
3. Mix kuzu well in water and add to the warm dill and milk with salt.
4. Gently bring to a boil. Serve over fish or millet-aduki croquettes (see Recipe 49).

138. HUMMUS
Serves a party

¾ *cup chick peas*
4 cups water
4 slices kombu, 1"×2" approx.
Pinch salt
2 tablespoons tahini
1 tablespoon fresh lemon juice
2 crushed cloves garlic
½ *cup water*
2 tablespoons umeboshi vinegar
Chopped parsley, to garnish

1. Wash chick peas and soak overnight in 2 cups water.
2. Discard water and add fresh (3 cups). Boil in pressure cooker with kombu for 1½ hours or in covered pan for 3 hours, adding more water if necessary.
3. When soft, add salt and boil another ½ hour.
4. Blend chick peas, kombu and any water left.
5. Place tahini in a pan and heat gently. Stirring well, add the lemon juice and garlic. Add a little water if necessary to keep it from sticking to pan. When it bubbles, remove from heat and add umeboshi vinegar.
6. Stir the tahini into the chick peas.
7. Garnish with parsley and serve.

139. GUACAMOLE (A MEXICAN SPREAD APPETIZER)
Serves a party

3 ripe avocados
Juice of 1 lemon
1 tablespoon tamari soy sauce
1 medium, red onion, chopped fine
1 crushed clove garlic

1. Peel and pit the avocados. Mash with a fork.
2. Add lemon juice and tamari soy sauce.
3. Mix the chopped onions and garlic thoroughly into the mixture.
4. Serve with corn chips.

   (Mexicans serve a hot chili pepper sauce with this spread.)

140. LEMON SAUCE
Serves 4

2 tablespoons whole corn flour
2 teaspoons safflower oil
1 cup soy milk
1 teaspoon soy sauce
Juice of ½ lemon
1 teaspoon lemon rind
1 teaspoon kuzu
½ cup cold water

1. Place corn flour in hot oil. Stir.
2. Gently mix in soy milk.
3. Add soy sauce, lemon juice and rind.
4. Mix kuzu in cold water. Pour in and stir. Serve over Millet-Arame Croquettes (see Recipe 50).

141. MISO DRESSING FOR SALADS

1 level teaspoon natto miso
1 level teaspoon genmai or buckwheat
  miso
½ cup boiled water
1 teaspoon olive oil
1 teaspoon rice vinegar

1. Mix misos with water.
2. Add olive oil and vinegar.
3. Stir well and serve over salads.

142. MOCHI AND ONION SAUCE

Mochi is made from cooked, pounded, sweet rice (see INGREDIENTS—MOCHI).

1½ cups water
1 medium, diced onion
¾ cup grated mochi
2 teaspoons light tahini
1 tablespoon umeboshi vinegar
Juice of 1 tablespoon fresh grated
  ginger (optional)

1. Bring water to a boil and add onion. Simmer for 5 minutes.
2. Add grated mochi and stir well until sauce thickens.
3. Add tahini, umeboshi vinegar and ginger. Stir and remove from heat.
4. Serve with buckwheat burgers or rice croquettes.

(See also Bechamel Sauce, Recipe 134.)

143. MOCHI-UMEBOSHI "MOCK CHEESE" SAUCE

3 cups water
1 medium onion, sliced fine (1 cup)
1 teaspoon light tahini
½ teaspoon caraway seeds or basil
¾ cup grated mochi
1 teaspoon white miso
½ cup hot water
2 tablespoons umeboshi vinegar

1. Bring water to a boil in a pan. Add onions and simmer 3 minutes.
2. Add tahini, caraway seeds or basil and grated mochi. Stir well.
3. Mix the miso in water to a smooth consistency. Add to the sauce and stir.
4. Add the umeboshi vinegar and stir. The "cheese" sauce is ready.
5. Serve over Aduki Pizza (see Recipe 127) or Aduki Rice and Sweet Corn Croquettes (see Recipe 128).

144. MUSHROOM AND PEPPER SAUCE WITH GINGER AND KUZU

3 cups water
1 teaspoon grated ginger
2 large, sliced mushrooms
½ sliced red pepper
½ cup tamari soy sauce
2 teaspoons kuzu
½ cup water

1. Bring water to a boil with ginger.
2. Add mushrooms and pepper.
3. Add tamari soy sauce.
4. Dissolve kuzu in ½ cup of water, add to mixture and stir until it thickens to a smooth sauce.
5. Serve over grains or noodles.

145. OATMEAL SAUCE
Serves 4

1 tablespoon whole-wheat flour
1 tablespoon oat flakes
3 cups water (vegetable or cabbage
    water)
1 teaspoon grated ginger
1 tablespoon umeboshi vinegar
Breadcrumbs

1. Mix flour and oat flakes in water. Bring to a boil.
2. Add ginger and umeboshi vinegar, stirring well. Add more water if necessary.
3. Pour sauce over Stuffed Cabbage (see Recipe 42) and sprinkle with breadcrumbs. Brown in oven for 5 minutes or so and serve.

146. ONION AND SQUASH SAUCE
Serves 4 to 6

1 finely chopped Spanish onion
2 regular onions, finely chopped
½ teaspoon sesame oil
½ teaspoon corn oil
1 teaspoon grated ginger
1 teaspoon tekka condiment
2 cups baked pumpkin or butternut
    squash
½ cup tamari soy sauce
1 cup water

1. Sauté onions in oil, stirring for 5 minutes over low heat.
2. Add ginger and tekka. Simmer another 20 minutes.
3. Blend baked pumpkin or squash with tamari soy sauce and 1 cup water.
4. Add squash to onions, bring to a boil and simmer gently for 25 minutes. Add more water if needed.
5. Serve over Millet-Azuki Croquettes (see Recipe 49), Buckwheat Burgers (see Recipe 39) or soba noodles (see INGREDIENTS—NOODLES).

147. ROAST "CRISPY" DUCK PANCAKE SAUCE

3 tablespoons water
1 tablespoon barley malt
2 teaspoons tahini
1 tablespoon mirin or sake
1 teaspoon hacho miso
Juice of half an orange

1. Mix water, barley malt, tahini and mirin or sake in a heated pan. Using a wooden spoon, stir well. Mixture should be smooth. Add more water if necessary. Turn off heat.
2. Mix miso in orange juice and stir into the sauce. Serve with Crispy Duck (see Recipe 172) or Pancakes (see Recipe 78).

148. PESTO SAUCE

2 cups fresh basil
2 sliced cloves garlic
½ cup water
1 teaspoon miso
½ cup water
2 tablespoons olive oil
2 tablespoons roasted pine nuts

1. Blend basil and garlic with ½ cup water and place in pan.
2. Mix miso in water and add the oil. Blend.
3. Add roasted pine nuts to miso liquid and blend.
4. Bring basil and garlic to a boil. Simmer for 2 minutes only. Add miso mixture, bring to a boil and remove from heat.
5. Serve with soba noodles (see INGREDIENTS—NOODLES).

149. SALAD DRESSING: APPLE JUICE AND TAMARI SOY SAUCE

An "oil and vinegar" mixture.

½ cup apple juice
2 tablespoons sesame oil
2 teaspoons tamari soy sauce
1 umeboshi plum (pitted and sliced) or
1 tablespoon umeboshi vinegar
½ teaspoon sesame salt (see
  INGREDIENTS—SESAME)

1. Mix apple juice, sesame oil and tamari and add umeboshi pieces.
2. Sprinkle on sesame salt and serve over salad.

150. SWEET AND SOUR BARLEY MALT AND GINGER SAUCE
Serves 4

2 teaspoons brown rice vinegar
2 teaspoons tamari
2 teaspoons brown sesame oil
2 teaspoons barley malt
2 teaspoons ginger juice
1 teaspoon roasted sesame seeds
¾ cup water

1. Warm brown rice vinegar, tamari and sesame oil in a pan over low heat, mixing well.
2. Stir in barley malt, ginger juice, sesame seeds and water.
3. Serve over swordfish or other fish and top with pink ginger.

(This sauce can also be served with chicken.)

151. SWEET AND SOUR SAUCE WITH MUSHROOMS AND SCALLIONS (SPRING ONIONS)
Serves 4 to 6

2 tablespoons sweet brown rice vinegar
4 teaspoons barley malt
1 tablespoon tamari soy sauce
1 cup water
1 chopped scallion (spring onion)
2 sliced mushrooms
¼ sliced red pepper
1 teaspoon kuzu
½ cup water

1. Heat vinegar and stir in barley malt and tamari.
2. Add water and almost bring to a boil.
3. Add vegetables and simmer 2 minutes.
4. Mix kuzu well in half cup of water and add to mixture; stir until it thickens. Remove from heat.
5. Serve over fish.

152. TAHINI, GINGER AND SCALLION (SPRING ONION) SPREAD

1 teaspoon grated fresh ginger
1 finely sliced scallion (spring onion)
1 teaspoon toasted sesame oil
½ cup tahini
1 cup water
2 teaspoons white miso
½ cup boiled water or vegetable water

1. Roast ginger and scallion (spring onion) in the sesame oil for 2 minutes over low heat.
2. Add tahini and water and stir constantly until it bubbles. Remove from heat.
3. Mix miso in water and add to the spread; mix thoroughly. Allow to cool.
4. Refrigerate after use. Add a little water and stir each time before serving. Good on bread, toast or rice cakes. Can also be mixed with 1 tablespoon soft, cooked whole oats and used as spread.

153. TAHINI, LEMON AND TAMARI DRESSING

1 tablespoon tahini
Juice of 1 lemon
½ cup boiled water or vegetable water
1 tablespoon tamari soy sauce
1 tablespoon chopped dill or parsley

1. Mix tahini and lemon.
2. Slowly add the water until smooth.
3. Add tamari and dill or parsley.
4. Serve with salad or over rice.

154. TAHINI AND SOY SAUCE

2 tablespoons tahini
2 tablespoons tamari soy sauce
1 cup water or vegetable water
1 teaspoon kuzu
½ cup cold water

1. Mix the tahini and soy sauce in a small saucepan.
2. Add the vegetable stock and heat gently. Stir.
3. Mix kuzu in cold water and add to the mixture.
4. Almost bring to a boil, until mixture becomes creamy.
5. Serve over croquettes or rice, fish or tempeh (see Recipe 131).

155. TAHINI, RICE VINEGAR AND MISO DRESSING

1 tablespoon tahini
1 tablespoon white miso
1 tablespoon rice vinegar
½ cup water

1. Heat tahini gently until it bubbles. Remove from heat.
2. Mix tahini with white miso and rice vinegar.
3. Add water to the mixture — this should be a fairly thick dressing. Serve on salad.

156. TOFU CHEESE

1 teaspoon genmai rice miso
1 teaspoon white rice miso
2 tablespoons boiled water
2 cups tofu, crumbled,
   or 1 half-pound block tofu

1. Mix misos with water.
2. Cover the tofu surface with the miso.
3. Leave to ferment at room temperature for 24 hours. If block tofu is used, leave for two days.

Add chopped herbs (chives, tarragon, etc.) if desired. Delicious served with hot bread, toast or crackers.

157. TOFU-DILL SALAD SPREAD

2 cups tofu
1 tablespoon chopped green pepper
1 tablespoon chopped celery
1 tablespoon chopped dill-salted pickles
   (see Recipe 112)
1 tablespoon lemon juice
1 teaspoon safflower oil
1 tablespoon umeboshi vinegar
1 tablespoon chopped dill
½ teaspoon natural mustard
Pinch salt

1. Blend ingredients together and serve with whole-wheat bread or whole-wheat sesame crackers.

158. TOFU SAUCE TARTARE

2 tablespoons tofu
½ cup water
3 teaspoons grated, fresh ginger juice
2 umeboshi plums pitted and crushed
½ cup soy milk
1 tablespoon safflower mayonnaise
   (optional)
½ cup finely chopped, fresh scallions
   (spring onions) or chives or 1
   chopped, pickled cucumber (see
   Recipe 112)

1. Parboil tofu in water for 5 minutes.
2. Blend tofu in a suribachi with ginger juice and umeboshi.
3. Add soy milk and mayonnaise (optional). Mix to a creamy consistency.
4. Add scallions (spring onions), fresh chives or pickled cucumber, and serve with fish.

159. UMEBOSHI AND KUZU SAUCE

1 cup vegetable water
1 medium onion, diced
2 umeboshi plums, pitted and sliced
   fine
1 teaspoon kuzu
½ cup cold water
1 teaspoon mirin
¼ cup chopped parsley

1. Bring water to a boil. Add onion and sauté for 4 minutes.
2. Add umeboshi plum and simmer for 1 minute.
3. Mix kuzu in water and add to the mixture with mirin and parsley. Stir until sauce thickens.
4. Serve over vegetables or cooked, chopped vegetables can be added to it and it can be served with rice or noodles.

160. UMEBOSHI-MUSTARD SAUCE

1 tablespoon natural or Dijon mustard
½ tablespoon umeboshi paste
or 2 umeboshi plums, pitted and
   mashed
1 cup vegetable water
1 teaspoon kuzu
1 tablespoon arrowroot
2 teaspoons tamari soy sauce
½ cup cold water

1. Mix mustard and umeboshi in vegetable water and heat gently in a pan.
2. Mix kuzu, arrowroot and tamari in cold water and add to the pan. Simmer for 3 minutes, stirring well. Add a little more water if necessary to make sauce and add to Prawns and Lotus Root (Recipe 170).

(If using mustard powder, mix it with a little umeboshi vinegar.)

Safflower plant

animal

5% ANIMAL QUALITY *foods*

Once or twice a week 5% ANIMAL QUALITY *foods* can be included in your menu — rather as CONDIMENTS. Shell *fish*, fish (cooked or eaten RAW), wild or free range birds are preferred to MAMMAL meats (*pork*, *beef* etc.) which are usually CHEMICALLY *produced* or treated. Always serve with VEGETABLES and GRAINS for balance.

Animal Food

161. CHICKEN AND CASHEW NUTS IN SWEET AND SOUR SAUCE
Serves 6 to 8

4 deboned chicken breast filets
¾ cup cashew nuts
1 tablespoon toasted sesame oil
2 cups water
2 cups apple juice
1 tablespoon barley malt
1 tablespoon tamari soy sauce
1 tablespoon umeboshi vinegar
1 tablespoons mirin
2 teaspoons kuzu in ½ cup apple juice

1. Skin the chicken breasts and place with the nuts in an oiled pan. Sauté for 5 minutes.
2. Pour in water and apple juice, barley malt, tamari soy sauce, umeboshi vinegar and mirin. Stir. Lower heat. Simmer 35 minutes.
3. Mix kuzu in ½ cup apple juice. Add to the mixture and stir. Remove from heat before mixture boils.
4. Serve with rice and vegetables.

162. CHICKEN AND MANGO ROAST
Serves 6 to 8

8 slices dried mango
¾ cup water
4 chicken breasts (free-range birds)
2 cups cranberry juice
2 tablespoons tamari soy sauce

1. Soak mango in water for 10 minutes.
2. Remove any fat from chicken and place chicken in a shallow oven dish.
3. Pour cranberry juice over the chicken and a little tamari soy sauce on each piece.
4. Place 2 mango slices on each portion and pour in soaking water from mango.
5. Cook in a 400°F oven for 30 minutes, turn pieces and cook another 20 minutes.

(Fresh mango or any dried fruit such as apricot can be used.)

163. CHICKEN IN BECHAMEL SAUCE WITH GRAPES
Serves 4

2 chicken breasts (free-range birds)
1 small, sliced carrot
1 small, sliced onion
1 stalk celery
½ cup chopped parsley
3 cups water
2 teaspoons kuzu
½ cup soy milk
1 cup seedless green grapes
1 tablespoon sake or dry white wine
  (optional)

1. Remove skin from chicken.
2. Bring water to a boil and add chicken and vegetables. Simmer over low heat for 20 minutes or until chicken is tender.
3. Remove chicken from stock and slice into small pieces. Return to pot.
4. Mix kuzu in soy milk and add to the chicken and vegetables. Stir until sauce thickens.
5. Add grapes and sake or white wine.
6. Serve with rice.

164. COD FILETS WITH MISO, SHALLOT AND SCALLION (SPRING ONION) SAUCE
Serves 4

1½ pounds cod
2 teaspoons light miso
Juice of 1 lemon
2 teaspoons sesame oil
1 large, diagonally sliced shallot
1 crushed clove of garlic
2 sliced scallions (spring onions)
8 snow peas (mangetout peas)
2 tablespoons fresh, chopped dill
Parsley, to garnish

1. Slice cod into filets. Remove back skin.
2. Mix miso and lemon juice.
3. Place oil in a pan and heat. Sauté shallots, garlic and one scallion (spring onion) for 2 to 3 minutes over medium heat.
4. Add cod filets, the rest of the scallion (spring onion), snow peas (mangetout) and dill. Pour on the miso and lemon. Cover and cook for 10 minutes.
5. Garnish with parsley and serve with brown rice.

165. CRAB AND SWEET CORN SOUP
Serves 4

4 cups water
2 fresh ears of corn
1 cup sliced fresh, cooked crab pieces
1 tablespoon kuzu
¾ cup soy milk
Pinch salt
¼ cup freshly chopped parsley

1. Bring water to a boil and cook ears of corn for 10 minutes. Remove kernels and keep water.
2. Place corn kernels and crab meat in corn water. Bring to a boil and simmer 2 minutes.
3. Mix the kuzu in the cold soy milk and add to the soup to thicken it gently. Heat until liquid clears.
4. Add pinch of salt. Stir.
5. Decorate with parsley and serve.

(Tamari soy sauce can be added to taste.)

MEAT is an elaborate
and expensive way to
obtain PROTEIN.

166. FISH "BOUILLABAISSE" SOUP
Serves 6 to 8

8 cups water
1 slice kombu, 2"×6"
2 cups salmon pieces
2 cups white meat fish
1 cup squid, cleaned and sliced in rings
2 bay leaves
6 coriander seeds, ground fine
Pinch salt
1 tablespoon sesame oil
2 medium onions
1 clove garlic
½ red pepper
1 small leek, sliced fine
1 teaspoon saffron powder or 8 saffron pieces
8 cooked prawns
1 tablespoon kuzu
1 cup water
3 slices whole-wheat toast

1. Bring water to a boil with kombu. Simmer for 3 minutes. Remove kombu and slice it into ½" squares.
2. Add salmon, white fish, squid, bay leaves, coriander seeds and salt. Simmer for 15 to 20 minutes. When fish is tender, remove it, take out bones and return to the soup.
3. Meanwhile heat oil in a pan and add onions, garlic, red pepper, leek and saffron. Sauté for 5 to 8 minutes.
4. Mix fish and vegetables and add the prawns. Simmer for 15 minutes.
5. Mix kuzu in water and add to the soup. Stir until it thickens.
6. Slice toasted bread into ½" squares and serve with the soup.

167. NEW ENGLAND FISH CHOWDER WITH CREAM OF TAHINI
Serves 6

1 tablespoon olive oil
1 clove chopped garlic
1 medium, sliced onion
2 pinches salt
¼ pound dark meat fish (bluefish or mackerel or tuna)
¼ cup carrot pieces
¼ cup sliced turnip
¼ cup red pepper pieces
¼ cup celery pieces
¼ teaspoon basil
4 cups water to cover
¼ pound white meat fish (sole or haddock)
½ cup rice flour
1 teaspoon tahini
1 cup water
¼ cup chopped parsley

1. Heat olive oil in pot over medium heat. Don't let it get too hot.
2. Add garlic to oil and sauté for 2 minutes.
3. Add sliced onion and salt. Stir well. Cover after 2 minutes and cook another 7 minutes.
4. Slice dark fish in small chunks. Add to onions and stir. Cook for 5 minutes.
5. Add carrots, turnip, red pepper, celery and basil. Cook 5 to 10 minutes.
6. Cover with water and cook 10 minutes.
7. Add white meat fish chunks and cook another 15 minutes.
8. Mix rice flour and tahini with enough water to make a creamy paste. Use this to cream the soup.
9. Decorate with chopped parsley and serve.

168. PAELLA
Serves 4 to 6

3 cups brown rice
6 cups water
1 tablespoon olive oil
2 large, finely sliced onions
1 clove garlic, crushed
½ teaspoon saffron powder or turmeric
½ red pepper, sliced
6 pieces chicken meat
Pinch salt
2 cups vegetable water
2 cups water
Pinch salt
6 scrubbed mussels (closed when fresh)
6 large prawns in their shells
1 cup fresh, sliced squid
1 cup fresh string beans
or 1 cup fresh green peas
½ cup water
1 cup fresh, chopped parsley
1 lemon (sliced)

1. Cook the rice in water over medium heat until water is absorbed (30 minutes). The rice should not be completely cooked.
2. Heat oil in heavy pan or skillet and sauté onions and garlic for 2 minutes.
3. Add saffron or turmeric, red pepper, chicken and salt. Sauté and stir well for 10 minutes over low heat.
4. Add vegetable water and simmer for 15 minutes, or until chicken is tender.
5. Mix the rice and the chicken mixture in a shallow ovenproof dish.
6. Bring 2 cups of water to a boil. Add salt and drop in mussels, prawns and squid. Boil over high heat for 5 minutes. Mussels should open.
7. Decorate rice and chicken with the various shellfish and squid and pour remaining fish water over it.
8. Cover paella well with a lid or foil and place in a preheated 300°F oven for 25 minutes, or until liquid is absorbed and the rice soft.
9. Cook beans (or peas) in water gently for 5 minutes (until water has evaporated).
10. Decorate paella with beans (or peas), parsley and lemon slices and serve.

(Note: Paella can be made by using 3 cups of diced tofu instead of chicken.)

169. PHEASANT CASSEROLE
Serves 4

1 tablespoon corn oil or sesame oil
2 medium, sliced onions
1 pheasant (plucked and cleaned)
1 sliced apple
1 cup chopped parsley
1 cup fresh cranberries
or ½ cup raisins
Pinch salt
1 bay leaf
Pinch coriander
2 cloves
2 cups apple juice or cider
2 teaspoons arrowroot
½ cup water
½ cup red wine (or to taste)

1. Heat a heavy casserole over medium heat. Add oil.
2. Sauté onions with the pheasant, apple, parsley, cranberries (or raisins), pinch of salt, bay leaf, coriander and cloves. Stir ingredients well for 10 minutes.
3. Add apple juice or cider.
4. Cover and place in preheated 300°F oven for 1 hour.
5. If gravy needs thickening, mix arrowroot in water and add to the casserole with red wine before serving.
6. Serve with rice, Red Cabbage (see Recipe 117) and Parsnips and Onion (see Recipe 110).

(Beware of lead shot when eating pheasant!)

170. PRAWNS WITH LOTUS ROOT AND UMEBOSHI-MUSTARD SAUCE
Serves 2

1 teaspoon toasted sesame oil
1 cup fresh lotus root, sliced fine
or 1 cup dried lotus root, soaked in
*   water for ½ hour (keep water)*
1 clove garlic, finely chopped
2 scallions (spring onions), sliced
*   diagonally*
6 large prawns, sliced
1 cup fresh snow peas (mangetout peas)

1. Place oil in preheated iron skillet, add lotus root, garlic and half the scallions (spring onions). Sauté, stirring well, for 15 minutes over medium heat.
2. Add prawns and the rest of the scallions (spring onions). Simmer for another 10 minutes. Stir well. Add snow peas (mangetout) and stir for 2 minutes.
3. Serve with Umeboshi-Mustard Sauce (see Recipe 160).

171. PRAWNS WITH MOCHI-LEMON SAUCE
Serves 4

3 cups vegetable water
1 large, finely chopped onion
4 teaspoons tahini
Juice of ½ lemon
2 teaspoons fresh lemon rind
1 tablespoon tamari soy sauce
¾ cup grated mochi
12 small prawns

1. Bring water to a boil. Add onions and simmer 10 minutes over low heat.
2. Add tahini, lemon juice and rind and tamari soy sauce.
3. Add grated mochi and stir until sauce is smooth.
4. Add prawns. Stir for 2 minutes.
5. Serve on noodles or whole wheat spaghetti.

172. ROAST "CRISPY" DUCK IN PANCAKES

The preparation of Peking duck or crispy roast duck can take time. You will need to begin this version only 24 hours before your meal!

1 duck (3 or 4 pound), cleaned and
*   plucked*
½ teaspoon salt
2 cups water
3 tablespoons barley malt
*   or rice syrup*
2 tablespoons tamari soy sauce
¾ cup mirin or sake
1 lemon sliced
2 teaspoons kuzu dissolved in ½ cup
*   water*

1. Pour boiling water over the duck inside and out. Allow to stand for 5 minutes and dry off with paper towels. Sprinkle salt inside.
2. Heat the water in a pan.
3. Add barley malt or rice syrup, tamari soy sauce, mirin (or sake) and lemon. Bring to a boil.
4. Turn heat to medium-low and simmer for 30 minutes. Add kuzu and stir. Allow this syrup to cool.
5. Using a ladle or brush, cover the duck inside and out with the syrup until the skin is thoroughly coated with it.
6. Use a meat hook and hang the bird by the neck, with a pan underneath to catch the drops. Leave it for 4 or 5 hours in a cool place during which time brush some more of the syrup over the skin (at least two or three times).
7. The duck now needs to hang in a cool place overnight or preferably for 24 hours. The skin will become textured like parchment. An electric fan on it is a good idea.
8. Place duck on a rack in a roasting pan and pour 1 cup water in the pan to catch the fat. Place pan in preheated 450°F oven for 15 minutes.
9. Turn oven down to 350°F and roast for 1 hour. Turn oven down to 200°F and roast for 1½ to 2 hours, longer if preferred more crisp.
10. Remove duck from oven and let stand for 10 minutes before carving it. Slice meat and skin into pieces and arrange on a warm plate, or serve duck at the table with the pancakes and vegetables.

THE VEGETABLES:
Serves 4 to 6

2 scallions (spring onions)
1 cucumber, about 8" long

1. Wash onions and cucumber and cut crosswise into 2" lengths.
2. Slice cucumber pieces and onion pieces lengthwise into very fine slivers.
3. Layer these with slices of duck on the Pancakes (see Recipe 78) with Roast Duck Sauce (see Recipe 147).

173. SALMON ROE AND AVOCADO
Serves 4

2 avocados
3 teaspoons salmon roe "caviar"
*   or lump fish "caviar"*
1 small onion, finely chopped
1 pitted umeboshi plum, each sliced
*   into four sections*
Chopped parsley to garnish

1. Slice avocados in half. Remove pits.
2. Place a teaspoon of chopped onion in each.
3. Drop in ½ teaspoon salmon roe and top it with ½ slice of umeboshi.
4. Serve garnished with chopped parsley and Salad Dressing (see Recipe 149).

174. SCALLOPS WITH RICE OR NOODLES
Serves 4

1 teaspoon corn oil
1 small, diced onion
½ clove garlic, finely chopped
1 cup small scallops
3 teaspoons kuzu
¾ cup soy milk
¼ cup chopped parsley
1 tablespoon sake or white wine
*   (optional)*

1. Heat oil in iron skillet or pan. Add onion and garlic. Stir-fry for 5 minutes.
2. Add scallops. Stir-fry for 3 minutes.
3. Dissolve kuzu in soy milk.
4. Mix kuzu and milk. Add to scallops and onions. Stir well until sauce thickens. Add parsley with sake or wine.
5. Stir and serve over rice or noodles. Decorate with parsley.

175. SUKIYAKI, UDON NOODLES AND SEAFOOD
Serves 4

THE BROTH:
4 cups udon noodles, cooked and
*   strained (see INGREDIENTS—*
*   NOODLES)*
6 cups kombu and shiitake mushroom
*   broth with tamari soy sauce (see*
*   INGREDIENTS—DASHI)*

1. Heat dashi or noodle broth in the iron skillet (a little can be placed in small side dishes to use as a dipping sauce).
2. Arrange the fish and other ingredients decoratively in the broth, adding them according to the time they take to cook. Simmer 5 or 10 minutes.

THE SEAFOOD:
6 scallops
6 clams in their shells (scrubbed)
8 shrimps
1 cup watercress (washed)
8 fresh mushrooms
4 scallions (spring onions), finely sliced
  diagonally
4 Chinese cabbage leaves, sliced into
  ½" pieces
Sliced lemon

This dish can be cooked in the kitchen or at the table by using a hot plate. Serve with slices of lemon.

176. SWORDFISH WITH TARRAGON

1 pound swordfish
½ teaspoon white miso
½ teaspoon mugi miso
¼ cup water
Juice of ½ lemon
1 teaspoon fresh, chopped tarragon
  or 1½ teaspoons dried tarragon

1. Place fish in ovenproof dish.
2. Mix misos with water and lemon juice.
3. Sprinkle chopped tarragon on fish and pour miso and lemon over it.
4. Bake in 375°F oven for ½ hour.
5. Serve. Good with boiled millet and Tahini and Soy Sauce (see Recipe 154).

177. TURKEY CROQUETTES AND ONION SAUCE
Makes 4 to 6 croquettes

2 cups finely chopped cooked turkey
  meat
1 chopped onion
1 cup chopped parsley
1 tablespoon mugi miso
½ cup warm water
1 tablespoon fresh, grated ginger
1½ cups soft, cooked brown rice (see
  INGREDIENTS—GRAINS)
1 cup oatmeal
1 cup breadcrumbs (or oatmeal)
1 tablespoon corn oil

1. Mix the turkey, onion and parsley.
2. Mix miso in warm water and add to the turkey mixture with the ginger.
3. Add cooked rice and oatmeal and mix.
4. Wet hands and roll croquettes in breadcrumbs (or oatmeal).
5. Pan-fry over gentle heat for 3 minutes on each side.
6. Place in a 300°F oven for half an hour and serve with Onion and Parsley Bechamel Sauce (see Recipe 134).

(Can also be made with salmon.)

178. WAKAME AND SHRIMP SOUP
Serves 4

½ cup soaked wakame
1 cup soaking water
4 cups vegetable water
6 or 8 shrimps, sliced
1 tablespoon tamari soy sauce
1 diagonally sliced scallion (spring onion)
4 slices lemon

1. Slice wakame into very small slices. They will expand, so do this thoroughly. Place in a pan with the soaking water.
2. Add vegetable water. Bring to the boil and then simmer 10 minutes.
3. Add the shrimps and tamari soy sauce and simmer another 10 minutes.
4. Sprinkle with scallion (spring onion) and serve with a ½ slice of lemon for each bowl.

Brussels Sprouts

Fruit & Nuts

5% FRUIT *in season* & NUTS *for your* DESSERT
which can include GRAINS & GRAIN PRODUCTS *(pastry,*
cakes, puddings, cereals, sweet rice) sweet VEGETABLES
such as **carrots, pumpkin, squash** — *even Azuki Beans.*
AGAR, CARRAGEEN, KUZU & TOFU *for jellies & whips.*

Desserts

179. ALMOND CREAM

1 cup peeled almonds
½ pint soy milk
1 tablespoon maple syrup
1 drop vanilla extract

1. Blend almonds.
2. Add soy milk, maple syrup and vanilla and blend until creamy. (Add more milk if necessary.) Refrigerate.
3. Serve over kanten and top with strawberries, cherries or grated nuts (see Recipe 206).

(Amazake milk can be used instead of soy milk and maple syrup.)

180. ALMOND AND CINNAMON COOKIES
Makes 12 small cookies

1 cup whole-wheat pastry flour
¼ teaspoon cinnamon
2 tablespoons corn or sesame oil
2 cups slivered or flaked almonds
1 tablespoon rice syrup or barley malt
¾ cup apple juice
1 tablespoon apple and pear spread or other sugarless jam (optional)

1. Mix flour with cinnamon and rub in oil.
2. Add almonds with rice syrup. Stir well.
3. Use enough apple juice to make a soft, not too wet, mix.
4. Place small cookie shapes on an oiled, lightly floured, baking sheet and press a small indentation on top of each one. Drop in ¼ teaspoon sugarless jam.
5. Bake in a preheated 350°F oven on a low rack for 10 minutes. Turn heat down to 300°F and bake for 30 minutes.
6. If using apple and pear spread, place a small quantity on top of each cake and bake another 5 minutes before taking out of the oven so that spread will set.

181. AMAZAKE, BLACKBERRIES AND KUZU
Serves 4

*2 cups amazake milk (see
    INGREDIENTS—AMAZAKE)*
1 tablespoon kuzu
1 cup apple juice
1 cup blackberries

1. Heat amazake gently in a pan.
2. Mix the kuzu in the cold apple juice.
3. Add kuzu to the amazake and stir well, until it's about to boil. The mixture should thicken.
4. Save 6 blackberries for garnish and place the rest in a bowl or in separate containers. Pour the amazake over them and let cool.
5. Garnish with rest of fruit. (This can also be made by substituting 2 cups soy milk and 1 dessertspoon barley malt for the amazake.)

182. AMAZAKE AND PEAR "BLANCMANGE"
Serves 4

*2 cups amazake milk (see
    INGREDIENTS—AMAZAKE)*
2 teaspoons kuzu
1 cup apple juice
1 sliced pear
2 tablespoons cashew nuts

1. Heat amazake gently in a pan.
2. Mix kuzu in the cold apple juice and add to amazake. Stir until it thickens and begins to boil.
3. Slice pear into dessert dishes and pour amazake cream over them.
4. Roast nuts in iron skillet. Chop fine and sprinkle over the top of the amazake.
5. Cool and refrigerate before serving. Serve with a dollop of Tofu Cream Whip (see Recipe 216).

(Blackberries can be used instead of the pear. Keep four to decorate the top. This can also be made by substituting 2 cups soy milk and 1 dessertspoon barley malt or rice syrup for the amazake milk.)

183. AMAZAKE KANTEN WITH ALMONDS AND STRAWBERRIES
Serves 6

4 cups amazake milk (see
  INGREDIENTS—AMAZAKE)
2 tablespoons agar-agar flakes
2 drops almond extract
½ cup chopped, roasted almonds
6 fresh strawberries

1. Heat amazake. Add agar-agar and almond extract. Bring to a boil.
2. Pour into a bowl or into separate containers.
3. Sprinkle with chopped almonds and top with strawberries.

(This can also be made by substituting 4 cups soy milk and 2 dessertspoons barley malt for the amazake.)

184. APPLE AND BLACKBERRY OR PEACH CRUMBLE
Serves 4 to 6

1 cup whole-wheat flour
1½ cups rolled oats (uncooked)
½ teaspoon salt
½ teaspoon cinnamon
¼ cup sesame oil
1 teaspoon fresh, grated lemon rind
¼ cup water
2 cups sliced apples
½ cup apple juice
2 cups blackberries
  or 2 cups sliced peaches
1 teaspoon sesame oil
1 tablespoon barley malt (optional)

1. To make crumble mixture, mix dry ingredients and add sesame oil, lemon rind and water. Stir well.
2. Apples should be peeled first (unless they are organically grown). Boil them in the apple juice for 5 minutes over low heat.
3. Mix with the blackberries or peaches.
4. Oil a shallow pie pan and pour in fruit.
5. Sprinkle crumble over the fruit and pour barley malt over the mixture.
6. Place in preheated 350°F oven for 35 minutes.

185. APPLE AND CINNAMON KANTEN DESSERT
Serves 2 to 4

2 cups water
2 sliced apples
2 tablespoons raisins
½ teaspoon cinnamon
Pinch salt
1 teaspoon kuzu
1 cup apple juice
2 teaspoons barley malt
1½ tablespoons agar-agar flakes

1. Bring water to a boil and add apples, raisins, cinnamon and salt. Simmer gently for 5 minutes, or until apples are soft.
2. Mix kuzu well in apple juice.
3. Add kuzu and barley malt to apples. Stir well over low heat.
4. Sprinkle in the agar-agar flakes and stir well.
5. Wet mold or pyrex dish and pour in kanten. Let set.

(This can also be made with apples and hunza (dried) apricots and a variety of fruits.)

186. APPLE "FAN" FRITTERS WITH BARLEY MALT SAUCE
Serves 4

2 tablespoons kuzu
2 cups cold mineral water
⅔ cup 85 percent whole-wheat pastry
   flour
⅓ cup cornmeal (maize flour)
Pinch salt
6 small, sweet apples

1. Mix kuzu in cold water with pinch of salt.
2. Mix pastry flour, salt and cornmeal (maize flour). Add kuzu water gently. Batter mixture should not be too runny. Let stand ½ hour.
3. Cut apples into quarters and remove cores, leaving some skin at one end.
4. Slice each quarter lengthwise into four slices. The skin should hold the sliced sections together. Then gently fan out the slices, which are held together by the section of skin.
5. Dip the apple "fans" into the batter to cover and deep-fry (see INGREDIENTS—TEMPURA). Serve with Barley-Malt Sauce.

BARLEY MALT SAUCE:

1 teaspoon kuzu
1 cup apple juice
1 dessertspoon barley malt
½ teaspoon miso
2 teaspoons grated ginger

1. Mix kuzu in 1 tablespoon of the apple juice.
2. Heat rest of apple juice with barley malt, miso and ginger. Stir and gently bring to a boil.
3. Add kuzu and bring to boil.
4. Pour over fritters to glaze.

187. APPLE (OR PEAR) PIE

3 to 4 medium sweet apples or pears
   (peeled and cored)
1½ teaspoons kuzu
1 cup apple juice
1 teaspoon agar-agar flakes

1. Slice the apples or pears.
2. Arrange them on the pie crust (see Recipe 72) and bake in preheated 375°F oven for 25 minutes.
3. Remove from oven and allow to cool.
4. Dissolve the kuzu in the apple juice and heat gently; sprinkle on agar-agar stirring until it thickens, to make a glaze. Remove from heat just before it boils.
5. Pour over the cool apples or pears.
6. Let set for an hour before serving.

188. APPLE JUICE AND PINE NUT KANTEN
Serves 4

3 cups natural apple juice
½ teaspoon cinnamon
2 tablespoons raisins
1 tablespoon roasted pine nuts
2 tablespoons agar-agar flakes

1. Heat apple juice with cinnamon, raisins and roasted pine nuts for 2 minutes.
2. Stir in agar-agar to dissolve and bring to a boil.
3. Pour into wet mold or separate containers and allow to cool. Refrigerate.
4. Decorate with Tofutti Cream (see Recipe 218).

189. APPLE AND NUT KANTEN
Serves 4

2 apples
1 tablespoon seedless raisins
1 cup water
Pinch salt
1 tablespoon barley malt
1 teaspoon light tahini
1 cup apple juice
1 cup roasted ground almonds or pecan
 nuts
1½ tablespoons agar-agar flakes

1. Slice apples and place in water with salt and raisins. Bring to a boil and simmer for 10 minutes, or until soft.
2. Add barley malt, tahini, apple juice and nuts to apples and mix well or blend if preferred. Return to the pan.
3. Add agar-agar flakes and stir over heat. Bring to a boil and turn off heat.
4. Allow to set. Refrigerate and serve.

190. APPLE-MANGO KANTEN
Serves 4

2 medium, red eating apples
1 cup water
Pinch salt
½ teaspoon agar-agar
1 sliced mango
4 fresh mint leaves or cherries

1. Peel and slice the apples. If organic, grate the peel.
2. Bring water to a boil and add salt, apples and grated peel. Lower heat and simmer for 10 minutes.
3. Slice fresh mango into pyrex dish.
4. Strain off stewed apples, leaving juice in the pot, and arrange in dish with mango pieces.
5. Add agar-agar to the juice and stir well over heat. Bring almost to a boil and then turn off heat. Pour juice over the apple and mango.

6. Let set. Place in separate containers if preferred.
7. Decorate with a mint leaf, cherry or dollop of Tofu Cream Whip or Tofutti Cream (see Recipes 216 and 218).

191. APPLE PIE FILLING

8 apples
1¼ cups apple juice
½ cup raisins
½ teaspoon cinnamon
½ teaspoon nutmeg
½ teaspoon vanilla extract
2 teaspoons agar-agar flakes
1½ tablespoons kuzu
½ cup apple juice

1. Peel apples, core and dice them.
2. Bring apple juice to a boil with raisins, spices and agar-agar flakes. Boil for half a minute.
3. Dissolve kuzu in ½ cup apple juice, add to the mixture and stir until it begins to boil. Remove from heat.
4. Roll out pastry (see recipes 73, 74 and 75). Place half on the bottom of pie dish.
5. Add apples, pour over the spice sauce and cover with pastry. Decorate and pierce pie crust and place in 350°F oven for 30 minutes, then in 400°F oven for 15 minutes.

192. APPLE-TAHINI PANCAKE FILLING
Serves 4

2 sweet apples peeled, cored and sliced
Pinch salt (optional)
Pinch cinnamon
½ cup raisins
½ cup water
2 teaspoons light tahini
1 teaspoon barley malt
½ teaspoon kuzu
½ cup water

1. Cook apples, salt, cinnamon and raisins in water for 10 minutes.
2. In another pan mix tahini and barley malt. Heat gently until tahini bubbles.
3. Mix kuzu in water and add to the tahini. Stir carefully until mixture is a creamy spread. Add a little more water if necessary.
4. Spread tahini mix then apples over Buckwheat Pancakes (see Recipe 71) and fold pancakes over it.

193. APRICOT KANTEN
Serves 4

1 cup hunza or dried apricots (pitted)
Pinch salt
3 cups water
Juice of 1 orange
2 tablespoons agar-agar flakes
½ cup roasted almonds or hazelnuts

1. Soak apricots 1 hour. Bring to a boil in water and salt. Simmer for half an hour.
2. Add orange juice.
3. Sprinkle on agar-agar. Simmer and stir until mixture is smooth.
4. Wet shallow pyrex dish or mold or individual containers. Pour in mixture and allow to cool. Refrigerate.
5. Decorate with grated almonds or hazelnuts or Tofutti Cream (see Recipe 218).

194. ADUKI AND RAISIN KANTEN
Serves 4 to 6

½ cup aduki beans
½ cup raisins
1 strip kombu
3 cups water
3 tablespoons agar-agar flakes
4 cups apple juice and water, mixed
½ teaspoon vanilla extract

1. Soak aduki for at least 2 hours or, if possible, overnight. Discard water.
2. Place aduki beans, raisins, kombu and water in a pan. Bring to a boil and cook 10 minutes (remember aduki will swell 5 times or more in volume).
3. Simmer gently for 1½ to 2 hours, or until beans are soft. Add more water if necessary. Let most of it evaporate during the last ½ hour of stewing.
4. In another pan heat the apple juice and water with vanilla. Sprinkle agar-agar flakes into it and stir.
5. Add the aduki and raisins. Stir well.
6. Place into containers or mold and let cool.
7. Decorate with Tofutti Cream (see Recipe 218) and a piece of fruit.

   (Aduki and raisins can be used as a side vegetable dish, for salad or can be added to rice croquettes.)

195. BROWN RICE PUDDING 1
Serves 4

1 cup apple juice
3 cups soy milk and water mixed
1 cup cooked brown rice (see
  INGREDIENTS—GRAINS)
1 tablespoon raisins
½ teaspoon cinnamon (optional)

1. Mix soy milk, apple juice and water in an ovenproof dish.
2. Add rice, raisins and cinnamon.
3. Bake in preheated 250°F oven for 2 hours.

(See also Recipe 201.)

196. BROWN RICE PUDDING 2
Serves 4

½ cup brown rice
1 cup water
2 cups soy milk
1 tablespoon barley malt
2 cups apple juice
2 tablespoons raisins
¼ teaspoon cinnamon
Pinch salt

1. Mix ingredients in an ovenproof dish. Cover and place in preheated 450°F oven for 45 minutes.
2. Turn oven down to 250°F and bake another 2 hours.
3. Remove cover and bake a further 30 minutes.

(See also Recipe 201.)

197. BAKED APPLES WITH TAHINI RAISINS AND LEMON (OR ORANGE) FILLING
Serves 4

4 apples
1½ tablespoons tahini
½ cup raisins
2 teaspoons grated, fresh lemon (or
  orange) peel
½ teaspoon cinnamon
1 tablespoon grated, roasted walnuts or
  hazelnuts
Juice of ½ lemon (or orange)
4 teaspoons barley malt

1. Cut a 1″ cone shape off the base of the apple. (This is to prevent the filling running out while cooking.) Remove centre and core of the apple with a knife, leaving a round hollow right through the apple.
2. Mix tahini, raisins, lemon (or orange) peel, cinnamon and grated walnuts with lemon (or orange) juice.
3. Stuff apples with the mixture. Replace cone in base.
4. Cook in 350°F oven for 15 minutes, or until tender. Remove from oven and pour a little barley malt over each apple. Return to oven for another 5 minutes and then serve.

198. BARLEY MALT AND KUZU CREAM
Serves 4

2 cups soy milk
2 tablespoons barley malt
1 dessertspoon kuzu
1 cup apple juice
½ satsuma or tangerine
½ cup chopped, roasted hazelnuts or almonds

1. Heat soy milk and add the barley malt, stirring well.
2. Mix kuzu and apple juice and add to the milk, continuing to stir. Almost bring to a boil.
3. Pour into bowls and leave to set.
4. Break the satsuma into small sections and place one on top of each portion. Sprinkle with chopped, roasted hazelnuts or almonds.

199. BOIL AND BAKE FRUIT CAKE

3 cups mixed fruit (seedless raisins, currants, dates, apricots, etc.)
Peel of ½ lemon grated
Peel ½ orange grated
½ diced apple
½ cup mixed nuts, crushed
½ cup sunflower seeds
2 cups apple juice
1 cup bancha tea
⅓ cup sunflower or sesame oil
1 teaspoon cinnamon
Pinch salt
2 teaspoons fresh, grated ginger
2 cups flour
1 egg or 1 tablespoon of kuzu mixed in
1 cup apple juice
2 teaspoons sesame oil
¼ cup whole-wheat flour
1 dozen peeled almonds

1. Mix the fruit, nuts, seeds, apple juice, bancha tea, oil, cinnamon, salt and ginger in a pan. Bring to a boil and simmer gently for 5 minutes.
2. Allow to cool (can stand overnight), then add the flour and egg or kuzu and apple juice. Save a tablespoon of kuzu liquid to glaze cake.
3. Stir well and pour mixture in an oiled cake pan (sprinkle inside pan with flour).
4. To peel almonds immerse in boiling water. Decorate top of cake with them and brush kuzu-apple juice mixture to smooth and glaze surface.
5. Bake in preheated 380°F oven, on low rack, for 1 hour 15 minutes.

200. CAROB "BLANCMANGE"
Serves 4

1 teaspoon kuzu
1 cup cold water
2 cups soy milk
Pinch cinnamon
1 tablespoon raisins
1 teaspoon carob flour
1 tablespoon barley malt

1. Dissolve kuzu in cold water until smooth.
2. Stand heatproof bowl in boiling water and add soy milk, cinnamon, raisins, carob flour and kuzu to bowl. Stir gently until hot.
3. Add barley malt and continue to stir.
4. Sprinkle on agar-agar and stir well.

1½ tablespoons agar-agar
6 or 8 pitted cherries

5. Add raisins and stir until the mixture is smooth and creamy. Allow to cool a little.
6. Pour into a wet mold. Let set. Turn out and decorate with the cherries.

201. CAROB-RICE PUDDING WITH CAROB SAUCE
Serves 4

2 cups cooked rice
2 cups water
1 cup soy milk
1 tablespoon barley malt
1 tablespoon chopped raisins
2 teaspoons tahini
½ teaspoon vanilla extract
1 heaping teaspoon ground cinnamon

1. Soak the cooked rice for an hour or so in 2 cups water. Mix rice with soy milk, barley malt, chopped raisins, tahini and vanilla extract.
2. Pour mixture into an ovenproof pyrex or ceramic dish.
3. Sprinkle with cinnamon and bake for an hour in 350°F oven.

CAROB SAUCE:

1 tablespoon carob flour
2 cups water
1 tablespoon grated orange rind
2 tablespoons kuzu
1 cup water
1 tablespoon barley malt
½ cup orange juice
1 heaping tablespoon chopped
   hazelnuts

1. Mix carob flour well in water with grated orange rind.
2. Bring to a boil and cook for 20 minutes, stirring well.
3. Dissolve kuzu in 1 cup water, add to barley malt and orange juice, simmer and stir until smooth.
4. Spread mixture over the rice pudding and sprinkle with hazelnuts and orange rind.
5. Cool and serve.

(This can also be topped with Cashew and Apple Cream.)

202. CASHEW AND APPLE CREAM

4 golden delicious apples
1 cup cashew nuts
1 teaspoon vanilla extract
Pinch salt

1. Peel and slice apples. Mash apples to a purée, but don't add liquid.
2. Roast cashew nuts 20 minutes. Add the apples, salt and vanilla and blend.
3. Use as cream (see Recipe 201).

203. COUS COUS CAKE

1 cup seedless raisins (or golden
* seedless raisins)*
Pinch salt
3 cups water
1 cup cous cous
2 teaspoons kuzu
2 cups water
2 tablespoons barley malt (or rice
* syrup)*
2 teaspoons fresh ginger juice
Pinch salt

1. Boil the raisins in salted water for 20 minutes.
2. Pour in the cous cous. It should be almost covered. Mix in with raisins.
3. Simmer 5 minutes (pan covered). Turn off heat. Cous cous will swell and rise. Let stand 20 minutes.
4. Place cous cous and raisins in shallow dish.
5. In another pan, mix kuzu in water. Heat gently.
6. Add the barley malt (or rice syrup), ginger and salt and bring to a boil to make a glaze.
7. Pour over cous cous and allow to set.

(As an alternative glaze use Apricot Kanten (see Recipe 193), or another fruit kanten can be spread over the top of the cake and allowed to set.)

204. FRUIT CAKE

3 cups whole-wheat flour
½ cup safflower or sunflower oil
1 tablespoon crumbled tofu
½ teaspoon cinnamon or nutmeg
1 cup muesli (see recipe 31)
1 cup puffed whole wheat (optional)
½ cup apple juice
1 cup bancha tea
1 grated apple
1 cup seedless raisins
½ cup chopped, mixed nuts
1 teaspoon sesame paste
2 teaspoons grated, fresh lemon rind or
* orange rind*
2 teaspoons grated ginger

1. Mix flour, oil, tofu, cinnamon, muesli and puffed wheat.
2. Add apple juice and bancha tea and apple.
3. Mix in raisins, nuts, sesame paste, grated lemon and ginger. Let stand for half an hour. Mixture should not be too wet.
4. Place mixture in an oiled cake pan and bake in preheated 350°F oven, on low rack, for 1 hour.

205. FRUIT COMPOTE
Serves 4 to 6

1 red delicious (sweet) apple
1 golden delicious (sweet) apple
1 Granny Smith (sour) apple
2 ripe pears
3 dried apricots
¼ cup seedless raisins
¼ cup apple juice
1 teaspoon pure vanilla extract

1. Peel, core and slice apples and pears and place in pot.
2. Slice apricots and add to apples with raisins and apple juice.
3. Bring to a boil and simmer ten minutes.
4. Add teaspoon vanilla extract. Serve with Muesli or topped with Tofu Cream Whip (see Recipe 216).

206. LEMON AND APRICOT KANTEN WITH ALMOND CREAM
Serves 4

4 cups apple juice
1 cup seedless raisins
1 cup sliced, dry apricots
Rind of 1 lemon, grated
Pinch salt
2 tablespoons agar-agar flakes

1. Heat apple juice and add raisins, apricots and lemon rind. Simmer for ½ hour. Add salt.
2. Sprinkle in agar-agar and stir into mixture. Bring to a boil and turn off heat.
3. Pour into individual dishes or a mold.
4. Top with Almond Cream (see Recipe 179), decorate with fresh fruit and serve.

207. OATCAKES WITH RAISINS

1 cup whole-wheat pastry flour
1 cup oat flakes
1 teaspoon cinnamon
½ cup seedless raisins
3 tablespoons oil
Pinch salt
2 tablespoons barley malt
½ cup soy milk

1. Mix the ingredients to make a soft dough. Use a little more soy milk if mixture is too dry.
2. Shape into cookies.
3. Brush oil on baking tray. Sprinkle with a little flour and place cookies on it. Flatten slightly.
4. Bake quickly in a 450°F oven, on low rack, for half an hour.

(Cookies can be rolled in sesame seeds before baking.)

208. OATMEAL, RAISIN AND WALNUT COOKIES

1 cup walnuts
¾ cup sunflower seeds
1½ cups oats
¾ cup apple juice
2 tablespoons maple syrup
½ cup barley malt
¼ cup mixed sesame and corn oil
¼ teaspoon salt
½ teaspoon vanilla extract
¾ cup rice flour
1 cup rye flour
½ teaspoon baking powder

1. Roast walnuts and sunflower seeds in a 400°F oven for 20 minutes and then blend or crush.
2. Soak oats in apple juice.
3. Mix maple syrup, barley malt, oil, salt and vanilla.
4. Mix rice flour, rye flour and baking powder.
5. Combine all ingredients, add nuts and stir well.
6. Place cookies on an oiled baking sheet and bake on middle rack in a 350°F oven for 35 to 40 minutes, or until golden brown. Do not overcook.

209. OATCAKES WITH PEAR AND APPLE SPREAD
Makes about 12

Dry ingredients:
2 cups oat flakes
  or 2 cups Muesli (see Recipe 31)
½ cup whole-wheat flour
½ cup chopped seedless raisins
¼ cup chopped hazelnuts
¼ cup chopped almonds

Wet ingredients:
3 tablespoons sunflower oil
3 tablespoons barley malt
2 tablespoons sunflower butter (or tahini)
1 tablespoon soy milk
2 tablespoons pear and apple spread or whole fruit jam (no sugar)

1. Mix dry ingredients.
2. Gently heat and blend with a wooden spoon, the oil, barley malt and sunflower butter (or tahini). Pour over dry ingredients.
3. Mix thoroughly. Add soy milk.
4. Form mixture into balls and place balls on an oiled baking sheet and press them flat.
5. Make an indentation in the top of each cookie and fill with a little pear and apple spread.
6. Bake in a preheated 375°F oven, on low rack, for 35 minutes, or until golden brown.

210. PEARS BELLE HÉLÈNE
Serves 4

4 pears (peeled)
2 cups water
Pinch salt
1 cup seedless raisins
1 cup water
Pinch salt
¾ cup grain or barley coffee
   or dandelion root coffee
3 cups water
1 cup freshly oven-roasted hazelnuts
2 teaspoons kuzu
½ cup water

1. Immerse pears in boiling water. Add pinch of salt.
2. Simmer gently for 15 minutes, or until pears are soft.
3. Remove pears (throw out water), and place pears in separate dessert dishes.
4. Soak the raisins for half an hour or longer. Boil in water and salt for 10 minutes.
5. Make the grain or dandelion root coffee — a thick brew — and strain; then add to the raisins.
6. Blend or chop the hazelnuts fine. Add to the mixture.
7. Mix kuzu in water. Add to the sauce and bring to a boil to thicken.
8. Serve on top of pears.

211. PECAN CREAM

For dessert toppings.

1 cup pecans
1 cup soy milk
1 cup barley malt
½ teaspoon vanilla extract
½ teaspoon agar-agar powder

1. Roast nuts in oven for 15 minutes.
2. Heat soy milk, stir in barley malt and pour over the pecans.
3. Place in blender with vanilla and agar-agar powder.
4. Bring to a boil, allow to cool and refrigerate overnight. Blend again. This should be a light, creamy texture and not too thick. If too thick, add a little water.

212. PUMPKIN OR SQUASH PIE FILLING

3 pounds pumpkin or squash
3 cups water
1 tablespoon raisins
1 teaspoon cinnamon
¼ teaspoon nutmeg
1 tablespoon maple syrup
1 teaspoon vanilla extract
2 free-range eggs or 1½ tablespoons
  agar-agar flakes
1 teaspoon kuzu

1. Remove seeds and dice pumpkin or squash.
2. Place in pan with water, bring to a boil and simmer for ¾ hour, or until soft. Remove peel.
3. Blend pumpkin and remaining water to a smooth cream and return to saucepan.
4. Add raisins, cinnamon, nutmeg, maple syrup and vanilla.
5. If not using eggs, mix kuzu in ½ cup cold water and add to mixture. Sprinkle on agar-agar flakes and stir until almost to a boil. Remove from heat. Let cool for ½ hour.
   Alternatively, beat eggs until fluffy and pour into mixture. Stir in thoroughly.
6. Press out Pastry Crust in a pie pan (see recipes 73 and 74) and pour mixture into shell, allowing ¼″ for rising.
7. Bake in a preheated 350°F oven for 30 minutes, then in a 450°F oven for 15 minutes.

213. ROLLED OATS, WHEAT FLAKES AND ROLLED BARLEY COOKIES

¾ cup rolled oats
¾ cup roasted wheat flakes or puffed
  whole wheat
¾ cup rolled barley
½ cup chopped, mixed nuts
½ cup raisins
3 teaspoons safflower oil
2 tablespoons barley malt
1 teaspoon rice syrup
1 cup pastry dough (see Recipe 75)

1. Mix oats, wheat flakes, barley, nuts and raisins.
2. Melt barley malt and rice syrup and mix with the oil over low heat.
3. Pour barley malt and oil into dry ingredients and stir together.
4. Roll pastry thinly onto a preferably rectangular tray 9″×12″.
5. Press mixture firmly into pastry. Mark out 3″×2″ slices with knife.
6. Bake on middle tray in preheated 400°F oven for 20 minutes, or until golden brown.
7. Remove from tray and cut or break into 3″×2″ slices.

214. SUGARLESS JAMS

A 'sugarless' jam can be made by cooking grape juice or apple juice with apples for ½ hour to 45 minutes until one-third of the volume of liquid is left. This can be strained if a clear jam is required or left as it is. The fruit is then added and the time it is then cooked depends on the fruit. Strawberries 5 minutes, apples 15 minutes, apricots 15 minutes, cherries 20 minutes, oranges 45 minutes.

SWEET ORANGE MARMALADE
Makes 2 jars

4 sweet oranges
4 cups pure, unsugared grape or apple
  juice
2 apples, cored and diced with skin
½ teaspoon salt
18" square piece of muslin or
  cheesecloth

1. Scrub oranges gently and wipe. Cut each in half and extract juice.
2. Add juice to grape, or apple juice.
3. Remove pips and pith from oranges and tie securely in the muslin.
4. Place this with fruit juices and apple in pan and bring to boil. Simmer for 45 minutes or until ⅓ of the liquid remains. Strain if clear jam is required. Add salt.
5. Slice orange skin fine or thick according to preference, add to the juice and boil for 30 to 45 minutes. Squeeze out muslin bag and remove. Marmalade is ready when a drop of the liquid sets on a cold plate.

Jars, with or without screw tops, can be used for storing the jam. Place them in a 212°F oven for 20 minutes. Ladle the jam into each jar and cover with a circular piece of grease proof paper, cut to the correct size to fit inside the jar. Screw on the lid or stretch cling film over the top of each jar and secure with an elastic band. Allow to cool and store. Once opened the jam must be refrigerated.

215. TAHINI AND APPLE CUSTARD
Serves 4

½ cup raisins
2½ cups apple juice
3 apples peeled and sliced
3 tablespoons tahini
Pinch salt
Pinch fresh-grated lemon peel
3 tablespoons agar-agar flakes
½ cup grated, roasted almonds

1. Soak raisins in apple juice for an hour or so before heating. Allow to simmer for 5 minutes.
2. Add the sliced apples. Bring to a boil. Remove some apple for decoration.
3. Add tahini, salt and grated lemon peel. Sprinkle agar-agar flakes over and stir well.
4. Remove from heat and allow to set.
5. Blend mixture. Serve cold in separate bowls. Decorate with apple slices and sprinkle grated almonds on top.

216. TOFU CREAM WHIP

1 pound tofu
2 teaspoons vanilla extract
2 tablespoons maple syrup
1 teaspoon dandelion or grain coffee
1 teaspoon tahini
½ cup apple juice
¼ cup soy milk

1. Blend tofu with vanilla, maple syrup, coffee and tahini.
2. Add apple juice and soy milk to mixture while blending. Take care when adding liquid or the whip may become milky.
3. Serve on top of kantens or pies.

217. TOFU, RICE AND APRICOT WHIP
Serves 4

1 cup hunza dried apricots (if available)
3 cups water
2 cups well cooked soft whole grain
    rice (see INGREDIENTS—GRAINS)
1 tablespoon barley malt
1 cup tofu
1 cup apple juice
½ teaspoon cinnamon
½ cup roasted pecan nuts

1. Soak apricots for an hour and boil until soft (half hour) and most of the liquid has evaporated. Remove pits.
2. Blend the rice, barley malt, tofu, apple juice and cinnamon. Place in a bowl and stir in apricots.
3. Decorate with chopped pecan nuts.

218. TOFUTTI CREAM

½ cup apple juice
2 fresh apples, diced
2 teaspoons barley malt
1 tablespoon kuzu
½ cup cold apple juice
½ cup roasted hazelnuts
3 cups tofu
½ teaspoon vanilla extract

1. Heat apple juice in pan. Add apple and barley malt. Bring to a boil.
2. Add kuzu in cold apple juice to fruit. Stir until mixture thickens. Remove from heat just before boiling. Allow to cool.
3. Blend the nuts and add the fruit mixture, tofu and vanilla. Blend to make a cream.
4. Refrigerate and use to decorate sweet dishes.

1½ cups of fruit in season — strawberries, blackberries, cherries, pears, grapes, etc., can be used instead of apple.

219. TOFU AND WALNUT PIE

1 cup ground, roasted walnuts or hazelnuts
2 cups tofu, crumbled
1 cup water and soy milk, mixed
2 tablespoons barley malt
½ teaspoon vanilla extract
1 cup apple juice
2 tablespoons agar-agar flakes

1. Blend walnuts (or hazelnuts) and add tofu, water and soy milk, barley malt and vanilla extract. Blend these ingredients.
2. Heat apple juice in pan and sprinkle on agar-agar flakes. Stir until dissolved. Bring to a boil and then turn off heat.
3. Add the walnut mixture and stir well.
4. Pour into a cooked pastry crust (see Recipes 73, 74, 75, 79). Allow to cool and then refrigerate.

220. VANILLA CUSTARD 1

2 cups soy milk
½ teaspoon scraped vanilla pod
1 tablespoon raisins
2 tablespoons rice syrup or barley malt
Pinch ground turmeric for color (optional)
1 tablespoon kuzu

1. Place 1½ cups soy milk and the vanilla in a pan with raisins, rice syrup and turmeric (if yellow color is desired). Heat and stir.
2. Mix the kuzu in ½ cup cold soy milk and add to the pan. Stir well, until the custard thickens.
3. Serve over sweet dishes.

VANILLA CUSTARD 2

2 cups soy milk
½ teaspoon vanilla extract or scraped
    vanilla pod
Pinch ground turmeric
    or 2 or 3 threads of saffron (to color)
    — optional)
1½ tablespoons maple syrup
1 tablespoon agar-agar flakes
1 teaspoon kuzu
1 teaspoon corn meal
½ cup soy milk

1. Heat soy milk, vanilla and turmeric or saffron.
2. Add maple syrup and agar-agar and gently bring to a boil.
3. Mix kuzu and cornmeal in ½ cup soy milk. Pour into custard and stir.
4. Bring to a boil and then remove from heat.
5. Allow to cool or serve hot over sweet dishes.

221. WALNUT OR PECAN COOKIES

2 cups whole-wheat pastry flour
2 tablespoons corn oil
1 cup ground, roasted walnuts or
    pecans
1 free-range egg
2 tablespoons barley malt or rice syrup
1 teaspoon cinnamon
¼ teaspoon vanilla extract

1. Mix ingredients to make a soft biscuit dough.
2. Brush a baking tray or cookie sheet with oil and dust with flour.
3. Spoon out dough onto tray or sheet. Flatten slightly.
4. Bake on middle rack in a 450°F oven for half an hour.

222. WHEAT FLAKE AND MALT COOKIES

½ cup sesame oil
2 tablespoons barley malt
1 tablespoon tofu
1 teaspoon vanilla extract
1 tablespoon soy milk
1 cup flour
½ teaspoon salt
2 cups whole-wheat flakes or puffed
    whole wheat
½ cup chopped raisins
¼ cup shredded coconut
1 teaspoon grated lemon rind

1. Mix first five ingredients.
2. Stir in the flour, salt, flakes, raisins, coconut and lemon rind.
3. Place on an oiled cookie tray or set out cookies on waxed paper and cook on middle rack in a 350°F oven for ½ hour.

Some Suggested Menus

⊙ $\quad$ *Spring menus* $\quad$ ⊙

1.

BREAKFAST: $\quad$ Miso soup (see Recipe 14) or
boiled brown rice with
miso soup added for flavor.

Five grain bread (see Recipe 69) with
hummus (see Recipe 138) or with
sweet orange marmalade (see Recipe 214).

Green tea.

LUNCH: $\quad$ Soba noodles with tofu "Alfredo" sauce (see Recipe 62) and
water sautéed cabbage (see Recipe 102).
Slice fruit cake (see Recipe 204).

Green tea or
Apple juice.

DINNER: $\quad$ Sushi (see Recipe 121).
Pancakes (see Recipe 77) with bechamel vegetable sauce (see
Recipe 109).
Kombu and carrots (see Recipe 104) or
Aduki and parsnip (see Recipe 126).

Spring greens, water sautéed (see Recipe 102).
Millet and cauliflower mash (see Recipe 51) or
boiled brown rice (see INGREDIENTS—RICE).
Daikon and umeboshi vinegar (see Recipe 97).

Carob and rice pudding with carob sauce (see Recipe 201).

Barley tea (mugicha).

2.

BREAKFAST: $\quad$ Whole-oat porridge (see Recipe 32) served with
stewed apricots and rice syrup (2 teaspoons) on top and soy milk.

Whole-wheat bread (see Recipe 81) served with
tahini and ginger spread (see Recipe 152) and/or
sweet orange marmalade (see Recipe 214).

LUNCH: $\quad$ Millet and baked parsnips with vegetables (see Recipe 53).
Wheat flake and malt cookies (see Recipe 222).
Bancha tea.

DINNER: Onion and dulse soup (see Recipe 21) with
          tamari soy sauce.
          Tempuraed vegetables tofu and prawns (optional) (see INGREDIENTS—
          TEMPURA and Recipe 111) with
          boiled brown rice (see INGREDIENTS—RICE).
          Chinese pressed cabbage (see Recipe 95, 96).
          Sliced dill cucumber pickles (see Recipe 113).

          Pears Belle Hélène (see Recipe 210).

          Roasted grain coffee.

Summer menus

1.

BREAKFAST: Breakfast muesli crunch (see Recipe 31) with
             stewed apples and raisins, and
             apple juice and soy milk.

             Corn, rye and wholewheat bread (see Recipe 68) with
             tahini, ginger and scallion miso spread (see Recipe 152) or
             sweet orange marmalade (see Recipe 214).

             Bancha tea.

LUNCH: Rice, avocado and corn salad (see Recipe 57).
             Wheat flake and malt cookies (see Recipe 222).

             Hojicha or Bancha tea.

DINNER: Crab and sweet corn soup.
             Oat and rice patties (see Recipe 56) with
             umeboshi-kuzu vegetables (see recipe 124).
             Carrot, scallion and mangetout salad (see Recipes 90 and 106), hijike-
             shiitake side dish (see Recipe 98) and tamari soy sauce.
             Tofu and walnut pie (see Recipe 219) with vanilla custard (see Recipe
             220).

             Dandelion or grain coffee.

2.

BREAKFAST: Puffed whole wheat or rice decorated with
fresh fruit in season (grated apple, sliced peach, stoned cherries or
strawberries) and apple juice or grape juice with a dash of soy milk.

Oat cakes or toasted whole-wheat bread (see Recipe 81) with
apple-pear spread.

Bancha tea.

LUNCH: Carrot, apple and onion salad with raisins (see Recipe 88) with
cold, boiled brown rice (see INGREDIENTS—RICE).
Oatcake or sour dough and onion bread (see Recipe 70) with
tofu-dill salad spread (see Recipe 157).
Sauerkraut (see Recipe 113).
Apricot kanten (see Recipe 193).

Genmaicha (see INGREDIENTS—GREEN TEA).

DINNER: Guacamole (see Recipe 139) served with
corn, rye and whole-wheat bread (see Recipe 68) or
corn chips (unsalted or with sea salt or tamari soy sauce flavor).
Cous cous (see Recipe 44) served with
aduki and summer squash (see Recipe 126).

Carrot, dulse and celery boiled salad (see Recipe 89) or
watercress and onion salad (see Recipe 125).

Carob "blancmange" (see Recipe 200).

Mint tea with fresh mint.

(S) *Autumn menus* (S)

1.

BREAKFAST: Whole-oat porridge (see Recipe 32) served with
blackberries and apples stewed with raisins and a little corn and
barley malt and soy milk.

Whole-grain bread (see Recipe 67) with
tofu cheese (see Recipe 156).

Mugicha (see INGREDIENTS—BARLEY).

LUNCH: Pumpkin and miso soup (see Recipe 23) with
boiled, whole-grain rice flavored with
tahini and shiso condiment (see INGREDIENTS—SHISO).

Oatcakes with raisins (see Recipe 207) or
oatmeal raisin and walnut cookies (see Recipe 208).

Bancha tea.

DINNER: Lentil pâté (see Recipe 105) served with
            corn and rye bread (see Recipe 68) or
            rolled oats and celery soup (see Recipe 24) with
            wholemeal bread croûtons.

            Udon noodles (see INGREDIENTS—NOODLES) with
            mushroom and red pepper sauce (see Recipe 144).

            Aduki and pumpkin (see Recipe 126).

            Carrot, scallion and mangetout (snow pea) salad (see Recipe 90) or
            mangetout and ginger salad (see Recipe 106) or
            broccoli with roasted pumpkin seeds (see Recipe 86).

            Pumpkin or squash pie (see Recipe 212) with
            pecan cream (see Recipe 211).

            Mu tea with a dash of apple juice.

2.

BREAKFAST: Whole-wheat flakes (unsugared) with
            compote of stewed apples and raisins with soy milk.

            Toasted whole-wheat bread (see Recipe 81) with
            tahini, ginger and scallion spread (see Recipe 152) or
            unsugared jam (see Recipe 214).

            Twig tea (see INGREDIENTS—BANCHA TEA).

LUNCH: Rice and bean croquettes (see Recipe 58) or served hot with
            mochi and onion sauce (see Recipe 142).
            Grated carrot, raisin and lettuce and
            salad dressing (see Recipe 149).

            Slice of fruit cake (see Recipe 204).

            Twig tea.

DINNER: Cold borsch soup (see Recipe 3).

            Paella (see Recipe 168) served with
            broccoli, steamed, with toasted pumpkin seeds.

            Radish flowers and umeboshi kanten (see Recipe 116) or
            Sauerkraut and radish kanten (see Recipe 119).

            Watercress, orange and onion salad (see Recipe 125).

            Apple and nut kanten (see Recipe 189) or
            lemon and apricot kanten (see Recipe 206) topped with
            almond cream (see Recipe 179).

            Mu tea and apple juice or
            roasted grain coffee.

Winter menus

1.

BREAKFAST: Whole-oat porridge (see Recipe 32) mixed with cooked rice served with sesame salt and tamari soy sauce.

Bread of five grains (see Recipe 69) with
tahini, ginger and scallion spread (see Recipe 152).

Bancha tea or twig tea.

LUNCH: Miso soup (see Recipe 14) with
bread (see Recipe 67) and tofu-dill salad spread (see Recipe 157).

Oatcakes with raisins (see Recipe 207).

Bancha tea or twig tea.

DINNER: Pumpkin soup (see Recipe 22) with
whole-wheat bread croûtons (see Recipe 28).

Buckwheat burgers (see Recipe 39) or
millet-aduki croquettes (see Recipe 49) with
mochi onion sauce (see Recipe 142) or with
onion and squash sauce (see Recipe 146).
Steamed broccoli (see Recipe 86) with
roasted pumpkin seeds.
Sweet boiled carrots (see Recipe 122) or
Carrot and turnip cooked salad (see Recipe 91).
Hijiki with onion, carrots and nuts (see Recipe 99).

Whipped aduki and raisins decorated with tofutti cream (see Recipe 218).

Mugicha (see INGREDIENTS—BARLEY).

2.

BREAKFAST: Whole-oat porridge (see Recipe 32) served with
sauerkraut (see Recipe 112) or
sliced dill cucumber pickles (see Recipe 112) or
tamari soy sauce and shiso condiment (see INGREDIENTS).

Bread (see Recipe 67) with
tahini, ginger and scallion spread or
apple and pear spread (available commercially with no sugar added; see also Recipe 214).

Bancha tea or twig tea or
roasted grain coffee.

LUNCH: Brown rice, aduki beans and vegetables (see Recipe 33) with
sesame salt and tamari soy sauce.

Slice of boil and bake cake (see Recipe 199).

Genmaicha (see INGREDIENTS—GREEN TEA).

DINNER: Watercress soup (see Recipe 28).
Tempeh and mochi layered stew (see Recipe 130) or
tempeh with tahini and miso cream sauce (see Recipe 131) with
boiled rice or millet.

Steamed brussels sprouts (see Recipe 86) or
kale and mushrooms boiled (see Recipe 101).

Kombu and carrots (see Recipe 104).

Dill cucumber pickles (see Recipe 112) or
cauliflower in umeboshi vinegar (see Recipe 93).
Baked apple (see Recipe 197) or
Apple pie (see Recipe 191).

Dandelion coffee or
roasted grain coffee.

I suppose I had now better admit that Ohsawa had a poor opinion of actors. They were low in his seven levels of judgment and health, as "sellers of pleasure," and were, in his opinion, "gourmands and greedy." Perhaps he didn't know many actors — or perhaps he did! But suggesting to an actor that he should be in bed, like everyone else, before midnight and should not eat three hours before getting there is rather difficult if the actor has to work in the theater at night! It is, though, generally a sound suggestion and worth remembering.

There is much that is wise in macrobiotics, and the traditional remedies and diagnoses which Ohsawa and Michio Kushi detail in their books are worth reading. They both make other suggestions for a "harmonious and healthy way of life."

The Unique Principle does provide a compass and a state of mind that is glad for life and natural things. Eating naturally can also help the appreciation of natural fibers in clothing and furnishings. Wearing a fabric such as cotton, for example, next to the skin is pleasanter and healthier than wearing synthetics. Too much metallic jewelry around the neck, wrists and fingers especially can affect the joints and skin.

Swimming in the ocean with its mineral content is naturally better for you than luxuriating in a chlorinated pool. When bathing or taking a shower use a loofa or brush on your skin and finish with a cold shower unless your doctor says otherwise. Try rubbing yourself down thoroughly with a hot, damp towel each day. This is especially good for the hands, fingers, feet and toes. Baths can be a relaxing yin treatment after a hard yang day's work, but soaking for hours in hot water is rather like soaking your vegetables for too long — the body can be drained of minerals! Most "bath salts" contain frothy detergents and strong, chemically perfumed cosmetics that not only smell harsh but are tough on the skin.

Take a half hour of fresh-as-possible air each day by walking or gently jogging — on grass if possible or on sand — even in bare feet if you can. San Francisco has a stretch of undeveloped beach that runs for a couple of miles to the Golden Gate. It is more by luck than town planning, I suspect, but it is a splendidly accessible place to walk or jog. Most cities, though, have a park where there are trees and grass.

Give plants space in your home. With care, plants can live with you for years and will become great friends. They look good and help keep the air fresh during the day. The temperature of your rooms needs to be kept as natural as possible, without too much reliance on central heating or air conditioning. Open the windows whenever you can, let in the air and enjoy the seasons.

Perhaps one of the most important health factors, next to food, is exercise. As "sellers of the physical," actors are probably more aware than most of how necessary it is to keep the body functioning as smoothly as possible. Sitting for long periods while writing this book has made me acutely aware of how uncomfortable desk work can be and how vital it is to do some sort of regular exercise. Any type of exercise is worthwhile, from yoga to gentle jogging or lifting light weights (Nautilus or Universal for example). Nan Bronfen says, "Exercise helps keep minerals in the bones and strengthens them. Lack of stress or weight-bearing movements causes bone resorption. Exercise that delivers rapid impact is more effective in generating the right kind of electrical stimulation. Walking is excellent exercise, and weight-lifting exercises are better than swimming" (in this respect).

"...Especially Macrobiotics! A Warning!"

While reading for the next sections on nutrition I came across several warnings concerning macrobiotics, which are well worth mentioning.

Carl C. Pfeiffer, PhD, MD, in *Mental and Elemental Nutrients*, seems to jump to a common conclusion about Regimen 7 — the brown rice only diet. He assumes, as did some others in the early days of macrobiotics, that the aim of all macrobiotics is to pass through the seven stages of eating, "reducing the variety of food ingested purportedly to help the individual achieve well-being, spiritual awakening or rebirth . . . until the last stage when all that one ingests is brown rice and tea." I quote Pfeiffer, who goes on to stress emphatically, and quite correctly, the dangers of making a habit of the brown rice only diet.

George Ohsawa, who claimed that "the happy man eats anything he wants with great joy and gratitude," was also of the opinion that most sickness was produced by excesses of food. He recommended a diet of brown rice only, which he called Regimen 7, from time to time to recover physically and mentally from the effects of such excesses. "Grain fasts such as Regimen 7 can include small amounts of seasoning, condiments and liquid, and the *whole* grains can be prepared in various ways — as porridge or gruel, pancakes, bread, noodles, chapatis, etc.," says Michio Kushi, who warns that grain fasts such as Regimen 7 should not last longer than two weeks at a time unless under experienced supervision. To eat nothing but rice for weeks on end is dangerous — and very boring! You may get away with it in a Zen monastery or on top of a mountain but not when living an average life in the middle of any large modern city, with all its strain, stress and pollution.

If, however, you are not feeling well — usually because of something you have eaten — just one day on brown rice, with a few vegetables and kuzu sauce makes all the difference. Try it!

Another interesting reference to macrobiotics is found in Frances Moore Lappe's excellent book, *Diet for a Small Planet*. A quotation from the Berkeley Trube in 1970 states, "Several cases of severe protein malnutrition (*kwashiorkor* — a disease native to North Africa) have been found in Berkeley. An unpublished University of California hospital report blames certain fasting, vegetarian and *especially macrobiotic* diets for this. These diets often result in clinically protein-deficient peoples."

Frances Moore Lappe deals with "Complementary Proteins," the combination of nonmeat foods producing high-grade protein equivalent to or even better than meat proteins. The combining of grains and beans, for example, to boost protein has been practiced for centuries by many different civilizations, and macrobiotics use beans and bean products (tofu, tempeh, tamari soy sauce and miso) for cooking. Tempeh also guarantees a supply of Vitamin B_{12} that can be lacking in a completely vegetarian diet.

In California during the sixties there were stories about young people practicing — or malpracticing — macrobiotics. Stories of dehydration, kidney failure, of a young man who drank a whole bottle of soy sauce to yangize himself, of others not drinking enough liquid or eating nothing but rice for weeks on end. Balance is the essence of yin and yang.

Common sense tells us that extremes can be dangerous, and we don't have to be philosophers to realize that.

More recently, however, in August 1982, *Life* magazine featured an article about a Dr Anthony Sattilaro, complete with photographs and oscilloscope pictures of his bone scan taken in May 1978. The scan showed dark shadows, cancerous lesions, at the top of his skull, right shoulder, left rib cage, back and sternum. Soon after this scan was taken Dr Sattilaro was to lose his father from the same disease. He was, in fact, driving back to Philadelphia from the funeral when he picked up two hitchhikers. Both men were in their early twenties and were macrobiotic students. One of them, Sean McLean, told this doctor who had practiced medicine for twenty years that a change of diet could reverse his condition — that he didn't have to die. "When you eat lots of red meat, dairy products, eggs, refined foods like sugar and white flour and foods high in preservatives, then you get cancer — if you don't die of a heart attack first!"

"I just looked at him," said Dr Sattilaro, "and thought he was a silly kid. What could a twenty-five-year-old cook know about cancer?" But in time he chose to think of those two kids as angels. Fourteen months later, after a strict macrobiotic regimen supervised by the Philadelphia East West Foundation, his bone scan showed that Dr Sattilaro was free of the illness. He admits that one case history is insufficient evidence, but since his recovery he has made many innovative changes at the hospital of which he is president and hopes to begin scientific studies exploring the role of nutrition in cancer and other degenerative diseases.

ᛞᛈᛋ   *Ten regimens to health and happiness*   ᛞᛈᛋ

To "achieve a state of well being," George Ohsawa recommended using vegetables and grains (instead of animal food) in various proportions. "Regimen 7 is the simplest, the easiest and wisest," he said, "try it for 10 days."

DIET NO.	CEREALS	VEGETABLES	SOUP	ANIMAL	SALADS FRUITS	DESSERT	BEVERAGES
7	100%						As little
6	90%	10%					as possible.
5	80%	20%					
4	70%	20%	10%				
3	60%	30%	10%				
2	50%	30%	10%	10%			
1	40%	30%	10%	20%			
−1	30%	30%	10%	20%	10%		
−2	20%	30%	10%	25%	10%	5%	
−3	10%	30%	10%	30%	15%	5%	

Adapted from George Ohsawa *Zen Macrobiotics.*

The body - a laboratory
or paralysis by analysis

"We human beings," said Carl C. Pfeiffer, "are biochemicals, if you'll pardon such a pragmatic definition. Everything in the universe is technically a chemical and some of the most beneficial biochemicals, by our standards, are contained in our food, air and water. These are the nutrients that evolved with life, the vitamins and minerals natural to our food and bodies."

The sun's energy is confined by plants with chemicals such as carbon dioxide, water, nitrogen and minerals to produce a naturally balanced supply of nutrients for our body's use. You might say we are motivated by solar power!

Robert S. Meldelsohn, MD, in *Confessions of a Medical Heretic* says that macrobiotics on the other hand incorporates diet in a "universal system of thought and behavior. It does not get caught in the trap of singling out cholesterol or vitamins or trace minerals or proteins. Macrobiotics is a synthesizing system. Modern nutrition in contrast depends on analysis . . . this often leads, as everyone knows, to paralysis by analysis."

However, as we aren't, many of us, familiar with eastern philosophy and the "oneness of Tao," the final chapter is for those of us who are concerned about the possibility of not eating a properly balanced diet which contains all the necessary nutrients. There are many books on the subject, but this will, I hope, give a cross reference to which we analytical westerners can refer.

The chemistry of carbohydrates

The words *carbohydrates* and *starches* have an ominous ring to the ears of most figure-conscious bodies, although unrefined complex carbohydrates are reckoned to be the healthiest and best energy source we can have. Nan Bronfen, nutritionist for the Pritikin Research Foundation, says that grains and legumes should be our main calorie supply and adds, "Let me stress grains should be whole."

There are two principal kinds of carbohydrates. *Complex carbohydrates* and *simple sugars*. To make them plants need sunlight, carbon dioxide and water.

Complex carbohydrates are constructed of many sugar units joined together. Before they can be used by the body, they must be broken down into one of the simplest sugars — *glucose*. This breaking down is done gradually by the enzymes in the mouth and digestive tract. This slow digestion means a steady, easily regulated flow of glucose into the bloodstream, for distribution as useable energy.

Simple sugars, however, are very different from complex carbohydrates in their effect on the body. They enter the bloodstream directly and quickly, causing a sudden rise in blood sugar and stimulating the pancreas to release insulin in large quantities. In time, as with an addictive drug, more and more may be needed to get that energy "high."

Some simple sugars are:
Sucrose: cane or beet, made up of glucose and fructose.
Fructose: found in fruit and vegetables.
Lactose: milk-sugar made up of galactose and glucose.
Maltose: freed by the digestion of starch. It consists of two glucose molecules.
Cellulose is a *complex carbohydrate.* Our body cannot use it for energy and it is often removed in food processing. However, although mainly indigestible, cellulose is vital to healthy digestion as a major part of roughage.

White Sugar

White sugar has been referred to as "pure, white and deadly" and a "source of empty calories," providing energy and nothing else. The chemical reaction white sugar causes in the body gobbles up B vitamins and can lead to a calcium-phosphorus imbalance. Because of powerful publicity campaigns we feel it supplies "instant energy," but all foods contain calories. White sugar we can and should do without. It rots our teeth, makes us neurotic — and fat!

"If you look for sweetness," said Buddha, "your search will be endless, you will never be satisfied. But if you seek the true taste you will find what you are looking for."

Molasses

Molasses is the residue left after the extraction of sugar — or most of it — from the cane. Blackstrap molasses contains concentrates of iron, calcium, zinc, copper and chromium as well as lead,l pesticides and sulfur—ingredients not always mentioned on the label or in the food charts! It is in some ways the least wholesome of the products extracted from the sugarcane plant.

Honey

Honey has less calories per weight than white sugar; otherwise it contains the same large amounts of fructose, glucose and sucrose — and only slightly more vitamins and minerals.

Many claims are made that honey will cure arthritis, rheumatism, sleeplessness and bedwetting, and that it will help sexual activities, restore sexual potency and retard the aging process. There is, however, no scientific or nutritional basis for any such claims.

Saccharine and Sugar Substitutes

Such commercial products bear no relationship to natural sugar sweeteners, and there is continued concern about their long term safety. (See also INGREDIENTS—BARLEY MALT, CAROB, RICE SYRUP, MAPLE SYRUP.)

Facts about fats

When we eat more food than we need — which is more often than not — our excess energy is stored as *fat.*

Fats are composed of the same three elements as carbohydrates: carbon, hydrogen and oxygen. They are, though, a more concentrated form of energy. The fats and fatty substances in the body are called *lipids.* These are mainly composed from among some seventy or more different *fatty acids* plus *glycerol.* Fatty acids are either *saturated* or *unsaturated. Saturated* fats are solid at room temperature. *Unsaturated* fats tend to be liquid (oils) at room temperature.

Fats are absolutely necessary to us, but a diet high in fats encourages the body to make too much *cholesterol.*

Cholesterol

Cholesterol is also a kind of *lipid.* The body produces plenty of its own cholesterol, and there is really no need to include it in the diet. Excess amounts can harden and block the arteries, which frequently leads to heart disease.

Cholesterol is found in most animal foods but never in whole foods from plant sources. It is in all meats — particularly organ meats. Four ounces of liver, for example, contain three and a half times the maximum daily allowance! Eggs have 250mg in each yolk, which is two and a half times this allowance. Full-fat dairy products are high in cholesterol. Whole milk is reputedly dangerous for anyone over two years of age!

Lecithin

Lecithin is a lipid very similar in chemical composition to other fats. It is made in the body by the liver and consists of fatty acids and phosphate, which makes it both water and fat soluble.

Some nutritionists now say that it could cause the same problems as other fatty substances in the body. The use of lecithin as a supplement and additive is therefore not advised.

Margarine

To make margarine, unsaturated fats are saturated by adding hydrogen so that they will resemble the texture of butter. These altered, artificial fats lack vitamin E and linoleic acid (an essential fatty acid) and may also tend to increase the cholesterol and fats in the blood. Nickel is sometimes used as a catalyst and can remain in the product with possible harmful effects. Palm and coconut oils are often contained in cheaper margarines. These oils can be 99 percent saturated — which is more saturated that beef fat!

Unsaturated Oils

Processed, refined oils have invariably been exposed to heat. Heat causes oxidation and destroys vitamin E. Such oils can oxidize easily in the body and thus destroy vitamins. When buying oils be sure they are as *un*refined as possible and are cold pressed. Use them sparingly when cooking. Sauté at lower temperatures with less oil, or use water instead (see also INGREDIENTS—OILS).

 Protein complements

To make proteins, plants again use carbon, hydrogen and oxygen with the addition of the important element nitrogen and sometimes sulfur. It is only by eating plants, or by eating animals that eat plants, that man and beast can obtain nitrogen.

And just as carbohydrates are built of sugar units and fats of fatty acids, proteins are made up of *amino acids. Amino* means "containing nitrogen in a certain form."

Amino Acids — Complete Protein

Proteins are not used in the form in which we eat them. They are first broken down into twenty-two amino acids. The body is able to synthesize all of these except eight, which are therefore known as *essential* amino acids. Protein containing all eight of these is called *complete* protein.

Complementary Proteins

Some foods are high in certain essential amino acids and low in others. However, by combining a food low in one with food high in that particular amino acid, a more complete protein supply results. Grains and beans eaten together complement each other and can actually increase the percentage of usable protein by up to 40 percent, providing more protein than meat. The whole can thus be greater than the sum of its parts!

Complementary grain and bean diets have evolved and have been traditionally practiced by people all over the world. American Indians eat their corn or wheat tortillas and frijoles. Rice and beans are a popular staple in Jamaican and other Carribean island diets. Middle Easterners have chick peas with their wheat cous cous, and India is the country of chapati or rice and lentils. Indonesians cook tempeh, a soybean ferment, with their rice, and in China, Japan and Korea other soy products — tofu, miso and tamari soy sauce — are served with rice. Macrobiotics uses all these various complements to boost protein supply.

Of all the nutrients in our diet, protein is probably the least likely to be deficient. Excessive amounts, on the other hand, can undoubtedly be harmful.

Meat as a Source of Protein

There is generally a look of alarm and despondency on the faces of meat eaters when grains are suggested as an alternative principal food, but nutritionists give some pretty convincing reasons for not eating too much of this form of protein. Even athletes are often advised these days to use complex carbohydrates as a main source of energy.

Meat contains complete protein but not as much as is generally thought. 70 to 80 percent of the calories in meat comes from fat, and meat is high in cholesterol.

These days many animals—cattle, pigs, chickens and turkeys, etc.—are treated with antibiotics to stimulate growth and resistance to disease in unsanitary, crowded conditions. It is estimated that meat tissue can contain the residues of up to 143 different drugs!

Meat is, in fact, an elaborate and expensive way to obtain proteins. One nutritionist says, "It is time to drop the notion that we need meat to survive." Another says, "Grains and legumes will provide sufficient protein without all that extra fat."

 Main minerals

It is interesting that our body fluids, the very blood in our veins, resemble the mineral content of the ocean from which, we are told, life evolved. The enzymes and cells of our bodies depend on the major salts of the sea.

The body cannot manufacture its own minerals as it can some vitamins. They must be supplied by, and are available, in a proper diet. They should be taken in food rather than in extracted form as pills. Dr William Strain of Cleveland has rather grimly likened element nutrition to a giant spider's web. If one strand of the web is pulled the whole structure is distorted!

Minerals are not destroyed by heat, light or air. They can be lost from food in the cooking water — so always use it! Minerals are usually extracted when foods are processed.

THE MACRONUTRIENT MINERALS

CALCIUM (Ca)

We have two to three pounds of calcium in our body — it is the most abundant mineral — but only 20 to 30 percent of the amount ingested is used. Excessive consumption of meat, rich in phosphorus, upsets the calcium-phosphorus balance. A fatty diet interferes with calcium absorption.

Calcium and Exercise

Exercise—or the lack of it—is an important factor as exercise helps keep minerals in the bones, and weight-bearing movements cause calcium absorption into bone. Walking, running and even light weight-training are recommended.

PHOSPHORUS (P)

This the second most abundant mineral in the body, makes up 1 percent of the human body weight — half that of calcium — 90 percent of which is combined with oxygen as phosphates deposited in the bones and teeth. It depends on vitamin D and calcium for its absorption.

Excess intakes of iron, aluminum and magnesium can interfere with phosphorus absorption, as they form insoluble phosphates. The calcium-phosphorus balance is disturbed by sugar intake or by high milk, fat or protein diets.

Nan Bronfen says that modern man is eating two or three times more phosphorus than calcium, which is the wrong balance. Plants and vegetables are fed with phosphate fertilizers and are sprayed with insecticides; phosphates are added to processed foods and sodas to give an acid flavor.

POTASSIUM (K)

Potassium is alkaline-forming and is the third most plentiful mineral in the body. Most of it is used inside the body cells, while sodium is found in the fluids outside the cells. It works in constant dynamic balance with sodium throughout the body.

The average American's intake has been estimated at anything up to 6,000mg, three times a suggested daily requirement, since the potassium content of many foods is high. Macrobiotics recommends moderate intakes with a sodium-potassium balance of 5:1 to 7:1 (see also YIN AND YANG).

SODIUM (Na)

The unprocessed "salt of the earth" of ancient times and provider of trace minerals is, unfortunately, now "refined" table salt — pure sodium chloride. Most of the other natural salts of the sea have been extracted, iodine then added, sometimes sugar to make it pour, even sodium bicarbonate as a bleach to keep it white! Unrefined sea salt has a slightly off-white "glow" because of its mineral "impurity" which can be up to 12 percent. Sodium taken with these minerals is not to be feared but respected.

Most people take far more than they need, especially of refined salt. According to the Manual of Nutrition, published in London by HMSO, adults need 4 grams each day in a temperate climate, which can be achieved by eating natural food. Most people take in from five to twenty grams. Such excess sodium may cause potassium to be lost and is strongly associated with high blood pressure.

SULFUR (S)
Since early times men have visited mineral springs, or spas, to "take" waters that smell strongly of sulfur. Such water contains hydrogen sulfide. Sulfur, like potassium, is found inside every body cell, especially in those of the hair. In fact, the smell of burning hair is due to a 15 percent sulfur content. Most of the peculiar odors of foods in the body laboratory are due to the presence of sulfur compounds! A diet containing enough protein will provide adequate sulfur.

CHLORINE (Cl)
Chlorine is usually found in the body in some compound form with sodium or potassium as *chloride*. The total amount present is around three ounces. It is essential for the acid-alkaline balance in the blood and the production of hydrochloric acid in the stomach for digestion.

As sodium chloride in the form of table salt is widely distributed in our food there is no problem in obtaining sufficient amounts. The chlorine in drinking water can destroy vitamin E and impair the intestinal flora that helps digestion.

MAGNESIUM (Mg)
Our body supply is approximately 21 grams, 70 percent of which is located in the skeleton. It does not leave the bones as readily as do calcium and phosphorus.

Heavy drinkers, people living on refined foods or those who drink soft water, are apt to have low magnesium supply. The milling of white flour can remove 86 percent of it, and refined grains increase the body's need for magnesium which is essential to carbohydrate metabolism.

The U.S. Research Council's recommended daily intake is 350mg for men, 300 for women, 450 during pregnancy, which the average refined food diet will barely provide.

 # The trace elements

IRON (Fe)
In your body there are a mere 3 to 4 grams of the same mineral used to make your cast-iron skillet, but without this iron life would cease in a few seconds! Iron lies at the centre of a large and complex protein molecule, *hemoglobin*, which transports oxygen to the cells of the body. Without oxygen no energy is released.

Poor eating habits and preserved foods that have been depleted of iron can lessen supplies, as can eating too many sweets. Eggs seem to decrease the amount of iron absorbed, taking alkaline indigestion cures, drinking too much coffee and tea all hinder absorption. Sea vegetables are an exceptionally rich source of iron.

There is so much attention given to iron deficiency, which is only one form of anemia, that iron overload, often caused by years of iron tonics or large volumes of iron-containing wines, tends to occur mostly in men over forty. Symptoms include loss of weight and a grey pallor to the skin.

IODINE (I)

The content of trace elements in foods often depends on the soil in which plants are grown. In the early 1900s, for instance, the soil of the Midwest and Great Lakes areas in the U.S. was deficient in iodine and this became known as the Goiter Belt. People living in certain areas around the world often had a high incidence of enlarged thyroid glands. Today food sold in markets is usually from many different areas. Sea vegetables, however, are always a rich and reliable source of iodine.

Iodine, as a constituent of *thyroxine*, assists in regulating the body's energy. Cretinism can be the result of a limited iodine intake by the mother during pregnancy.

MANGANESE (Mn)

Manganese is described as one of the "desirable" elements. It plays a role in activating numerous enzymes in the body. The main food sources of manganese are from whole grains, nuts and vegetables. Manganese is often removed from the soil by lime that is added to increase vegetable foliage. Milling of grain also removes manganese; corn, for instance, contains 1mg per 100g and corn flakes only 0.04mg.

COPPER (Cu)

There is evidence that copper should be classified as a "heavy metal," as are lead, mercury and cadmium. It is essential to the body, however, in very small amounts. As iron metabolism is highly dependent on it, copper is important for the proper formation of hemoglobin.

Copper is present in many foods, especially whole grains, beans, nuts and seafood. Deficiency is usually due to excessive intake of certain other minerals (e.g., by supplementation). The proportion of copper to these other minerals, particularly zinc, is important. High doses of vitamin C can interfere with its absorption.

Toxicity through excess copper is rare but copper cooking utensils should always be lined with stainless steel.

ZINC (Zn)

Zinc, which is related to the normal absorption and action of vitamins, especially the B complex, maintains about twenty enzyme systems in the body and is described as the "traffic policeman," directing and overseeing the efficient flow of these body processes. It is readily absorbed in the body and is found in the male reproductive fluid. The prostate gland contains more zinc than any other part of the body, and delayed sexual maturity in adolescents has recently been connected with zinc deficiency. Stretch marks on the skin and white spots in the finger nails may indicate zinc deficiency.

Apart from soil exhaustion, the most common cause of poor zinc supply is that food processing removes zinc — bugs cannot grow without zinc either! — while soluble zinc salts can go down the drain with the vegetable water. Pregnant women and those on "the pill" can have low zinc levels while foods high in copper can negate much of the zinc obtained. Oysters, for instance, are very high in zinc but are also high in copper!

How vital are vitamins?

Nature makes most vitamins from carbon, hydrogen and oxygen in differing proportions. In 1912 a substance was discovered in the polishings from whole-grain or "brown" rice that prevented beriberi. It was called *thiamine* — *amine* means "containing nitrogen." The word *vitamine*, as it was originally spelled, meant *vita* (life) and *amine* (nitrogenous). By the 1920s, however, the "e" was dropped as very few vitamins proved to contain nitrogen.

Although the thiamine in whole-grain rice has been known to prevent beriberi for many years, polished white rice, minus its supply of thiamine continues to be the staple human food of the Far East, and beriberi continues to be a widespread deficiency disease there. In the western world, white refined bread and white refined flour are our main cereal food. Vitamins and minerals are often completely removed from them and we are encouraged to make up the deficiencies in our diets by taking supplement tablets invariably manufactured, at huge profit, from the very nutrients that have been taken from our food in the first place!

Vitamins are essential factors needed for the healthy functioning of the body, but supplementation with *isolated* vitamins is regarded with suspicion. Nan Bronfen says categorically that vitamins, when used in their extracted forms rather than as parts of whole foods, are being used as drugs. An overdose of one vitamin can increase the deficiency of others because of their complex inter-relationships. Vitamins are interdependent, and nature knows best how to package them.

Some vitamins are soluble in water — the B complex vitamins and vitamin C — others are fat soluble — these are vitamins A, D, E, F and K. Some are resistant to heat, some are not; some are destroyed by storage, light, air, acid, alkali, pollution, processing and by cooking in copper or aluminium. Alcohol, smoking, stress and the pill can all deplete body stores or increase the body's need for vitamins. It is well to be aware of the losses that occur when cooking: prolonged boiling of vegetables in water leaches out water-soluble vitamins. Place vegetables in boiling water — not too much of it — to "seal" them. Keep the cooking water, and use it for soup stock or to make sauces — or drink it! It's usually delicious, particularly if seasoned with a little tamari soy sauce or miso. Avoid cooking vegetables for too long.

Around twenty vitamins have so far been identified, but not all are scientifically or officially accepted or understood.

VITAMIN A
The functions of vitamin A in the body are, it is generally admitted, not completely understood. Plant foods do not contain vitamin A, but a substance called *β-carotene* (as in carrots), which is readily converted into vitamin A by the body. Orange-colored or dark green vegetables and orange-colored fruit contain especially plentiful supplies of β-carotene. Carotene is stored in the body fat and overdosing can turn the skin yellow.

Vitamin A is good for eye conditions and proper night vision. Working in bright light, dim light or fluorescent light raises the body's demand for it as does TV, some drugs, smoking, car fumes and air pollution. Older people who especially need green vegetables often consume too few.

THE B-COMPLEX VITAMINS
Scientific understanding of the relationship between diet and nervous and psychotic disorders

is in its infancy, but it is realized that the B vitamins are related to mental health, nerve cell and tissue functioning, as well as the metabolism of carbohydrates, amino acids and fats. B vitamins are difficult to separate and, though seemingly independent, each has a specific, related function. They are supplied mainly by the same whole foods: whole grains, legumes, land vegetables, sea vegetables, nuts and seeds. Meats and liver, which are extreme yang, also contain B vitamins. Brewers yeast and molasses are also considered good sources, but they are extremely yin.

B vitamins are, as we have said, frequently removed from whole foods by refining processes to "improve" color and texture and to "curtail pest attraction." The pests, quite rightly, don't like refined foods! Sugar, alcohol and oral contraceptives also increase the need for B vitamins.

Vitamin B^1 (Thiamine)
Thiamine, the magic ingredient discovered in rice polishings, was the first member of the B complex to be chemically identified. It contains sulfur as well as nitrogen and is highly soluble in water, which means it has limited body storage and needs to be supplied daily.

Thiamine is part of an enzyme complex needed to metabolize carbohydrates into simple sugar for energy production. It is essential for the health of the nervous system and is consequently known as the morale vitamin because of its beneficial effect on mental attitudes. It can help prevent travel sickness.

Heat and hot water cause loss of vitamin B^1. Never overcook vegetables or throw out the cooking water. Body supplies are depleted by excessive sugar intake, smoking and drinking alcohol. Thiamine can also be destroyed by an enzyme present in raw clams and oysters. It is inhibited by caffeine, food processing methods and "the pill."

Vitamin B^2 (Riboflavin)
Vitamin B^2 is reported to be one of the most commonly deficient vitamins in America. Most common symptoms are: cracks and lesions in the corner of the mouth; inflamed, sore tongue; itching and burning of the eyes; eye fatigue; sensitivity to light; dermatitis around the nose, mouth, forehead and ears. Deficiency symptoms of various B vitamins are often so similar however that it is sometimes difficult to tell which is lacking. Large supplementary doses of any of them may result in high losses. Light, especially ultraviolet light, destroys it and alkaline solutions (baking soda), sulfur drugs, alcohol and "the pill" increase demands.

Vitamin B^3 (Niacin)
During famines caused by the Napoleonic wars, farmers in Europe, living almost entirely on corn, were stricken by an epidemic of a dreadful skin and nerve disease called pellagra. Even today corn is used mainly as animal food in Europe because of its grim association with the disease. The missing nutrient from corn proved to be *niacin*. Corn does contain all the B vitamins, but the niacin is not released in the body. Indians in Mexico and Peru have eaten beans with their corn since ancient times and have supplemented their diet in this way. Niacin is fairly stable but excessive consumption of sugar and alcohol, certain antibiotics and sleeping tablets deplete the body's supply — as does "the pill."

Vitamin B^5 (Pantothenic Acid)
The Greek word *panthos* means everywhere. *Pantothenic acid,* or vitamin B^5, occurs in all living cells and was first isolated in Texas in 1940. It affects all manner of bodily chemical functions, is water soluble and synthesized by bacterial flora of the intestines.

Pantothenic acid is so widely distributed that an isolated deficiency of vitamin B^5 from among other B complex vitamins is rare, and the means of detecting it are limited.

Vitamin B^6 (Pyridoxine)

In the 1930s a factor was discovered in animal liver which prevented skin disorders in rats and also in humans. Vitamin B^6 consists of three related compounds: *pyridoxine, pyridoxinal* and *pyridoxamine*. It is water soluble but stable to heat, light, air and acid and is needed for the proper absorption of vitamin B^{12}. Another of its functions is to help maintain the balance of sodium and potassium which regulates the body fluids.

The need for it increases during pregnancy, lactation, aging and if taking oral contraceptives. The consumption of protein also increases the demand for vitamin B^6. Deficiency symptoms are similar to those of vitamins B^2 and B^3: numbness and cramps in arms and legs, tingling hands, cracks around the mouth and eyes, nervousness and depression.

Vitamin B^{12} (Cobalamin)

Vitamin B^{12} is the first cobalt-containing substance found necessary for life and the only vitamin containing an essential mineral element. It cannot be made synthetically, but can be produced by fermentation.

Vegetarian diets are frequently high in folic acid, which may mask a vitamin B^{12} deficiency; serious nerve damage and pernicious anemia could result. Total vegetarians, who eat no animal food, fish or dairy products, need to be sure they have some sea vegetables, miso or tempeh as these are good sources of the vitamin (see INGREDIENTS—MISO AND TEMPEH). Absorption increases during pregnancy and decreases with age. Impaired memory and concentration in older people may often be caused by a lack of vitamin B^{12}. Amounts required are minute but essential.

Folic Acid: Folacin

Folic acid, also known as vitamin M or Bm was first isolated from the leaf vegetable, spinach. It works closely with vitamin B^{12} and excessive supplementation of it can disguise the symptoms of vitamin B^{12} deficiency and of pernicious anemia.

Folic acid is lost in food refining and processing. A major cause of folic acid deficiency is destruction during prolonged cooking, refrigeration or storage at room temperature in the light for long periods. Excess alcohol, chlorine in drinking water, antibiotics, "the pill" all increase requirements. Deficiency is common among the elderly and people who eat too few green leaf vegetables. Adequate folic acid consumption is important during pregnancy.

VITAMIN C (ASCORBIC ACID)

As early as 1747 a British physician, James Lind, MC, discovered that lime juice prevented the scurvy that had plagued sailors of that time. Boiling the lime juice with water destroyed the effect of the nourishing factor. This factor was vitamin C, a sugarlike substance that most animals can synthesize in their bodies from glucose, the exceptions being monkeys, guinea pigs, the Indian fruit bat, the red-vented bulbul bird apparently, and man! Scurvy is still found today in older people living on convenience and junk foods.

Ascorbic acid, available in synthetic form, is the subject of argument as a possible cure for the common cold. Massive doses of it are recommended by some nutritionists and suspected by others. "Vitamin C can perhaps reduce the severity of a cold, but it may make it last longer!" It is much better to get it from whole foods than from pills, because foods containing the vitamin provide bioflavanoids which protect it from oxidation. Vitamin C is the least stable vitamin; it is very sensitive to oxygen and its potency is lost through exposure to light, heat and air. It is very water soluble and, although readily absorbed, most of it is eliminated in three or four hours.

The body's ability to absorb vitamin C is reduced by smoking (one cigarette can use up to 25 mg), air pollution and alcohol. As vitamin C is needed for adrenalin production it is used up more rapidly under stress or shock. The ingestion of aspirin, pain killers, sulfur drugs, antibiotics and cortisone increases demands. Baking soda creates an alkaline medium, which destroys it, and cooking in copper or aluminum utensils is also destructive. Drinking too much water will deplete the body's vitamin C.

The recommended daily amount required is around 45mg for adults, preferably taken in frequent small doses.

VITAMIN D

This, the "sunshine vitamin," is really a hormone needed only in miniscule amounts and is made by the body. Ultraviolet light from the sun converts a type of cholesterol called ergosterol in the skin into vitamin D, which is absorbed into the circulatory system. The body can store sizeable reserves of it. Very small areas of skin need to be exposed, as 18 International Units per square centimeter can be manufactured in three hours! Pigmentation is a factor — the more pigment there is, the less vitamin D is produced. Deficiency can cause faulty mineralization of bones, which can lead to rickets. There is a risk that children of dark-skinned immigrants to a northern climate may develop rickets from lack of sunlight as their skin prevents them from producing vitamin D as readily as do light-skinned people. Vitamin D is not lost in the cooking water but is lost in the oil when frying! Provitamins D are found also in both plant and animal tissue. Foods containing vitamin A usually contain some vitamin D.

VITAMIN E (TOCOPHEROL)

This fat-soluble vitamin is composed of a group of seven substances called *tocopherols*. Of these *alphatocopherol* is the most potent and valuable form of vitamin E found in oil-containing foods such as grains, seeds and nuts as well as leafy greens and fish.

Fats and oils containing vitamin E are less susceptible to oxidation or rancidity than are those without it. The cosmetic industry claims that vitamin E can help retard the ageing process and it is often used, in ointment form, on the skin.

Vitamin E is destroyed by processing. White flour, for instance, no longer contains much vitamin E as the germ of the wheat, which is the richest known source, is removed. W. E. Shute, MD, a leading heart specialist, claims that "prior to the removal of natural wheat germ, with its vitamin E, from whole-wheat flour and bread there were no cases of coronary thrombosis; now it is one of the world's major killers." A diet high in refined vegetable oils and polyunsaturated fats and oils increases the demand for vitamin E. Chlorine in drinking water, rancid oil or fat, inorganic iron supplements, air pollution and mineral oil used as a laxative, all deplete supplies. "The pill" neutralizes the effect of vitamin E, and air pollution increases the need for it.

Women severely deficient in vitamin E are likely to have pregnancy problems, and men can be made sterile.

229

Appendix 1

Yin and yang

UNIVERSAL PRINCIPLES
— That which has a beginning has an end.
— Each thing is individual and unique.
— There can be no front without a back, no beauty without ugliness. Your opponent is your greatest benefactor. Sickness is the other side of health, for the back is the real meaning of the front.
— The greater and wider the front, the greater and wider the back. The greater the beauty, the greater the ugliness.
— All opposites are complementary and can be classified in two categories — yin and yang.

YIN AND YANG
— Yin and yang are the two arms of the Infinite, the Absolute, Oneness—God. The two poles of infinite expansion.
— Yin and yang are continuous, forever in motion and changing.
— Yin and yang together produce all energy.
— Yin attracts yang: yang attracts yin.
— Yin repels yin: yang repels yang.
— Yin-Yang components are always in different proportions and are constantly changing.
— Nothing is completely yin or completely yang.
— Nothing is neutral. Either yin exceeds yang or yang exceeds yin.
— Large yin attracts small yin: Large yang attracts small yang.
— Excess yin produces yang: Excess yang produces yin.

Adapted from G. Ohsawa's *Zen Macrobiotics* and Michio Kushi's *Book of Macrobiotics*.

Appendix 2

 *Acid- and alkaline-forming foods*

In an attempt to reconcile the western concept of acid- and alkaline-forming foods with the eastern Tao concept of yin-yang, Herman Ahara produced a chart (overleaf) of four categories balancing yin and yang acid- and alkaline-forming foods.

Yang alkaline-forming foods are high in *sodium.*
Yang acid-forming foods are high in *phosphorus, sulfur* and *sodium.*
Yin alkaline-forming foods are high in *potassium, magnesium* and *calcium.*
Yin acid-forming foods are high in *phosphorus* and *sulfur.*

A meal should contain a selection of one food from each category. Grains, of course, should be the principal food (yang, acid forming) with vegetables — including sea vegetables — (yin, alkaline forming) and beans (yin, acid forming) with sesame salt, tamari soy sauce and salted pickles (yin, alkaline forming). This menu should be a balance of the acid-alkaline factors. It is always advisable to avoid eating extremes of acid-alkaline or yin and yang too often.

Yin acid-forming foods

(High in phosphorus and sulfur)

sugar
sweets, candy
soft drinks
vinegar
saccharine
vodka   corn oil
some wine   olive oil
whisky   sesame oil
sake   peanut butter
beer   sesame cream
soybeans   cashews
green peas   peanuts
tofu   almonds
white beans   chestnuts
pinto beans
kidney beans
black beans
chick peas
red beans (aduki)
macaroni
spaghetti

Yang acid-forming foods

(High in phosphorus, sulfur and sodium)

corn, oats,
barley, rye
wheat
rice   shellfish
buckwheat   eel, carp
                            white meat, fish
                            cheese
                            fowl
                            meat
                            tuna, salmon
                            eggs

(S) Yin alkaline-forming foods (S)

(High in potassium, magnesium and calcium)

natural wine
natural sake
cola
cocoa
fruit juices
coffee
dyed teas
mineral waters
soda water
well water

honey
mustard
ginger
pepper
curry
cinnamon

tropical fruit
dates, figs
lemons, grapes
raisins, bananas
peaches
currants
pears, plums
oranges
watermelon

apples, cherries
strawberries

potatoes
eggplant
tomatoes
shiitake
taro potatoes
cucumber
sweet potatoes
mushrooms
spinach
asparagus
broccoli
celery
cabbage
pumpkin
onions
turnips
daikon
nori
hiziki
carrots

(S) Yang alkaline-forming foods (S)

(High in sodium)

kuzu tea

millet

dandelion tea
mu tea
Ohsawa coffee
yannoh
ginseng

sesame salt
soy sauce
miso
umeboshi
salt

wakame
kombu
lotus root
burdock
dandelion root
jinenjo

Bibliography

Abehsera, Michel, *Zen Macrobiotic Cooking,* Albyn Press, New York, 1971.

Abehsera, Michel, *Cooking for Life,* Swan House, Binhamton.

Agriculture, U.S. States Dept. of, *Handbook of Nutritional Contents Of Foods,* Dover Publications, New York, 1975.

Aihara, Herman, *Acid & Alkaline,* Ohsawa Foundation, Oroville, Cal., 1980.

Aihara, Herman, *Seven Macrobiotic Principles,* Ohsawa Foundation, Oroville, Cal., 1977.

Airola, Dr Paavo, *Are You Confused?,* Health Plus Publishers, Phoenix, Arizona, 1971.

Arasaki, S & T, *Vegetables from the Sea,* Japan Publications, Tokyo, 1983.

Bethel, Mary, *The Healing Power of Herbs,* Wilshire Book Co.

Bronfen, Nan, *Nutrition for a Better Life,* Capra Press, Santa Barbara, 1980.

Caine, Mary, *The Glastonbury Giants,* Helios Books.

Clark, Linda, *Know your Nutrition,* Keats, New Canaan, Connecticut, 1973.

Cooper, J. C., *Yin & Yang,* Aquarian Press, Wellingborough, 1981.

Detrick, Mia, *Sushi,* Chronicle Books, New York.

Dieno, Konrad, edited, *Documenta Geigy Scientific Tables,* Geigy Pharmaceutical (Aust) Pty Ltd.

Douell & Bailey, *Cook's Ingredients,* W. Morrow & Co. Inc., New York, 1980.

Esko, Wendy, *Introducing Macrobiotic Cooking,* Japan Publications, Tokyo, 1983.

Esko, Edward & Wendy, *Macrobiotic Cooking for Everyone,* Japan Publications, Tokyo, 1980.

Ford Heritage BSME, *Composition & Facts About Foods,* Health Research, Mokelumne Hill, Cal. 1971.

Holford, Patrick, *The Whole Health Manual*, Thorsons, Wellingborough, 1983.

Horn, Ken, *Chinese Cookery,* BBC, London, 1984.

Kinsman, Lisa, *Chinese Delights*, Norman & Hobhouse.

Kirschmann, John D., *Nutrition Almanac (Revised Edition),* McGraw Book Company, New York, 1979.

Kushi, Michio, *Cancer Prevention Diet,* St. Martins Press, New York, 1983.

Kushi, Michio, *Macrobiotics Experience,* East West Foundation.

Kushi, Michio, *The Order of the Universe Magazine*, Order of the Universe Publications, Boston, Mass., 1967.

Law, Donald, *You are How You Eat*, Turnstone, Wellingborough, 1977.

Levine Gelb, Barbara, *Food & What's in it for you*, Paddington Press.

Mackarness, Dr Richard, *Not All in the Mind*, Pan, London, 1976.

Magnin, Pierre, *Macrobiotic Health Food,* Lima Publications.

Mervyn BSc, PhD, Leonard, *Dictionary of Vitamins,* Thorsons, Wellingborough, 1984.

Mindell, Earl, *Vitamin Bible,* Warner Books, New York, 1979.

Moore Lappe, Francis, *Diet for a Small Planet,* Ballantine Books, New York, 1975.

Ohsawa, George, *Zen Macrobiotics*, Ohsawa Foundation, L.A., N.Y., 1965.

Ohsawa, George, *Book of Judgement*, Ohsawa Foundation, L.A., N.Y., 1966.

Ohsawa, George, *Guide Book for Living*, Ohsawa Foundation.

Ohsawa, George, *Macrobiotics an Invitation to Health & Happiness*, Ohsawa Foundation, San Francisco, Cal.

Oles, Shayne, *The New Zen Cookery,* Shayfer Corporation, Woodlands Hill, Cal.

Peterson, Vicki, *The Natural Food Catalogue*, Macdonald & Co., London & Sydney, 1984.

Pfeiffer PhD MD, Carl C., *Mental & Elemental Nutrients*, Keats Publishing, Inc., New Canaan, Connecticut, 1975.

Polunin & Huxley, *Flowers of the Mediterranean*, Chatto & Windus.

Rawson & Legeza, *Tao*, Thames & Hudson, London, 1973.

Rombauer, Irma and Marion Rombauer Becker, *Joy Of Cooking*, Bobbs-Merrill Co. Inc., Indianapolis, Indiana, 1963.

Sams, Craig, *About Macrobiotics*, Thorsons, Wellingborough/Rochester, Vermont, 1983.

Scott, David, *Middle Eastern Vegetarian Cookery*, Rider, Melbourne, Aust., 1982.

Sekules, Veronica, *Friends of the Earth Cookbook*, Penguin, Harmondsworth, Middx. 1981.

Shurtleff & Aoyagi, *The Book of Tofu*, Autumn Press, United States, 1975.

Shurtleff & Aoyagi, *The Book of Miso*, Autumn Press, Kanagawa-Ken, Japan, 1976.

Shurtleff & Aoyagi, *The Book of Tempeh*, Harper & Row, New York, 1979.

Smith MD, Loudon, *Feed Yourself Right*, McGraw-Hill, New York.

Thorpe, Susan, *The Four Seasons Wholefood Cookbook*, Thorsons, Wellingborough/Rochester, Vermont, 1983.

Weber, Marcea, *Whole Meals*, Prism Press, Chalmington, Dorset, 1983.

Wheatley, Michael, *A Way of Living as a Means of Survival*, Corgi Books, London, 1977.

Index